100 THINGS
BILLS FANS
SHOULD KNOW & DO
BEFORE THEY DIE

Jeffrey J. Miller

TRIUMPH
B O O K S

Library of Congress Cataloging-in-Publication Data

Miller, Jeff (Jeffrey J.)
    100 things Bills fans should know & do before they die / Jeff Miller ; [foreword by] Marv Levy.
        p. cm.
    ISBN 978-1-60078-728-7 (pbk.)
    1.   Buffalo Bills (Football team)—History. 2.   Buffalo Bills (Football team)—Miscellanea. I. Title. II. Title: One hundred things Bills fans should know & do before they die.
    GV956.B83M55 2012
    796.332'6409747—dc23

2012023538

This book is available in quantity at special discounts for your group or organization. For further information, contact:

    Triumph Books LLC
    814 North Franklin Street
    Chicago, Illinois 60610
    (312) 337-0747
    www.triumphbooks.com

Printed in U.S.A.
ISBN: 978-1-60078-728-7
Design by Patricia Frey
Photos courtesy of AP Images unless otherwise indicated

100 THINGS
BILLS FANS
SHOULD KNOW & DO
BEFORE THEY DIE

To Cathaline and Benjamin, my home team

Contents

Foreword

What a captivating look into the heart, the soul, the workings, the fans, and the moments of celebration and despair that have gone into fashioning the history and the character of the Buffalo Bills. While Jeff Miller has succeeded in awakening some fond memories in us all, he has also brought onto the stage much of what we really didn't know before.

This book isn't just about final scores or who won the division title 27 years ago. Oh, no! It is about people. You may know Jim Kelly's number or Thurman Thomas' statistics, you may know that Darryl Talley and Kent Hull were noted for their leadership abilities, and you may know that Ralph Wilson has been the team's only owner since the team came breezing into the Rockpile more than 50 years ago. But do you really know what went into fashioning the personality and the character of these fine men and of so many others like Billy Shaw, Tom Sestak, Doug Flutie, Cornelius Bennett, and Jack Kemp?

Some of the fascinating stories that Jeff brings forth in this book help you to feel as if you are enjoying a lunch out—or perhaps having a friendly argument with fellow Bills personalities. Besides the cast of characters who you will read about in this book, there is an engrossing roller coaster of Buffalo Bills–related subjects that Jeff portrays so engrossingly. Never-to-be-forgotten plays, moments of elation or desolation, fandemonium, draft days, tailgate revelry, a visit to a Bills bar on game day (I always wondered what that was like), and many other triumphant moments in Buffalo football history are portrayed herein.

It was my privilege a few years ago to collaborate with Jeff in writing a book about the Bills titled *Game Changers*. It was then that I learned what an astute and dedicated authority he is in matters pertaining to the team and to other intriguing sports-related subjects. Jeff is a member of the Professional Football Researchers Association and, among his many other accolades, he was the recipient in 2004 of the PFRA's Ralph E. Hay Award for career achievement in pro football research and historiography. I can see why.

And so, as you delve into the contents of *100 Things Bills Fans Should Know & Do Before They Die*, be aware that you will come away not just better educated about Buffalo Bills lore, but also wonderfully entertained (and maybe even revved up) as well. You may even want to belt out a few choruses of the fight song "Go Bills!" that I composed in collaboration with Cole Porter (yeah, sure) a few years ago.

Collaboration with Cole Porter and Jeff Miller—you can't top that. Well, maybe Jeff just did in writing this latest tome about our beloved Buffalo Bills.

—Marv Levy

Acknowledgments

Thanks first and foremost to my wife Cathaline and our son Benjamin for putting up with my frequent and sometimes prolonged absences while writing this book. I love you two more than you will ever know.

Special thanks to the members of the Bills family for sharing their memories and observations: Eddie Abramoski, Al Bemiller, Bobby Burnett, Chuck Burr, Butch Byrd, Wray Carlton, Don Chelf, Elbert Dubenion, Booker Edgerson, George Flint, Wilmer Fowler, Pete Gogolak, Johnny Green, Harry Jacobs, Jack Kemp, Daryle Lamonica, Marv Levy, Denny Lynch, Ron McDole, Van Miller, Lou Saban, Bob Schmidt, Billy Shaw, Mike Stratton, LaVerne Torczon, Jim Wagstaff, Ralph Wilson, and Mack Yoho.

My undying gratitude to author John Maxymuk for his help and encouragement throughout this project (you are a credit to football writers everywhere!); to Greg Tranter, the world's foremost collector of Buffalo Bills memorabilia, for his feedback and for sharing items from his vast collection; and to Mr. Eddie Weihing, for his thoughts and words of inspiration. Thanks also to Mike Burns, Jimmy Cerrito, Deb and Bill Connelly, Dan Dilandro, and Peggy Hatfield of the Butler Library at Buffalo State College, Jeff Mason, the Miller family, Lud and Judy Sternad, and John Turney, all of whom offered help and support during this project.

To Adam Motin, Tom Bast, and Katy Sprinkel at Triumph Books—it's always a pleasure to work with the best in the business!

And last, but certainly not least, a special thank you to Marv Levy for providing the foreword and sharing so many wonderful memories of his days with the Bills!

1 The Boss

Ralph J. Wilson Jr. gave the gift of professional football back to Western New York when he took a flyer on the renegade American Football League in 1959. Since that time, he has shared the same highs and lows as the fans who bleed red, white, and royal blue out of loyalty to their team. It is to Wilson's credit that the Bills are one of just two of the original eight AFL franchises that have never relocated out of their original territory (the other being the Denver Broncos). Since as far back as the 1960s, Wilson has endured rumors that he planned to sell the Bills or move the franchise to a more lucrative municipality, but through it all, the Bills have remained in the area and have thrilled, angered, excited, disappointed, and—most of all—captivated fans over the course of more than five decades.

Wilson was born in Columbus, Ohio, on October 17, 1918, but grew up in Detroit, Michigan, becoming an avid follower of the Detroit Tigers baseball team. He learned to appreciate football when the NFL's Portsmouth Spartans moved to the Motor City in 1934 and became the Detroit Lions.

Wilson enlisted in the Navy in 1941 and spent five years minesweeping in both the Mediterranean and the Pacific. In 1948, Wilson and his father, Ralph Sr., threw in with a group of Detroit-based businessmen to purchase shares in the Lions from their Chicago-based owner Fred Mandel.

"They were not going to sell a majority interest," Wilson said. "There was going to be 2 or 3 percent to 60 businessmen. My father and I—being residents here—went over. He used to take me to the games, or I'd go with somebody else when the Lions moved to Tiger Stadium. I had nothing to do with the management [and] was not on the board of directors of the Lions. I was just a big fan of the game, and in those days the Lions had a great team. They had Bobby Layne and Doak Walker."

As the game of professional football gained popularity throughout the 1950s, so did Wilson's desire to own a team of his own. "In those days, there were only 12 teams in pro football," Wilson observed. "When they went on national television, the sport became very popular because people all over the country where they didn't even have teams could see the games. Besides liking it very much, I could see that the game was becoming very popular, so I tried to buy a franchise—expansion or existing team, mostly an existing team. George Halas was the chairman of the expansion committee for the NFL, but they weren't looking to expand."

Wilson recalled the momentous day when he learned about a new football league being formed by a young man from Dallas, Texas. "I was up in Saratoga, New York, at the races, and I read in the *New York Times* that there was a young man named Lamar Hunt in Dallas who wanted to start a new league," Wilson recalled. "He went to the NFL and wanted an expansion team for Dallas, and they said no.

"In those days," he continued, "the Hunt family was one of the richest in the world. So Lamar said he'd start his own league. He was much younger than me—I was about 40, he was in his late twenties. He and Barron Hilton in Los Angeles and Bud Adams in Houston got together and they started the American Football League. They already had a franchise in Denver, and they hoped to have a franchise in Miami."

Wilson flew down to Florida to meet with the city of Miami's power brokers but came away disappointed. "We got a lot of opposition from the city council and the University of Miami. They didn't want the competition, and the city council said, 'We had a team down here [the AAFC Miami Seahawks] that went broke.

We're gonna wait for the NFL. Maybe someday they will expand and come down here.' So I came home and forgot about it."

There were other cities out there hungry for football, and Hunt kept after Wilson in hopes that he would be interested in placing a team somewhere else. "A few days later, Lamar called me and said, 'Ralph, we need an eighth team…to even out the league,'" said Wilson. Hunt suggested Wilson consider a few other cities, including St. Louis, Cincinnati, Louisville, and Buffalo.

After mulling it over, Wilson called a couple of friends whom he thought might be able to provide some sage counsel. "I called Nick Kerbawy, who had been the general manager of the Lions," said Wilson, "and he recommended Buffalo. He said there was a lot of fan interest over there, and they weren't taken in with the Browns and 49ers when the All-America [Football] Conference folded. I also called Edgar Hayes, who was the sports editor of the *Detroit Times*, and he said the same thing. Ed said, 'Listen, Ralph, let me set up a luncheon meeting with you and a man named Paul Neville, the editor of the *Buffalo Evening News*.' I said, 'Gee, don't bother with that—I'm really not interested. I don't know anybody over there.' He said, 'Just go over and have lunch with him.' I said, 'All right.' So he set up a lunch, and I flew over there.

"Paul Neville was a big football fan, as practically everybody in Buffalo is. He took me around downtown and showed me old War Memorial Stadium [at that time known as Civic Stadium]. It had a seating capacity of 30,000 to 35,000, which was certainly good enough for a new league. We had lunch and went back and forth, and I said, 'Listen, Paul, if I give you this franchise and place it in Buffalo, will your newspaper support me? I'll give you a team for three years, and we'll see what happens. Maybe the league will go bust, maybe *I'll* go bust!' He said, 'Oh yeah, we'll support you.' And I always kidded because after the three years was up, that was the last time they supported me."

That November, Wilson signed a lease with the city of Buffalo, and the Buffalo Bills were born. The league—like the many other American Football Leagues that came before it—was initially scoffed at by observers. There was even some doubt within their own ranks, for it was Wayne Valley, an executive with the Oakland Raiders franchise, who dubbed the group of owners "the Foolish Club."

"It was just a wild gamble, because bucking the NFL was a major task." Wilson observed. "It was like starting an automobile company and bucking General Motors."

Early on, Wilson was one of only three owners to maintain solid financial footing (along with Hunt and Adams). To his credit and the good fortune of the AFL, he recognized that the league's ultimate success depended on the success of each of the individual franchises. He backed up that understanding by loaning significant cash to two struggling franchises (Oakland and Boston) just to keep the overall venture afloat. In addition, he was instrumental in formulating AFL policies that ensured long-term success, such as gate and television revenue sharing. Often referred to today as "the conscience of the NFL," it was Wilson who lobbied most strenuously to have AFL games postponed on the Sunday after President John F. Kennedy's assassination. (The NFL chose to play.)

Wilson's mid-1960s Bills were an AFL powerhouse that delivered two league titles to Buffalo and established a physical style of play that forever endeared the team to the city and region. The franchise's success on the field has risen and fallen over the years, but the connection of the team to its home has remained strong.

Wilson has served on several league committees over the past half-century, but perhaps none were more important than his participation in the AFL-NFL merger negotiations. He has been an ardent promoter of the team's charitable endeavors and received the Seymour H. Knox III Humanitarian Award in 2003. Wilson and his wife, Mary, established the Ralph Wilson Medical Research

Ralph Wilson Jr. and the members of the "Foolish Club" gather in 1961. Posing seated from left are: K.S. "Bud" Adams Jr. (Houston Oilers) and AFL Commissioner Joe Foss. Standing left to right: Bill Sullivan (Boston Patriots), Cal Kuntz (Denver Broncos), Wilson (Buffalo Bills), Lamar Hunt (Dallas Texans), the League's founder, Harry Wismer (New York Titans), Wayne Valley (Oakland Raiders), and Barron Hilton (Los Angeles Chargers).

Foundation in 1999 and have contributed millions to that worthy cause, which benefits, among other organizations, Buffalo's Roswell Park Cancer Institute.

For more than five decades, the hallmark of Wilson's ownership has been loyalty—not only to Western New York and the fans, but also to his employees. Numerous are the stories describing some humanitarian act on his part, creating jobs within the organization, or coming to the rescue of a former player in need. He knows everyone in the organization by name and even receives hugs from some of his employees when he arrives from out of town.

The Wilsons reside in Grosse Pointe, Michigan. He is one of only three major sports-franchise owners who has owned the same team for more than 50 years (George Halas of the Chicago Bears and Bud Adams of the Houston Oilers/Tennessee Titans are the others). Wilson's daughter, Christy Wilson Hoffman, has been involved with the team since 1991, serving as a merchandising consultant. Another daughter, the late Linda Bogdan, became the league's first female scout when she joined the organization in 1986. In 2006, she was named vice president and assistant director of college and pro scouting, the position she held at the time of her passing in 2010.

In 1989, Mr. Wilson's name was placed on the Wall of Fame in Rich Stadium (which was, of course, renamed in Wilson's honor in 2000). In 1992, he was inducted into the Greater Buffalo Sports Hall of Fame. He received the ultimate gridiron honor when he was inducted into the Pro Football Hall of Fame on August 8, 2009, going in with Bruce Smith, one of his team's all-time greats. Although there continues to be concern over the viability of small-market teams like Buffalo in the multibillion-dollar world of today's NFL, Ralph Wilson's ongoing efforts have provided the city with more than 50 years of pro football thrills and success that has fallen just shy of a Super Bowl championship.

2 The Coach

Marv Levy is undeniably the most successful coach in the history of the Buffalo Bills. Not only does he hold the club record for most wins by a coach (112) and overall winning percentage (61.5), he also holds the record for most playoff appearances (eight) and division titles (six). He is also the only coach in NFL history to take his team to four straight Super Bowls.

Very impressive credentials, to be sure, but anyone who has had the pleasure of meeting Levy in person is more likely to walk away thinking he has just met a professor rather than a football coach. That shouldn't come as a surprise, though, since Levy was a member of the Phi Beta Kappa Society at Coe College and holds a master's degree in English history from Harvard. He is known to quote Winston Churchill, Dwight Eisenhower, or even Charles Dickens to inspire not only football players but those with whom he comes into contact in everyday life.

Levy's unlikely journey to pro football immortality began in Chicago, Illinois, where he was born Marvin Daniel Levy on August 3, 1925. The day after his graduation from South Shore High School in 1943, Levy, along with a bunch of school chums, enlisted in the Army Air Forces. Upon being discharged in 1946, he entered the University of Wyoming but quickly transferred to Coe College in Cedar Rapids, Iowa. At Coe, Levy lettered in football, track, and basketball while obtaining a degree in English literature. In 1950, Levy entered Harvard University to pursue his master's.

In 1951, Levy was hired as an English and history teacher at St. Louis Country Day School, and his position included the responsibilities of coaching the school's football and basketball teams. Two years later, he returned to Coe College as an assistant football coach under Dick Clausen, who had been Levy's head coach while he played there. When Clausen moved on to the University of New Mexico in 1954, he took much of his staff, Levy included. Levy was elevated to head coach at UNM in 1958 and over the next two seasons guided the Lobos to a 14–6 record, earning Skyline Conference Coach of the Year honors in both years. Off that success, Levy was hired in 1960 as the head coach at the University of California at Berkeley. Despite having a young, innovative assistant named Bill Walsh on his staff and also recruiting star quarterback Craig Morton, Levy's record over the next four seasons was a dismal 8–29–3.

In 1964, Levy moved on to the College of William and Mary in Williamsburg, Virginia, where he twice earned Southern Conference Coach of the Year honors and guided the Indians to a Southern Conference championship in 1966 during his five-year stint. The Tribe's 27–16 win against Navy in 1967, led by future Bills quarterback Dan Darragh, is considered one of the greatest upsets in college football history.

Levy found he missed the hustle and bustle of metropolitan living. He got his chance to return to big-city life when he was offered his first job at the professional level as a special teams coach under Jerry Williams, the new head coach of the Philadelphia Eagles. "Special teams is a designation I detest," wrote Levy in his autobiography, *Where Else Would You Rather Be?*. "To me, there are no special teams; they are kicking teams." At the time, Levy was only the second such assistant to be hired by an NFL team. Only a month earlier, George Allen of the Los Angeles Rams made history when he hired a young Dick Vermeil as the first-ever special teams coach.

When Vermeil left the Rams in 1970, he recommended Levy as his replacement. Allen took Vermeil's advice and hired Levy in February 1970, but after a single season with the Rams, Allen and his staff were fired. When Allen took over the Washington Redskins in 1971, he called on Levy to coach his kicking teams. Levy had his first taste of football's ultimate game not with the Bills, but with the Redskins. Unfortunately, Washington fell to the Miami Dolphins in Super Bowl VIII.

By this time, Levy's reputation was gaining traction throughout the pro football world, and teams saw him as a potential head coach. In 1973, he accepted an offer to become the head man of the Montreal Alouettes of the Canadian Football League. His five seasons up north proved very successful, including three Grey Cup appearances and two championships. He also won Coach of the Year honors in 1974.

Levy accepted his first NFL head coaching job in 1978 with the Kansas City Chiefs. The Chiefs had finished with a 2–12 record the year before Levy arrived, and in the rebuilding phase that predominated Levy's first season, he installed a ball-control offense known as the Wing-T, which he had employed to great success while head coach at the University of New Mexico. (The Wing-T is a blend of the single-wing and standard T formation, employing the motion and power of the single-wing while having the quarterback taking the snap directly from center as in the T formation. The modern version of the Wing-T employs two wing backs and a single halfback and relies on having an option quarterback.) The decision to use the Wing-T drew criticism, but it did help the Chiefs to double their number of wins in Levy's first year. The Chiefs improved in each season under Levy's watch, but after going 3–6 in the strike-shortened 1982 season, Levy was fired.

After interviewing for the head coaching job with the Bills (which ultimately went to Kay Stephenson) in 1983, Levy spent a season above—instead of on—the sideline, analyzing United States Football League games for ABC Radio. In 1984, he was offered the opportunity to return to his hometown of Chicago to coach the Blitz—the team representing the Windy City in the USFL.

"I had missed coaching," Levy recalled. "I yearned to organize a staff, to work with young men, to teach fundamentals, to plan strategy, to pore over films and scouting reports, and to compete every week against worthy opponents. I had heard and read about coaches having experienced 'burnout,' but I knew I wasn't afflicted with that malady."

Levy was joined in the Blitz front office by Bill Polian (with whom he had become acquainted while with the Alouettes), the team's director of player personnel, and John Butler, then serving the club as a scout. But after the season, the Blitz folded and Levy, again a coach without a team, briefly returned to broadcasting. A year later, he accepted an offer to return to the Alouettes as the team's director of football operations. In the meantime, Polian had taken over as the general manager of the Buffalo Bills and was endeavoring to reverse the fortunes of the moribund franchise that was mired in its third straight losing campaign in 1986. Polian convinced Ralph Wilson that Marv Levy was just the man they needed to lead the charge on the field.

After his Bills were embarrassed by the 1–7 Buccaneers in Week 9, Ralph Wilson fired then–head coach Hank Bullough and replaced him with Polian's old friend. Levy arrived at Rich Stadium on Monday, November 3, ushering in a bright new era in Buffalo Bills history.

"I came rushing down from Montreal, where I was when the phone call came," Levy remembered. "It was a windy day when I arrived in Buffalo. I walked into the team meeting room my first day, and sitting in it were fellows like Jim Kelly, Bruce Smith, Andre Reed, Darryl Talley, Kent Hull, Jim Ritcher, Fred Smerlas, Will Wolford, Jerry Butler, Mike Hamby, Pete Metzelaars, and many others whom I would come to like and admire. They were nine games into the season and had won only two of them. In each of the previous two years they had finished 2–14—and yet I perceived a sense of optimism among the young men in that room. In just six days they'd be taking the field against one of the best teams in the league—the Pittsburgh Steelers."

The Bills defeated the Steelers 16–12 in Levy's debut, and despite going 2–5 down the stretch, it was clear they were headed in the right direction. But the task that lay before Levy wasn't an easy one. "What the team needed was realism," he said. "This was a weary football team, beaten down mentally by losing. I never mentioned the word *win*. I talked about performance."

Rather than try to implement a system and make his players adjust to it, Levy decided to allow the team's strengths to dictate the direction it would take. After all, he had an abundance of talent on the squad; he just needed to find a way to best utilize it.

In 1987, Levy's first full season with the Bills, the team improved to 7–8, barely missing the playoffs in a season shortened by a players' strike. A year later, the Bills drafted Thurman Thomas, giving them a running back to complement Kelly's passing. The results were immediate as the team went 12–4 and captured their first AFC East title since 1980 and Levy was named NFL Coach of the Year.

But things started unraveling in 1989 as the team favored by many to win the AFC crown became known as the "Bickering Bills," as players began to let their egos get the better of them. The Bills finished a disappointing 9–7, but it was good enough to win the AFC East, and they went on to play the Cleveland Browns in the divisional playoffs. After falling behind 31–21 after three quarters, the Bills were forced to use their two-minute offense almost exclusively throughout the fourth quarter. The Bills ultimately came up short, but the explosiveness of their two-minute offense inspired the head coach. The man once accused of being ultraconservative was about to shatter that perception.

"On the trip back home to Buffalo after the game," Levy recalled, "our offensive coordinator, Ted Marchibroda, and our offensive line coach, Tom Bresnahan, stopped by my seat on the airplane. They needed to tap me on the shoulder in order to get my attention since I was deep in thought, mulling over some off-the-wall idea. When I looked up, Ted spoke. 'Marv, Tom and I have been talking. What would you think about our making that no-huddle, hurry-up scheme something that we feature right from the opening kickoff next season?' I was stunned. Not because of their 'outlandish' suggestion, but because Ted had just echoed the thought that had me so engrossed. And so was born the Buffalo Bills' style of offense that would propel us, beginning the following season, to four consecutive AFC championships."

Fueled by the no-huddle, the Bills began an unprecedented run in 1990 that saw them earn four straight trips to the Super Bowl. From 1990 to 1993, the Bills won an imposing 76.6 percent (49–15) of their regular-season games and 69.2 percent (9–4) of their postseason contests. And despite their failure to win any of their four Super Bowls, the fact that the Bills were able to repeat three times proves them to be one of the most resilient teams the league has ever seen.

During Levy's 11½ seasons in Buffalo, the team recorded 112 regular-season wins against 70 losses for an overall percentage of 61.5, appeared in the postseason eight times, and won six division championships. Between 1988 and 1997, the Bills were the winningest team in the AFC and second only to San Francisco league-wide. For his efforts, Levy was named NFL Coach of the Year in 1988 and AFC Coach of the Year in 1988, 1993, and 1995.

He was voted into the Pro Football Hall of Fame in 2001, and though this honor is often seen as the final chapter in a storied NFL career, Levy proved he wasn't finished. On January 5, 2006, at the age of 80, Levy was hired as the Buffalo Bills' general manager. While his two-year tenure overseeing the Bills' football operations was not nearly as successful as his stint as head coach, at least two players he brought in (Fred Jackson and Kyle Williams) are contributing in a big way to the team's recent resurgence.

Now fully retired from the game, Levy continues to stay active as a motivational speaker and as a color commentator. He also has delved more seriously into the literary sphere. His first book, an autobiography called *Where Else Would You Rather Be?* (the title based upon one of Marv's most famous catchphrases), was published in 2004. In 2009, he produced a collaborative effort with this author called *Game Changers: The Greatest Plays in Buffalo Bills Football History*. In 2011, Levy published his first fictional work, *Between the Lies*, which features a team based loosely on the Bills (including a quarterback named Kelly James). The book was very well received, and the very active octogenarian hints that other books may follow.

3 The Champs

The 1964 AFL title game was the culmination of the most successful season in the Buffalo Bills' five-year existence. Buffalo's 12–2 record was the best in the league that year, and the defense, the centerpiece of the team, was one of the most dominant ever fielded, yielding a league-low 242 points and going the last eight games without giving up a rushing touchdown. Their opponent, the San Diego Chargers—winners of the Western Division crown with an 8–5–1 record—were favored, and why not? They had played in three of the previous four title games and had won in 1963. Their offense was a veritable constellation of stars, featuring the likes of Keith Lincoln, Paul Lowe, Ron Mix, Tobin Rote, and Lance Alworth (although Alworth was sitting this one out with an injury).

They were intimidating on defense, too, featuring a front wall appropriately dubbed "the Fearsome Foursome," anchored by

6'9", 290-pound defensive tackle Ernie Ladd and 6'5", 270-pound defensive end Earl Faison. But they were also guilty of being a little overconfident, as evidenced by a brash gesture by Faison during pregame warm-ups.

"San Diego was on one side of the field, and we were on the other," said Bills cornerback Butch Byrd. "We were huddled up, and Lou Saban was giving us a 'rah-rah' speech. From out of nowhere, Faison leaned into our huddle and said, 'You guys better play—I'm gonna kill somebody today!' And Faison was huge—I just looked at him. Everyone looked at him. He was just wide-eyed."

The Chargers received the opening kick and immediately established that they planned to pound it out on the ground. Keith Lincoln went 38 yards on a first-down draw then carried again for five more. Two plays later, quarterback Tobin Rote hit tight end Dave Kocourek for a 26-yard touchdown and the game's first lead.

The Bills went nowhere with their first possession and were forced to punt, and the Chargers went right back to work. But their drive came to an abrupt halt at 6:41 when linebacker Mike Stratton nailed Lincoln with perhaps the most famous tackle in AFL history. Facing a second-and-10 at their own 34, the Chargers called a play that the Bills' All-League defender knew he had seen before.

"They seemed to have a pattern that they ran where they would flare the back out of the backfield behind the line of scrimmage," Stratton recalled. "At the same time, they would run the wide receiver on a curl, and then they would key on the linebacker. If the linebacker came up to cover the back, they would automatically throw to the curl. If the linebacker went back to cover the curl, they would throw to the back."

After seeing the play a couple of times, Stratton responded. "When the pattern came again, I just turned my head and started running for the outside receiver. After I ran about four or five steps, I turned around and looked back and started back toward the flare back. I had run far enough to discourage them; I'd better go for the back."

"Rote was looking for someone else and then dumped it off to Lincoln," Byrd recalled. "It looked like Lincoln had clear sailing. The ball kind of floated out there, and Mike, with his great speed, just closed on Lincoln. I was watching the ball, and I was watching Lincoln, and I could see they were going to get there at the same time."

"I saw the ball in the air," said Stratton, "and I was running like the devil to get to the back before he caught the ball and was able to juke me and pick up the first down. I knew it was going to be close. I got to Lincoln about the same time the ball did, and that was that. I knew it was a substantial collision."

"It was a fantastic hit," recalled Bills longtime trainer Eddie Abramoski, who saw the play unfold up close from the Buffalo sideline. "He just timed it perfectly. Lincoln broke three ribs on the play and had to leave the game."

According to All-Pro guard Billy Shaw, the Stratton hit completely changed the complexion of the game. "When Mike made this play, that turned things around. Up until that point, [the Chargers] had the momentum. They had already scored. Because Keith was gone, we had a chance."

Coach Saban agreed: "The Stratton hit actually turned the key. From that point on, we felt we did have a chance to win it. Mike's hit was a display of defensive strength. It lit the flame."

On their next possession, the Bills drove 64 yards in six plays to set up a 12-yard Pete Gogolak field goal. Buffalo took a 10–7 lead midway through the second quarter on a four-yard plunge by Wray Carlton. Gogolak added a 14-yarder later in the period to make it 13–7. The Chargers drove into Buffalo territory on their next possession and were threatening to score with time winding down in the half. But Stratton made another brilliant defensive play, picking off Rote at the Buffalo 15 and protecting the Bills' six-point lead.

The third quarter was a defensive stalemate, with neither offense able to produce points, but the Bills broke through early in the fourth after forcing a San Diego punt and taking possession at their own 48. On first down, Kemp threw a look-in to Glenn Bass at the San Diego 35, and the fleet receiver broke free for a spectacular 51-yard gain, taking the Bills down to the 1. Two plays later, Kemp snuck in to make it 20–7 Buffalo.

But the proud Chargers weren't ready to throw in the towel just yet. Speedy Duncan returned the ensuing kickoff to the Buffalo 46, giving his team a momentary lift. John Hadl—in for the ineffective Rote—drove the Chargers to within five yards of the Bills end zone, but his fourth-down pass was incomplete and the Bills took over. The Chargers forced the Bills to punt on the following drive, but former Charger Paul Maguire put the nail in the coffin when his kick rolled out of bounds at the San Diego 2-yard line with two minutes remaining. The Bills held off the Chargers' last effort and claimed a 20–7 victory and the AFL championship.

There was no doubt that Buffalo was the better team that day, as they outgained San Diego 387 yards to 259, collecting 21 first downs to the Chargers' 15. Even the Chargers knew it. "It was such a totally dominated game," recalled Chuck Ward, who covered the game for the *Wellsville Daily Reporter*. "The Chargers locker room was fine. They got the crap kicked out of them, and there wasn't much they could do about it. They said, 'Boy, they were good today.' It was a huge thing for us. It just confirmed that Buffalo was big-league."

"We all pulled together," said Buffalo's Booker Edgerson. "There was no selfishness on the team, and I think that that's where our success was. It was a very jubilant time."

4 Super Bowl XXV

"The Bills are going to the Super Bowl!"

"I don't believe it!"

"I never thought I'd see the day!"

"Next year has finally arrived!"

"I told you so!"

"Holy cow!" (Or some not-so-family-friendly variation on that theme.)

These are just a few examples of what Western New Yorkers were saying after the Bills clinched their first-ever Super Bowl berth by crushing the Oakland Raiders 51–3 in the 1990 AFC Championship Game. Fans and casual observers alike were astounded, whether by disbelief or elation, that their team had finally made it to the pinnacle of the National Football League.

It had been three decades in the making. But to fully understand how the Bills had finally gotten to this point, one need look no further than 1986. Hank Bullough, the Bills' decidedly unpopular head coach at the time, had the team off to a 2–7 start despite a roster that contained such names as Fred Smerlas, Bruce Smith, Andre Reed, Darryl Talley, Kent Hull, and Jim Kelly. The players, frustrated with the team's lack of direction and culture of losing, were ready to revolt.

Despite a reputation for stinginess, Bills owner Ralph Wilson had demonstrated his commitment to winning by loosening the purse strings enough to sign Kelly, but with each passing week Wilson saw his investment swirling down the drain. When his Bills were embarrassed by the 1–7 Buccaneers in Week 9, Wilson had seen enough. That evening, the exasperated owner informed Bullough that his services were no longer required.

To replace Bullough, Wilson and general manager Bill Polian tapped Marv Levy. Levy arrived in Orchard Park on Monday, November 3, ushering in the greatest era in the history of the franchise.

The reenergized Bills defeated the Steelers in their first game under Levy and, despite a losing record going down the stretch, appeared to finally be heading in the right direction. During the off-season, several more talented players were acquired, including linebacker Shane Conlan and cornerback Nate Odomes. But the high hopes that greeted the squad as they returned to camp were dashed during the strike-shortened season that saw the Bills finish out of the playoffs at 7–8.

Things really started clicking in 1988, however, and the team appeared to be on the verge of local sports history when they finished 12–4 and made it all the way to the AFC Championship Game. But the Bills, for the second time in their existence, fell one game short of the Super Bowl, losing 21–10 to the Cincinnati Bengals.

It all appeared to be unraveling in 1989 as the team favored by many to win the AFC crown was overcome by petty locker-room squabbling that boiled over into public mudslinging and backbiting. Given the enormity of talent present in that locker room, perhaps it was only a matter of time before egos would start to clash. The Bickering Bills limped to a 9–7 finish, but it was enough for a playoff berth against Cleveland. But when they met the Browns in that fateful game, they fell behind by 10 points after three quarters. They were forced to use their two-minute offense almost exclusively in the fourth quarter, and despite coming up short, the fast-paced approach proved effective. Levy planned to use the new strategy going forward.

The Bills opened the next season with their new no-huddle offense and ran roughshod over Jeff George and the Indianapolis Colts for a 26–10 triumph. A Week 2 loss to Miami proved little more than a speed bump on the road to the promised land as the Bills rebounded for a 30–7 destruction of the Jets in Week 3, kicking off a string of eight straight victories. The explosive Bills finished the season at 13–3 and held home-field advantage throughout the playoffs.

The Bills faced Miami in the AFC divisional playoff. Jim Kelly, after missing the last two regular-season games, returned with a vengeance (19 completions on 29 attempts, 339 yards, and three touchdowns) to outgun Dan Marino (23 of 49, 323 yards, and three touchdowns) and guide the Bills to a 44–34 victory in the highest-scoring non-overtime playoff game in NFL history. A week later, the Bills hosted the Los Angeles Raiders in the AFC Championship Game, a game that was over almost from the moment it began. Buffalo built up a 21–3 lead by the end of the first quarter and rolled to an easy 51–3 victory. Kelly gave another brilliant performance, completing 17 of 23 passing attempts for 300 yards and two touchdowns, while Thurman Thomas picked up 199 yards from scrimmage (138 rushing, 61 receiving).

The Buffalo Bills were going to their first Super Bowl! (Holy ——!)

The Big Game itself is remembered as one of the most exciting Super Bowls ever played, particularly with Operation Desert Storm going on at the same time. The Giants employed a plodding, ball-control offense designed to keep the ball away from Kelly and the Bills' high-octane offense. That strategy worked beautifully, as the Giants were able to hold on to the ball for 40 minutes and 33 seconds (a Super Bowl record) compared to Buffalo's 19 minutes and 27 seconds.

New York grabbed the game's first lead on a 28-yard Matt Bahr field goal midway through the first quarter. Buffalo stormed back to take a 12–3 advantage on a 23-yard kick by Scott Norwood, a one-yard run by Don Smith, and a two-point safety when Bruce Smith sacked quarterback Jeff Hostetler in the end zone. But the Giants defense stiffened, forcing the Bills to punt in back-to-back possessions. Hostetler then led a drive that culminated with a 14-yard touchdown toss to Stephen Baker, cutting Buffalo's lead to two points at the half.

The Giants burst from their locker room with the most time-consuming drive in Super Bowl history, which O.J. Anderson—the game's MVP—capped with a one-yard plunge, giving New York a 17–12 bulge. Early in the fourth quarter, Thurman Thomas broke free for a stunning 31-yard touchdown run, and suddenly the Bills were back on top by two. The Giants then put together a drive that ate up more than seven minutes of the clock and resulted in another Bahr field goal, putting them up by a point with 7:20 left in regulation. After an exchange of possessions, Kelly led the Bills offense onto the field with 2:16 to go and the ball resting at their own 10. He drove them as far as the New York 29 and then spiked the ball to stop the clock with eight seconds left.

It all came down to a 47-yard field-goal attempt by Scott Norwood. What happened next inspired what has become the most painful two-word phrase in Buffalo sports history (which, in the interest of good taste, will not be repeated here). It was a bitter pill to swallow, but the Bills would be back.

5 The Arm

Rugged swashbuckler Jim Kelly was a quarterback with a line-backer mentality, and if legendary Penn State coach Joe Paterno had his way, Kelly would have been a seek-and-destroy specialist at Linebacker U. However, the cocky young signal-caller from East Brady, Pennsylvania, would have none of it, and the Buffalo Bills and their fans should be forever grateful.

At East Brady High School, about 55 miles northeast of Pittsburgh, Kelly won All-State honors at quarterback and also led the school basketball team to the state semifinals. Jim was eager to play for Paterno at Penn State, but when he learned that Joe Pa was intent on turning him into a linebacker, Kelly balked. He instead enrolled at the University of Miami, becoming the first in a string of great quarterbacks (Vinny Testaverde, Bernie Kosar, Steve Walsh) to emerge from the school in the 1980s, finishing his career with 5,233 passing yards and 32 touchdowns despite suffering a severe shoulder separation as a senior.

When the Buffalo Bills selected Kelly with their first pick in the 1983 draft, however, the 6'2" 217-pounder balked again. "You can't be a great quarterback in snow and 30-mile-per-hour wind," he said. Kelly instead cast his lot with the Houston Gamblers of the upstart United States Football League and, after rehabbing his injured shoulder, became that circuit's top passer. In two seasons playing in the Gamblers' run-and-shoot offense, Kelly passed for 9,842 yards and 83 touchdowns and completed better than 63 percent of his throws. In 1984, he set USFL records by passing for 5,219 yards and 44 touchdowns and was named the league's Most Valuable Player. Because the Gamblers folded after Kelly's second season, he signed on with Donald Trump's New Jersey Generals in 1986. Fortunately for Bills fans, the USFL collapsed before Kelly could play a down with the Generals. Buffalo still held his NFL rights, and after three days of heated negotiations, Kelly signed a five-year, $7.5 million contract on August 18, 1986, to play for the team he once shunned.

He arrived in Western New York later that day to a welcome that would have made the Beatles proud. As the limo transporting everyone's new favorite Bill made its way toward downtown Buffalo, screaming fans lined the streets waving flags, pennants, and signs; snapping photos; and boisterously toasting his arrival. A press conference was held at the Hilton and was broadcast live over every local television and radio station. Immediately, ticket sales took off. Without playing a single game, Kelly had almost single-handedly saved the franchise from financial ruin.

Jim was an immediate hit with Buffalo fans, who saw in him the very embodiment of the blue-collar, never-say-die toughness for which their city was known. Here was a quarterback who simply refused to accept losing, and that attitude was contagious. Aided by GM Bill Polian's transition of the roster, the Bills improved to 4–12 in Kelly's first year, and in 1987, the team's first full season under head coach Marv Levy, they barely missed out on the play-offs with a 7–8 mark in that strike year.

Things finally came together for the Bills in 1988, the year they drafted halfback Thurman Thomas. With the multitalented Thomas taking much of the heat off Kelly and the passing game, the Bills finished at 12–4, claimed their first division title since 1980, and made it all the way to the AFC title game, only to fall short of the ultimate goal by losing to the Bengals.

But the dream appeared to be evaporating as the 1989 season unfolded into Bickering Bills drama. The loss of focus and cohesion was reflected on the field, as the team barely made the playoffs. Despite losing 34–30 to the Browns in the divisional playoff round, Kelly finished the game with 405 passing yards and four touchdowns and nearly pulled off a miraculous come-from-behind victory in the game's dying moments. Head coach Marv Levy was convinced that the two-minute offense, later called the "no-huddle" or "K-Gun" (not for Kelly but rather tight end Keith McKeller) should be the Bills' primary offensive attack in the upcoming season.

With Kelly at the controls of the no-huddle offense—the only quarterback at that time calling the majority of his own plays—the Bills dominated the AFC, finishing 13–3 to claim not only the Eastern Division title but also home-field advantage throughout the playoffs, as they led the league in scoring. Kelly enjoyed a monster season, leading the league with a 101.2 passer rating and a

Jim Kelly celebrates a touchdown completion—something the beloved Bills quarterback did 237 times in his Hall of Fame career.

63.3 completion percentage while throwing 24 touchdown passes and only nine interceptions. He led Buffalo over its first two playoff opponents by a combined 95–37 score to earn the franchise's first Super Bowl berth. Against the Giants in Super Bowl XXV, Kelly had a strong game, completing 18 of his 30 passes for 212 yards and driving the Bills to within field-goal range in the game's dying seconds, but a tortuously close missed field goal cost the team their best chance to date at a Super Bowl victory.

Kelly came back strong in '91, leading the league in touchdown passes with 33 and guiding the Bills to a second straight 13–3 finish. But the Bills lost a second consecutive Super Bowl, this time against the Washington Redskins, 37–24, in what was easily the low point in Kelly's otherwise phenomenal year, as he connected on less than 50 percent of his passes (28 of 58) and threw four interceptions.

He would have the Bills back in the Super Bowl twice more, but the results were the same in both: humiliating losses to the Dallas Cowboys. As a result, the Bills were the first, and still only, franchise to make four straight Super Bowl appearances. Unfortunately, they are also the first and only team to *lose* four straight.

After missing the playoffs in 1994 for the first time in seven years, the Bills returned in 1995 and '96 but were no longer a serious Super Bowl contender.

Kelly retired after the 1996 season. During his 11 seasons with the Bills, Kelly completed 2,874 of 4,779 passes for 35,467 yards and 237 touchdowns, all of which are Buffalo records. Behind Kelly's leadership, Buffalo outscored the league average by 11 percent, appeared in the postseason eight times, and won four AFC championships. Jim also registered 29 fourth-quarter comeback victories, placing him 12th in league history. (Denver's John Elway is the all-time leader with 42.) Kelly's numbers, however, begin to look a lot more impressive when you consider that his 29 comebacks occurred in 160 regular-season starts, giving him an overall percentage of 18.1. That places him just a hair shy of Elway, who registered 42 comebacks in 231 starts for a percentage of 18.2. To honor its greatest quarterback, Buffalo both retired Kelly's jersey number and added him to its Wall of Fame in 2001.

Shortly after his retirement from the football field, Kelly and his wife, Jill, were met with a challenge far greater than anything he had ever faced on a football field. On Jim's 37th birthday (February 14, 1997), Jill gave birth to a son, Hunter James Kelly. Shortly after his birth, Hunter was diagnosed with Krabbe leukodystrophy, an inherited and fatal nervous system disorder. Hunter died as a result of the disease on August 5, 2005, at the age of eight.

Ever since Hunter's diagnosis, the Jim and Jill have dedicated their lives to raising awareness and supporting research into finding a cure, beginning with the founding of their Hunter's Hope Foundation in 1997. The Kellys' tireless advocacy on behalf of Krabbe patients has promoted national awareness of the disease.

When Jim was inducted into the Pro Football Hall of Fame in 2002, his presenter, coach Marv Levy, noted of Kelly, "He inspired others with his work ethic and with his indomitable competitive spirit. He exuded confidence and he transmitted that quality to all of his teammates. He was a morale builder, a man who truly loved the game."

Kelly dedicated his induction to Hunter in a heartfelt, moving speech:

Then there is my only son, Hunter, born on February 14th, Valentine's Day, my birthday. The son I've always wanted. I've dreamt what every father dreams about: playing catch in the backyard, going fishing, camping, everything that fathers and sons do. But within four months my son was diagnosed with a fatal disease called Krabbe leukodystrophy. They told us to take him home and make him comfortable. And from that day, my wife and I decided to fight this disease. And so, we made it our lifelong commitment to make sure that kids all over the world don't suffer like my son does. Since the day I was selected, I prayed to God that my son would be here with me today. God has granted me that blessing. It has been written throughout my career that toughness is my trademark. Well, the toughest person I've ever met in my life is my hero, my soldier, my son, Hunter. I love you, buddy.

On and off the field, there has been no finer representative of the Buffalo Bills than Jim Kelly.

6 The Quest

It's always easy to say "I told you so" in hindsight, but Reggie McKenzie can speak those four words without fear of equivocation. After all, the Bills guard saw his friend and teammate O.J. Simpson come into his own in 1972 to win the NFL rushing title after putting up disappointing numbers in his first three pro seasons. McKenzie watched as Lou Saban, the mastermind behind the Bills' AFL championships of the 1960s, returned to Buffalo after a six-year hiatus and designed his offense around the former Heisman Trophy–winning halfback. Saban built a mobile and powerful offensive line (McKenzie and fellow guard Joe DeLamielleure, tackle Dave Foley, center Mike Montler, and tight end Paul Seymour to complement holdover tackle Donnie Green and center Bruce Jarvis) designed to give Simpson the room he needed to reach the lofty peaks reserved for only the greatest runners in the game. McKenzie was convinced that Simpson was on the verge of a greatness no other back had ever reached. He wasn't kidding when he confidently predicted that Simpson—behind Saban's strategic plan and a solid offensive line—could become the first man to break the 2,000-yard barrier.

But as every cliché-uttering athlete reminds us, pro football is played one game at a time. So before McKenzie could say "I told you so" to those who scoffed at his brash prediction, the Bills would have to play 14 games—and Simpson, for his part, would need to average almost 143 yards in each. While the rest of the team felt it was attainable, Simpson himself wasn't so sure. After all, the single-season rushing record was 1,863, set by Jim Brown in 1963, and he averaged *only* 133 yards per game in that season. Simpson settled on a goal of 1,700 yards for the year. It was McKenzie who upped the ante to 2,000. Thus, a quest was born.

Week 1 found the Bills at Foxborough, Massachusetts, facing the New England Patriots. Simpson left little doubt that he was the top rusher in the entire league, and—if his record-setting performance that day was any indication—among the top backs of all time. Simpson erupted for 250 yards, breaking the old mark of 247 set two years earlier by Willie Ellison of the Los Angeles Rams. The play that set the tone—not only for this remarkable performance but for the rest of the season—came late in the first quarter, when Simpson took a handoff from rookie quarterback Joe Ferguson, swept around the right end, broke into the clear along the right sideline, and sprinted his way to a dazzling 80-yard touchdown run.

Simpson followed up his spectacular opening-day performance with a 103-yard effort against the Chargers in Week 2 and 123 yards in Week 3 against the Jets. After gaining 171 yards against the Eagles in Week 4, Simpson had 647 yards for an astounding per-game average of 161.75! Every football writer and fan had one eye trained on Simpson's compelling story, and Brown's "unbreakable" record suddenly seemed attainable. Simpson kept up the unbelievable pace with 166 yards against the Colts but tailed off against the Dolphins in Week 6, held to just 55 yards by the vaunted "No Name Defense."

Game 7 was a Monday night affair at home against Kansas City. With a national television audience tuned in, Simpson returned to form with 157 yards and surpassed the 1,000 mark at the halfway point of the season—the earliest the plateau had been reached by any back in history. Not only was he ahead of Brown's record pace (averaging 146 yards per outing), he was on pace to reach McKenzie's bold prediction of 2,000 yards.

But Simpson fell into a two-game slump in Weeks 8 and 9, gaining just 79 yards against the Saints and 99 yards versus the Bengals. He got back above the century mark with a 120-yard performance against the Dolphins, 124 yards against the Colts, and 137 against the Falcons, but even at that fast pace he still was losing ground in the quest for 2,000. After 12 games, Simpson had amassed 1,584 yards—an average of 132 yards per game. He would need to average 140 yards in the remaining contests to surpass Brown's record; it would take 208 yards per game to hit the magic mark of 2,000.

In Week 13, a wintry December afternoon at Rich Stadium against the Patriots, "Juice" rushed for 219 yards to pull within 60 yards of Brown but 197 shy of the ultimate goal.

The season finale had the Bills facing Joe Namath and the New York Jets at Shea Stadium. It was another cold, snowy day, but as Simpson had proved the week before, field conditions were of no consequence to him.

"I can't fail to mention how amazing Simpson played in bad weather," said DeLamielleure. "While other guys were slipping and sliding in an inch of water—or half a foot of snow—on the field, O.J. could plant and cut as if it were dry as a bone."

After gaining 57 yards on Buffalo's first possession, Simpson

Rushing Superlatives

It would be another 11 years before Eric Dickerson of the Los Angeles Rams became the second man to reach 2,000 yards. He shattered Simpson's record with 2,105 in 1984. By that time, the NFL had expanded its regular season to 16 games, so Simpson's accomplishment was perhaps more meaningful. Since then, only four other backs have topped the 2,000-yard mark: Barry Sanders (2,053 in 1997), Terrell Davis (2,008 in 1998), Jamal Lewis (2,066 in 2003), and Chris Johnson (2,006 in 2009).

Great backs all, of course, but Bills fans will always remember the one who did it first.

eclipsed Brown's mark with a six-yard run to the left behind DeLamielleure. The game was stopped, and referee Bob Frederic presented Simpson with the ball he had lugged for the record. After a short celebration, the game resumed. The record now in the books, the Bills focused on realizing the prediction that McKenzie had made back in training camp. But Simpson, perhaps distracted from the task at hand, fumbled the ball away on the very next play.

Early in the fourth quarter, the Bills were up 31–7 and the offense knew Simpson was close. "Joe Ferguson came in and said I needed 50 yards for 2,000," recalled Simpson. "We broke 20 off right away, and we were going after it then." At 8:32, Simpson reached the milestone with a seven-yard run through the left guard. Another celebration ensued, but this time Simpson did not return to the game. What else was there to prove?

Simpson's final total of 2,003 yards led the NFL and gave him his second consecutive rushing title. The event thrust Simpson into the national limelight, and one of our own Buffalo Bills became— along with boxer Muhammad Ali—one of the two most famous athletes in the world.

7 The Comeback

As the Buffalo Bills trudged into their locker room at halftime of the 1992 AFC Wild Card Game against the Houston Oilers, it looked as if the team's string of Super Bowl appearances would be ending at two. After 30 minutes of play, the Oilers looked to be in total control, leading 28–3, with a time-of-possession advantage of better than two-to-one (21:21 to 8:39). Warren Moon had been as close to perfect as a quarterback could be, completing 19 of 22 pass attempts for 220 yards and four scores.

It wasn't much of a surprise that the game was going so well for Houston, since the Oilers had clobbered the Bills 27–3 in the regular-season finale just one week earlier. The Bills were playing without starting quarterback Jim Kelly (who had been hurt in the previous Houston game) and star linebacker Cornelius Bennett and would lose halfback Thurman Thomas to injury before the first half was over. Even some of those hardy Bills fans had their doubts, as evidenced by the fact that this playoff game failed to sell out.

The Oilers established their dominance early, as Moon moved the famed run-and-shoot offense up and down the field almost at will. On Houston's first possession, he engineered a beautiful 80-yard drive that ended with a three-yard touchdown toss to receiver Haywood Jeffires, giving the Oilers a 7–0 lead. Bills quarterback Frank Reich, filling in for Kelly, responded with a drive that took the Bills to the Houston 18. Steve Christie then nailed a 36-yard field goal to make it 7–3 at the end of the first quarter.

The Oilers struck back in the second quarter when Moon put together another 80-yard drive, this time ending with a seven-yard touchdown strike to Webster Slaughter. After forcing Buffalo into a three-and-out, the Oilers added another touchdown when

Moon connected with Curtis Duncan for a 26-yard score. Moon continued to pour it on, extending the Houston lead to 25 points when he hit Jeffires from 27 yards out with less than two minutes remaining in the half. The Oilers strutted off the field at halftime with a 28–3 lead.

"In the somber locker room, I did not resort to any pep-talk theatrics," said Bills head coach Marv Levy. "All I recall saying was, 'You are two-time defending AFC champions. When you walk off the field 30 minutes from now, don't let anyone be able to say you quit, that you gave up.' Then I walked over to Frank Reich and said, 'Frank, I understand that you led the greatest comeback in collegiate football history. Today you are going to lead the greatest comeback in NFL history.' Frank didn't say anything. He merely nodded his head." During his college days at the University of Maryland, Reich came off the bench to lead the Terrapins back from a 31–0 deficit to a 42–40 victory. It was, at the time, the greatest come-from-behind win in the history of NCAA football. But could lightning that powerful strike the same player twice?

The Bills received the kickoff in the second half and began a drive at their own 36. On third-and-9, Reich dropped back to pass. His pass, intended for tight end Keith McKeller, bounced off the big TE's hands directly into the mitts of Oilers defensive back Bubba McDowell, who then raced 58 yards for another Houston touchdown. Less than two minutes into the second half, the Oilers held a seemingly insurmountable 35–3 lead.

The Bills caught their first real break of the game when the wind shifted just as Al Del Greco was approaching the ball on the ensuing kickoff. The kick became an unintentional squib that caromed off the chest of Mark Maddox, who was stationed in the front line of Buffalo's return team. Maddox then fell on the ball to give the Bills excellent field position at midfield. Reich then drove the Bills to their first touchdown, a one-yard plunge by Kenneth Davis that cut the deficit to 35–10 with 8:52 left in the third.

Levy then instructed Steve Christie to attempt an onside kick, which the first-year Bill executed beautifully, recovering the ball himself and again giving the Bills excellent starting field position, this time from their own 48. Three plays later, Reich connected with Don Beebe on a 38-yard touchdown strike (although videotape clearly shows Beebe's left foot went partially out of bounds, which would have nullified the play had it been seen by one of the on-field officials or if there were instant replay in place at the time).

The Bills defense forced the Oilers to punt on their next possession, but all punter Greg Montgomery could muster was a 25-yard effort that gave Buffalo possession at their own 41-yard line. Meanwhile, Reich was cool as a cucumber, connecting with James Lofton for 18 yards and then on a screen pass to Kenneth Davis for 19 more before hitting Andre Reed for 26 yards and a touchdown. At 35–24, even the most pessimistic fan was beginning to believe.

The Oilers began their ensuing drive from their own 15. On first down, safety Henry Jones intercepted a Moon pass and returned it to the Houston 23. After gaining just five yards on the first three downs, the Bills were faced with a fourth-and-5 at the 18. Buffalo called timeout to discuss whether to attempt a field goal, which would bring the Bills to within eight, or go for the touchdown.

"As we conferred along the sideline," said Levy, "Frank convinced me that he had the play that would work. 'Go for it,' I told him, while the pundits slapped their foreheads with the heels of their hands." Granted, it was a risky call. If the play failed, all the momentum the Bills had built up during the quarter would evaporate. If they succeeded, however, it could leave the Oilers totally demoralized.

Reich then returned to the huddle and called his play. The offense came to the line and Reich barked the signals. He dropped back and fired a strike over the middle to Andre Reed, who hauled it in at the 7 and went into the end zone untouched. The extra point pulled the Bills to within four as the quarter ended. In a span of 6:52, the Bills had scored four touchdowns and had the Oilers, at one time holding a commanding 32-point lead, searching desperately for a way to hold back the Buffalo stampede.

After an exchange of punts to open the fourth quarter, the Oilers began a possession from their own 10. Finally settling down, they put together a methodical 15-play drive that took them deep into Buffalo territory. Houston appeared to be on the verge of another score, one that would extend their lead to 11 points, but then defensive end Phil Hansen came through with what Levy considered to be the play of the game.

On second-and-10 at the Buffalo 31, Moon called a screen pass to running back Lorenzo White. Hansen rushed in to pressure Moon, and as he jumped in the air in an attempt to block the pass, he was cut-blocked by a Houston lineman and fell to the turf. Moon's pass found its target, and White turned upfield with a convoy of blockers clearing the path toward a sure touchdown. But Hansen had not given up on the play. He leapt to his feet and took off after the Houston runner. At about the 20, Hansen dove forward in an effort to trip White, catching just enough of his heel to cause White to stumble and go down. The Bills then held on downs, forcing the Oilers to settle for a field-goal attempt. But the snap was muffed, and the Bills took possession at their own 26 with the score holding at 35–31.

"So much is remembered, as the years pass, about key plays that occurred in the great comeback game," said Levy, "but hardly anyone ever points out that touchdown-saving—and game-saving—tackle made by Phil Hansen on that early January afternoon. For me, it will remain fresh in my mind forever."

Moments later, the Bills were faced with a third-and-4 at their own 32. Offensive coordinator Jim Shofner called for a run that Kenneth Davis, playing brilliantly in Thurman Thomas' absence, broke off for a scintillating 35-yard gain. Davis might have gone all the way were it not for a diving tackle made by defensive back Steve Jackson at the Houston 33. Four plays later, Reich hit Reed for their third touchdown-pass hookup of the game, this time from 17 yards out, and the crowd went ballistic. The extra point was good, and the Bills had overcome a 35–3 deficit to take a 38–35 lead!

There was, however, still 3:08 left in regulation, and Moon wasn't giving up. He engineered a textbook 13-play, 63-yard drive that culminated in a game-tying 26-yard field goal with 15 seconds left, sending the game into overtime.

Houston won the toss and got the ball at their own 20-yard line. After picking up seven yards on two pass plays, Moon threw his 50th, and final, pass of the day. His throw was picked off by Bills cornerback Nate Odomes near midfield. A 15-yard face-mask penalty by Haywood Jeffries placed the ball at the Oilers 20. After two short Davis runs, Steve Christie—with Reich holding—booted a 32-yard field goal to win it for Buffalo, 41–38, and culminate the greatest comeback in the history of the National Football League.

Reich finished the game having completed 21 of his 34 passes for 289 yards and four touchdowns. "Without question, it's the game of my life," Reich observed. I was pretty emotional when I got back to the locker room. I couldn't hold the tears back. Your thought is to take it one play at a time and don't try to force anything. In thinking back to the experience in college, we only threw 15 times in the second half and we were down 31–0, so I knew it could be done. When we scored to make it 35–24 late in the third quarter, that's when I thought it was really within reach."

Andre Reed played spectacularly for Buffalo, catching eight passes for 136 yards and three touchdowns. For Houston, Warren Moon recorded 36 of 50 completions for 371 yards and four touchdowns—but his two interceptions were fatal.

A week later, the Bills, with Reich still calling signals, defeated the Pittsburgh Steelers 24–3 in the AFC divisional playoff round, earning the right to play in their third consecutive AFC

Championship Game against the Miami Dolphins. After dispatching the Dolphins with Jim Kelly back under center, Buffalo faced the Dallas Cowboys in Super Bowl XXVII. But there were no miracles left for the Bills or their fans, as the Cowboys rolled to a 52–17 victory.

8 Bruce Almighty

Bruce Smith is arguably the greatest Buffalo Bill of all time. In 15 seasons with the Bills, Smith appeared in 11 Pro Bowls, was chosen First-Team All-Pro nine times (and Second-Team twice more), was twice named the NFL Defensive Player of the Year, was AFC Defensive Player of the Year four times, and appeared in four Super Bowls.

Not convinced? There's more. Smith's 171 sacks are nearly 100 more than the next-closest Bills player (Aaron Schobel, 78), and his 12 seasons with 10 or more sacks tied him for the all-time NFL lead (until he assumed sole possession of the No. 1 spot with another double-digit sack season as a member of the Washington Redskins).

By the time his playing days were through, Smith was the NFL's all-time sacks leader with 200. He was enshrined in the Pro Football Hall of Fame in 2009, his first year of eligibility. He has also been named to the NFL's All-Decade Teams for both the 1980s and 1990s.

Point made?

Smith certainly lived up to the expectations the Bills had for him when they selected him with the first overall pick in the 1985 draft. He had a spectacular tenure at Virginia Tech, becoming the most honored player in the school's history. He totaled 46 career sacks with the Hokies, including 22 in his junior season alone. In 1984, Smith capped off his collegiate career by winning the Outland Trophy as the nation's top lineman and being a consensus selection to the All-America Team.

At the time, the Bills were banking on Smith being the agent of change for a franchise that had just suffered through a dreadful 2–14 season. Reporting to his first camp at 310 pounds, however, Smith struggled early on. But he was able to rebound to record six and a half sacks and recover four opponents' fumbles, earning AFC Defensive Rookie of the Year honors from the NFL Players Association. The following year, Smith reported in top physical condition and produced his first of 13 career double-digit sack seasons, notching 15 to finish fifth in the league. He earned his first Pro Bowl berth in 1987 and was named AFC Defensive Player of the Year after recording 12 sacks despite losing four games due to a players' strike.

Smith had his finest year in 1990, recording 19 sacks and 101 tackles to lead the Bills to a 13–3 record and the team's first-ever Super Bowl appearance, a performance that earned him NFL Defensive Player of the Year honors. In the Super Bowl, Smith sacked Giants quarterback Jeff Hostetler for a safety that gave Buffalo a 12–3 lead in the second quarter.

He repeated as Defensive Player of the Year in 1996, compiling 13.5 sacks and 120 tackles while forcing four fumbles.

For 15 seasons, Smith represented the cornerstone of the Bills defenses that propelled the team to 10 postseason appearances—including six straight between 1988 and 1993—and four Super Bowls. But after the Bills lost to the Tennessee Titans in the 1999 playoff game known simply as "the Music City Miracle," the Bills decided it was time to clean house and released Smith along with longtime teammates Thurman Thomas and Andre Reed.

Smith signed with the Washington Redskins and played four more years before retiring as the league's all-time leader in sacks, eclipsing longtime rival Reggie White by two (200 to 198). Since Bruce spent most of his career playing in a 3-4 defensive front, a scheme not geared toward creating sack opportunities for defensive ends, many observers consider his record all the more impressive. Proving wrong the detractors who dared to say he didn't play well against the run, Smith's career totals also include 1,225 tackles, 46 forced fumbles, and 15 fumble recoveries.

In 2005, Smith was inducted into the Virginia Sports Hall of Fame, and a year later the College Football Hall of Fame. He received dual awards in 2008, being voted into the Hampton Roads Sports Hall of Fame and the Buffalo Bills' Wall of Fame. The ultimate honor, of course, was his induction into the Pro Football Hall of Fame in 2009. Joining Smith in that year's class was Bills owner and founder, Ralph Wilson Jr.

Sadly, the only thing missing from Bruce Smith's résumé is a Super Bowl championship. Nonetheless, he was instrumental in reviving a moribund Bills franchise and driving the team to unprecedented heights.

9 Home Run Throwback

Well, some people refer to it as "Home Run Throwback." Others refer to it as "the Music City Miracle." Then there are those, like the late Tim Russert—the legendary political commentator, proud Buffalonian, and avid Bills supporter—who call it "a crime, a fraud perpetrated on the streets of Nashville." Whatever one chooses to call it, the Tennessee Titans' last-minute touchdown play that ended the 1999 AFC Wild Card Game and eliminated the Bills from the playoffs stands as one of the most controversial calls in

NFL history, and one of the most painful moments in the annals of Buffalo sports.

The Bills had made the playoffs that year mainly on the arm—and feet—of quarterback Doug Flutie, who had won 10 of 15 regular-season starts. But head coach Wade Phillips took a gamble and decided to start Rob Johnson instead of Flutie after Johnson played well in the season finale against Indianapolis. And though Johnson would play just well enough for the Bills not to lose, a special-teams snafu proved to be the Bills' undoing.

The Titans dominated the first half, their defense holding Buffalo to just 64 yards and providing the first points of the game early in the second quarter when Javon Kearse (a.k.a. "the Freak") forced Johnson to fumble out of the end zone for a safety. Titans quarterback Steve McNair extended the lead to nine points midway through the period with a one-yard touchdown run, and a 40-yard field goal by Al Del Greco as the half ran out put the Bills in a 12–0 hole at intermission.

The Bills finally came to life in the second half. Johnson led a five-play, 62-yard drive that took them to the Tennessee 4, from where Antowain Smith bulled over the goal line to make it 12–7. Early in the fourth, Johnson engineered a nine-play, 65-yard drive that Smith capped with a one-yard plunge, putting Buffalo on top for the first time in the game. Coach Phillips opted to go for a two-point conversion, but Kevin Williams dropped Johnson's pass in the end zone and the score stood at 13–12 with 11:08 remaining in regulation. But the Titans continued to fight, eventually reclaiming the lead when Del Greco made good from 36 yards out with 1:48 left. Williams brought the ensuing kickoff out to the Buffalo 39. Johnson, with no timeouts remaining, led a six-play drive to the Tennessee 23, playing the final snap with only one shoe, having lost the other on the previous play, with no time to put it back on. Christie then kicked a 41-yarder to put the Bills up by a single point with just 16 seconds showing on the clock.

The Buffalo sideline was jubilant as the Titans took the field to receive Christie's kickoff, which, barring any major breakdowns, should be a mere formality. All they had to do was keep the return as short as possible and then, if there was enough time left, defend against an improbable Hail Mary pass. Simple. But as Marv Levy, Wade Phillips' predecessor, was wont to say, "What it takes to win is simple, but it isn't easy."

Levy also preached the importance of preparation, but it seems the Titans were paying more attention to that lesson than the Bills. Alan Lowry, the Titans' special teams coach, had his squad preparing for just such a contingency by practicing a special play—dubbed "Home Run Throwback" for its employment of laterals to keep the ball alive—at least once a week all season. Until now, they had not had reason to use it. But there was one problem—Derrick Mason, Tennessee's regular return man, was out with a concussion. That forced wide receiver Kevin Dyson into the picture. Dyson had never practiced the play before, but he received an abridged lesson from Lowry before trotting onto the field.

Instead of squibbing the kickoff, Christie served up a short kick that was hauled in on the right side of the field by fullback Lorenzo Neal, who immediately handed off to tight end Frank Wycheck. Wycheck advanced forward to the 25-yard line before pulling up, pivoting to his left, and throwing the ball across the field to Dyson, also standing at the 25. "I took a hard step out and made sure it was a lateral," Dyson said later. "Once I caught it, I thought, *Get a touchdown, or good position for a field goal.*"

Dyson proceeded up the left sideline, escorted by a convoy of blockers who guided him untouched down the remaining length of the field for an incredible 75-yard touchdown and a 21–16 lead with three seconds left.

The stunned Bills desperately scanned the field for flags, but there were none to be found. However, a replay official in the press box was not satisfied that the play had not been the result of a forward pass—illegal on a kick return—and called for a review. Referee Phil Luckett spent several excruciating minutes reviewing the return from every available angle on the on-field monitor before emerging to declare his findings: "After reviewing the play on the field, it was a lateral [pass]."

The extra point made it 22–16. Bills fans, watching from the warmth of their living rooms back in Buffalo, prayed their team had a miracle of their own in store for the ensuing kickoff, but it wasn't to be.

The loss eliminated the Bills from the playoffs and ultimately cost special teams coach Bruce DeHaven his job after 13 years with the club. The game also was the last for all-time greats Thurman Thomas, Bruce Smith, and Andre Reed, as the team released all three for salary-cap reasons during the off-season.

The Titans advanced through the playoffs with subsequent victories over the Indianapolis Colts and Jacksonville Jaguars, earning a trip to Super Bowl XXXIV, which they lost to the St. Louis Rams. Buffalo fans took heart as they watched Tennessee's Kevin Dyson come up one yard short of scoring the winning touchdown in the game's dying seconds.

The AFL's Man

Like most other top prospects entering the pros during the early 1960s, Georgia Tech tackle/defensive end Billy Shaw was drafted by two teams—the Dallas Cowboys of the NFL and the Buffalo Bills of the AFL. The Cowboys selected Shaw with their 14th pick while the Bills chose Shaw with their second pick. Shaw gave serious consideration to both teams but credits

Bobby Dodd, his coach at Georgia Tech, with helping him make his final decision.

"I went to [Coach Dodd] and said, 'Coach, here are my options. Help me,'" Shaw recalled. "He said, 'There is a place in football for a new league, and you have a chance to be part of history, because if done correctly, it won't fail. It will enhance football.' And he was exactly on cue. I actually signed with Buffalo before the NFL Draft, and the reason that I did that was that Dallas had made contact with me before the draft and they wanted to play me at linebacker, and I had never played linebacker. Coach Dodd recommended that I go to Buffalo because they wanted me to play on either side of the ball."

Buster Ramsey, the Bills head coach at the time, had the rookie starting at left guard from day one, but when Lou Saban took over for Ramsey in 1962, Shaw began to wonder if he had made the right choice after all.

"I was concerned about myself [in 1962]," said Shaw. "I was struggling. When Lou came, he brought Red Miller in as his offensive line coach, and Red singled me out as his project. He said that as they reviewed the films that I was a finesse, noncontact guard, and they were going to make a player out of me. I tried to position myself at angles, because that's the way I was taught in college—that angle was more important than anything else. But Red helped me to develop into whatever level I accomplished. He was very instrumental in putting me on the right foot."

When Shaw was named All-AFL at the end of the 1962 season, there was never again any doubt that he had chosen wisely. Within a year he was considered among the best offensive linemen in the league and was the cornerstone of the forward wall that served as the foundation for the unprecedented success the team would enjoy in the mid-1960s. While the AFL became known for its progressive use of the forward pass, the Bills relied on a ball-control, NFL-style attack, which suited Shaw just fine. Although equally adept at pass blocking, Shaw was an excellent run blocker who possessed the foot speed to lead sweeps and stay in front of the runners far downfield. With Shaw and fellow linemen Al Bemiller and Stew Barber blazing the trail, the Bills became the dominant team in the AFL, making the postseason every year from 1963 to 1966 and claiming the league championship in 1964 and 1965.

For much of the decade, Shaw was the premier guard in the AFL, appearing in eight All-Star Games while being voted First-Team All-AFL five times (1962–66) and Second-Team twice more (1968–69).

But he made the surprising decision to retire on the eve of the historic merger between the AFL and NFL in 1970, despite the fact that he was only 31 and healthy enough to play for several more seasons. Shaw's early exit can be attributed to John Rauch, who had taken over as head coach in 1969.

"At the end of the '69 season he was going to move me to tackle, and I have never played anything except guard. And I really retired a year or two years early because I didn't want to go to offensive tackle."

As a Bill, Shaw was the team's most decorated player, and even in retirement the laurels continued to pour in. In 1970, he was chosen to the All-Time All-AFL Team, and he is an honoree of the Georgia Tech Athletics Hall of Fame (1979), the Bills Silver Anniversary Team (1984), the Georgia Sports Hall of Fame (1985), the Bills' Wall of Fame (1988), the Greater Buffalo Sports Hall of Fame (1994), the Mississippi Sports Hall of Fame (1996), and the Bills 50th Anniversary Team (2010). But without a doubt, the greatest honor came in 1999 when he was enshrined in the Pro Football Hall of Fame, becoming the only player so honored who spent his entire career in the American Football League.

"It took a while for it to sink in," Shaw said of the induction. "As an individual, it was the culmination of a career. Perhaps it's sad in a way, but as the only player in the Pro Football Hall of

Fame that played his whole career in the AFL, it was a sense of representing every guy that ever toiled or made an obscure team in the beginning of the AFL. And guys have called over the last few years to relay that message. It has been somewhat of a resurrection of our league. I get kidded a lot because a lot of people think it's the 'NFL Pro Football Hall of Fame' and 'you never played in the NFL' and 'why are *you* in it?'"

Ask anybody who saw him play, and you will have your answer.

11 Visit Bills Greats in Canton

Since 1963, the Pro Football Hall of Fame in Canton, Ohio, has served as both a shrine and a museum dedicated to honoring and preserving the legacy of the all-time greats of professional football. The decision to place the Hall in the relatively small northeastern Ohio city of Canton was based mainly on the fact that it was the site of the formative meetings of the American Professional Football Association (renamed the National Football League in 1922) and that the league's first president and star player, Jim Thorpe, played for the Canton Bulldogs for several years.

It is only fitting, then, that the first thing visitors notice upon entering the facility is a stunning, seven-foot bronze statue of Thorpe. From there, visitors are treated to exhibits covering literally everything about pro football from the creation and history of the NFL to individual accomplishments (such as O.J. Simpson's 2,000-yard season), the racial integration of the league, game officiating, the Super Bowl, the evolution of protective equipment and uniforms, rival professional leagues (like the AAFC, WFL, USFL, XFL, and four different AFLs), and much, much more.

The facility has seen many changes and expansions since its opening, staying in step with technological advancements. The Hall features a plethora of interactive, high-tech exhibits including a Teletrivia game, Call-the-Play Theater, a throwing cage, and a Madden EA Sports video game display. Then there is the Super Bowl Theater, which features a 20-foot-tall screen that brings the fan closer to the game with its state-of-the-art projection and sound equipment.

A feature of the Hall that researchers and historians find essential is the Archives and Information Center (AIC), located in the lower level of the fifth building. The AIC's collection contains nearly 20 million documents and more than 2 million photographs. Some items in the collection date to as far back as the 1860s. There is a separate file for every NFL team, and nearly every player, dating back to 1920. The only catch is that one must have an appointment to access and use the library.

The Future 50 expansion, opening in 2013, will feature the Ralph Wilson Jr. Pro Football Research and Preservation Center, which will enable the proper preservation and storage of the Hall's growing collection of pro football artifacts, documents, and archival materials.

For the majority of Hall patrons, the central exhibit in the entire facility is the Hall of Fame Gallery, where bronze busts of all enshrinees are displayed. Visitors can learn about each of the legends of the game through touch-screen kiosks that display biographical sketches, photos, and video footage. Buffalo fans will find nine busts relating to their beloved Bills:

- Joe DeLamielleure, Guard, Class of 2003 (Bills, 1973–79, '85; Cleveland Browns, 1980–84)
- Jim Kelly, Quarterback, Class of 2002 (Bills, 1986–96)
- Marv Levy, Head Coach, Class of 2001 (Bills, 1986–97; Kansas City Chiefs, 1978–82)

Longtime coach Marv Levy celebrates his induction into the Pro Football Hall of Fame on August 4, 2001.

- James Lofton, Wide Receiver, Class of 2003 (Bills, 1989–92; Green Bay Packers, 1978–86; Los Angeles Raiders, 1987–88; Los Angeles Rams, 1993; Philadelphia Eagles, 1993)
- Billy Shaw, Guard, Class of 1999 (Bills, 1961–69)
- O.J. Simpson, Running Back, Class of 1985 (Bills, 1969–77; San Francisco 49ers, 1978–79)
- Bruce Smith, Defensive End, Class of 2009 (Bills, 1987–99, Washington Redskins, 2000–03)
- Thurman Thomas, Running Back, Class of 2007 (Bills, 1988–99; Miami Dolphins, 2000)
- Ralph C. Wilson Jr., Owner, Class of 2009

The Pro Football Hall of Fame is located in Canton, Ohio, just off Interstate 77, at 2121 George Halas Drive NW.

For the air traveler, Akron-Canton airport is located just 10 minutes from the Hall. Several major airlines provide daily service. Additionally, Cleveland Hopkins Airport is less than an hour away.

The Hall opens every day at 9:00 AM and closes at 5:00 PM. From Memorial Day through Labor Day, the Hall remains open until 8:00 PM. The only day it is closed is Christmas Day. There are special admission prices for seniors and children younger than 14.

12 The Rematch

On December 26, 1965, exactly one year to the day after beating the Chargers at War Memorial Stadium for their first AFL championship, the Bills were scheduled to meet them again—this time in San Diego—for another go-round. Despite having throttled the Chargers 20–7 the previous year, and once again possessing a better regular-season record, the Bills were seven-point underdogs. As always, the flashy boys in powder blue were the darlings of the media, and that year's team had the advantage of playing at home and having their star wide receiver, Lance Alworth, back in the lineup.

"The Chargers, both years, were the best team, on paper, in the AFL," recalled Bills cornerback Butch Byrd. "They had Hadl as the quarterback, Lincoln and Lowe as running backs, Dave Kocourek was the tight end, and they had Ron Mix at tackle. They were loaded, but I think we were better. We were absolutely confident that we could beat the Chargers."

Fellow defensive back Booker Edgerson concurred. "The practices we had were very upbeat. Everybody was relaxed. We had a defense that didn't give up too much yardage, and we didn't allow too much scoring that year. We figured if our offense could get two touchdowns, then we were going to win the game."

But scoring two touchdowns with Buffalo's patchwork offense would not be easy. With the receiving corps depleted by injury (Elbert Dubenion, Glenn Bass, and Charley Ferguson were all out), coach Lou Saban and his offensive coordinator, John Mazur, devised a game plan predicated on the extensive use of double-tight-end formations. The hastily put-together strategy proved effective, however, as reserve tight end Ernie Warlick (who had lost his starting job to Paul Costa earlier in the season) played a major role in the Bills' offensive success that day, leading the team with three receptions.

Unlike the previous year's game, which was played on a muddy, cold War Memorial Stadium field, the 1965 title game was played in ideal conditions, with game-time temperatures hovering around 60 degrees. The sun shone brightly, with a very mild breeze barely moving the flags. It was a beautiful day for football, but for the Bills, the game started under a dark cloud as All-League guard Billy Shaw was knocked unconscious on the opening kickoff and had to be helped off the field. Reserve guard George Flint came off the bench and faced the unenviable task of going up against Ernie Ladd, the largest man in the entire league.

"George was outweighed by a hundred pounds," said Shaw. "George didn't weigh more than 235 soaking wet, and Ernie was 330 to 335. But George's heart was as big as a No. 3 washtub, and he held in there."

"I came in and played over Ladd," Flint recalled. "I didn't feel that good. I had an intestinal flu, and I think they were a little worried because I was down to about 225. I got a little playing time in and Saban switched me over to right guard."

Joe O'Donnell then moved over to left guard.

After a scoreless first quarter, Buffalo took the lead late in the second when Kemp capped a 60-yard drive by hitting Warlick with an 18-yard strike. It was on San Diego's ensuing possession that Byrd made the play of the game. The Bills forced the Chargers into a three-and-out, and quarterback John Hadl was called on to punt. Byrd fielded the kick at the Buffalo 26 and, after receiving a key block from Ed Rutkowski to free him to the outside, found daylight as he headed up the right sideline. Former Charger Paul Maguire took out Hadl and Dave Kocourek—the last two Chargers—with a single momentous block at the San Diego 20. Byrd coasted into the end zone for the score, giving the Bills a commanding 14–0 lead.

It seemed the game was going to be a blowout when middle linebacker Harry Jacobs blunted the Chargers' next possession by intercepting Hadl at the San Diego 32. The offense stalled, however, and Gogolak was sent in to try a 24-yarder. The Chargers dodged a bullet when Speedy Duncan broke through and blocked the kick, leaving them trailing by two scores instead of three as the teams retired for intermission.

The Bills received a lift when Billy Shaw returned to the field at the beginning of the second half. "I had a knot in the side of my head about the size of a big egg," Shaw explained, "and I couldn't get my helmet on. They weren't going to let me play until I got my helmet on. We had the bands on the inside, and I don't know if Eddie Abramoski knows about this, but Tony Marchitte got two pairs of scissors and I clipped that band so that my helmet would go on over that knot. So I had my helmet on."

An 11-yard Gogolak field goal early in the third extended the lead to 17. Byrd later intercepted a Hadl pass and brought it back to the Chargers 23, setting up Gogolak's second field goal, a 39-yarder that gave the Bills a 20–0 lead going into the fourth. Gogolak added a 32-yarder early in the period to make it 23–0 and put the game out of reach. It was then simply a matter of killing the clock before the celebration could begin.

For the second straight year, the Bills were AFL champs, and the fact that it was the second straight over the favored Chargers, on their home field—and a shutout to boot—made it impossible for anyone to question just how deserving they were.

"It was really a thrill to beat the Chargers two years in a row," recalled Kemp, the game's MVP. "But I can't overemphasize what our defense did to help us win the whole thing. They were just stupendous."

"I don't think Hadl or the coaching staff ever figured out what the heck was going on," added Mike Stratton. "Tom Day would be down on the line, and they'd start the count, and he'd just stand up and back off. [Defensive coordinator] Joe Collier put in one defense where we didn't have a down lineman. We had the entire line, all seven of us lined up across the line of scrimmage, and everybody standing up on two legs and nobody down in a three-point stance. They didn't know whether to wind their watch or what. But that one didn't go over too well. We had to move out of it."

"Before today's game," observed Collier afterward, "San Diego was the best team in pro football. Now what does that make us?"

13 The Thurmanator

That Thurman Thomas, one of the most versatile tailbacks in NFL history, ended up in Buffalo is solid evidence that the league draft is more of an art than a science. Thurman had enjoyed an outstanding collegiate career at Oklahoma State University, where he was the school's all-time leading rusher. He even managed to keep Barry Sanders on the bench while there. Thomas had 897 rushes for 4,595 yards, 43 touchdowns, and 5,146 total yards, including 21 100-yard rushing games for OSU, and was First-Team All-America in 1985 and '87. Yet a knee injury sustained during his junior season made NFL scouts nervous, and Thomas was overlooked in the first round of the 1988 draft. The Buffalo Bills, who didn't have a first-round pick that year, were thrilled to see Thomas' name on the board when they were ready to make their first pick in the second round and immediately tapped him with the 40th overall pick.

"The condition of my knee is going to be [questioned] throughout the rest of my career," Thomas said at the time. "I don't even worry about it." Instead, he internalized the fact that he had been rejected by every other team and used it to motivate himself whenever he went on the field.

Thomas was the team's featured back on opening day of 1988 and made an emphatic statement with a solid debut in which he picked up 86 yards and a touchdown on 18 carries while leading the Bills to victory over Minnesota. By year's end, he had shown just how shortsighted all those personnel gurus had been, gaining 881 yards on 207 attempts and playing a major role in the Bills' first playoff season since 1981.

The following season was Thomas' breakout year as he rushed for 1,244 yards on 298 carries and caught 60 passes for 669 yards to lead the league in total yards from scrimmage and earn his first Pro Bowl selection. The Bills made the playoffs again and were matched up against Cleveland in the divisional round. When they entered the fourth quarter trailing by 10, the Bills went to a hurry-up offense. The fast-paced approach proved effective, and Thomas finished the game with 13 receptions for 150 yards and two touchdowns. Head coach Marv Levy made the decision to implement the "no-huddle" as the team's primary offense in the upcoming season.

Thomas' versatility was a key ingredient to the explosive offensive attack. Buffalo improved to 13–3 in 1990, and No. 34 led the NFL in all-purpose yards, picking up 1,297 on the ground (along with 11 touchdowns) and catching 49 passes for 532 yards. He then rushed for more than 100 yards in each of the team's playoff games (117 against Miami and 138 against the Raiders) as the Bills marched all the way to Super Bowl XXV. Thomas played one of the greatest games of his life, rushing for 135 yards and a touchdown, while catching five passes for 55 yards in the Bills' heartbreaking 20–19 loss to the Giants. Most observers agree that had Buffalo won, Thomas would have been the game's MVP instead of Giants running back Ottis Anderson, who took home the honors after rushing for 102 yards and one touchdown.

"The Thurmanator," as he was dubbed by ESPN's Chris Berman, again led the NFL in all-purpose yards in 1991, surpassing the two-millennium mark for the first time with 2,038 en route to being named the NFL's Most Valuable Player. The Bills reached the Super Bowl again but were crushed by the Redskins, 37–24. Washington proved to have an answer for Thomas, who had one of his most miserable games as a pro, picking up just 13 yards on 10 carries.

He came back strong in 1992, eclipsing his overall output from 1991 by gaining 2,113 yards from scrimmage (1,487 on 312 carries and 626 more on 58 receptions) to lead the league for the fourth straight year. For the second year in a row, however, Thomas was disappointing in the Super Bowl. Despite scoring the first points of the game on a two-yard run, Thomas managed a paltry 19 yards in the Bills' humiliating loss to the Dallas Cowboys.

After leading the league in yards from scrimmage for four straight years, only Thurman Thomas could call rushing for 1,315 yards, catching 48 balls for an additional 387 yards, and finishing second in the league in scrimmage yards a disappointment. Still, it was enough to earn his fifth straight trip to the Pro Bowl and help take his team to the Show for the fourth consecutive year. It would prove to be yet another disappointing Super Bowl performance for Thomas and the Bills, who fell to Dallas again—this time 30–13. Thomas scored the Bills' only touchdown of the game, but he was limited to just 37 rushing yards. He also coughed up two fumbles that led to 10 Dallas points.

Thomas rushed for more than 1,000 yards in each of the next three seasons, but the Bills' Super Bowl era had faded into memory. He remained with the team through the 1999 season, at which time he was unceremoniously released—along with Bruce Smith and Andre Reed—to clear room under the salary cap.

Hurt by what he perceived as a lack of respect and appreciation for what had done for the Bills organization, Thomas signed on with the Miami Dolphins, Buffalo's most hated rival. It was unsettling to see one of the team's all-time greats emerge from the tunnel on October 8, 2000, sporting a Dolphins uniform, and though he wasn't spectacular that day, his 24 yards on seven carries and three catches for 26 more were enough to help the Dolphins prevail

22–13. He played in nine games for the Dolphins before suffering a season-ending knee injury against San Diego on November 12.

Thurman returned to football on February 27, 2001, signing a one-day contract with Buffalo so that he could retire as a Bill. The gesture was a fitting tribute to the man who even today makes the team's media guide look like his own personal stat sheet. Among the team records Thomas holds are career rushing yards (11,938), career rushing touchdowns (65), career rushing attempts (2,849), and total touchdowns scored (87—tied with Andre Reed). In addition, Thomas is the only player to lead the NFL in total yards from scrimmage for four straight years and is one of only five backs to rush for more than 1,000 yards in eight straight seasons (Curtis Martin, Barry Sanders, Emmitt Smith, and LaDainian Tomlinson are the others).

Despite three disappointing Super Bowl performances, Thomas holds the NFL playoff records for most career points (126), touchdowns (21), and consecutive games with a touchdown (9). He is third on the all-time playoff rushing list with 1,442 yards in 21 postseason games. He is also the only player to score a touchdown in four straight Super Bowls.

Thomas was voted into the Greater Buffalo Sports Hall of Fame in 2003 and was enshrined on the Bills' Wall of Fame in 2005. He received the ultimate honor when he was voted into the Pro Football Hall of Fame in 2007, his second year of eligibility, joining former teammates Jim Kelly and James Lofton and head coach Marv Levy. A year later, he was inducted into the College Football Hall of Fame.

He is one of several former Bills who has chosen to live in Western New York. He has his own Bills-focused TV show (called, appropriately enough, *The Thurman Thomas Show*) and is the owner of Thurman Thomas Sports Training in Elma.

14 Chairman of the Electric Company

Joe DeLamielleure thought playing guard in the NFL was going to be a piece of cake. After all, in his first regular-season outing as a pro, he saw his running back shatter the single-game record for yardage gained. And by the end of his first year, he had seen his running back shatter the single-*season* record. Piece of cake!

But what seemed to come easy for DeLamielleure almost didn't happen at all. The Bills had selected DeLamielleure, an All-American and three-time All–Big 10 guard at Michigan State, with their second of two first-round selections (26th overall) in the 1973 draft. However, a routine physical examination given shortly after the draft indicated that he had a condition that could keep him from realizing his dream of playing pro ball.

"His career with the Bills almost ended before it began," recalled Eddie Abramoski, the Bills' veteran athletic trainer. "When he reported after the draft we gave him the usual physical, and an abnormality showed up on his EKG."

"When I told [Michigan State head coach] Duffy Daugherty," said DeLamielleure, "he was convinced that I was fine to play. Duffy sent me to see his friend, Dr. Segul, at the Cleveland Clinic. The Cleveland Clinic gave me a clean bill of health. I couldn't get to Buffalo fast enough."

Lou Saban, who had coached the 6'3" 258-pounder in the Senior Bowl, wasted little time in proclaiming the rookie the second coming of one of the team's most storied figures. "After our first practice, when the team was gathering at midfield," wrote DeLamielleure in his autobiography, "he looked right at me and said to the whole team, 'Here is my next Billy Shaw.' Probably no one else knew who Billy Shaw was. I knew, though."

Little could Saban have known that both would one day be enshrined in the Pro Football Hall of Fame.

DeLamielleure impressed throughout the preseason and was rewarded with the starting right guard position for the season opener. He returned the Bills' faith with a solid performance that allowed O.J. Simpson to make NFL history. "[O.J.] rushed for 250 yards that day," he remembered, "which was an indication of what was to come. Not every game was going to go that smoothly, of course, but I didn't know that. I thought playing in the NFL was going to be easy."

By the end of the season, Simpson had set a new standard for running backs by becoming the first to gain more than 2,000 yards, and his offensive line, dubbed "the Electric Company" for its role in "turning on the Juice," had become one of the most famous forward walls ever assembled. Despite being the youngest member, the man known simply as "Joe D" emerged as the line's leader and was selected to the NFL All-Rookie Team.

DeLamielleure was named to his first Pro Bowl in 1975 and went on to play in a total of five (1975–79) in his initial seven-year stint in Buffalo. He was also extremely durable, never missing a start in 102 regular-season games during that stretch.

But DeLamielleure became disenchanted with the direction the team was taking after Chuck Knox took over as head coach in 1978. He lobbied for a trade and was eventually dealt to the Cleveland Browns in exchange for two draft choices.

He enjoyed five fine seasons in Cleveland and earned one return trip to the Pro Bowl, but by 1985, DeLamielleure was 34 years old and no longer the player he once was. He was released by the Browns during the preseason and re-signed with Buffalo, appearing in 10 games with the Bills that year before deciding his time had finally come. "I always felt lucky to have started my career there and very lucky to have been able to go back and end my career in Buffalo—the city that I love," he recalled.

DeLamielleure never missed a game due to injury in his entire 13-year career. In all, he was selected All-Pro eight times and appeared in six Pro Bowls. He was also named to the 1970s All-Decade Team by voters from the Pro Football Hall of Fame. Capping off an incredible career, he was enshrined into the Hall of Fame in 2003.

15 Action Jackson

Fred Jackson's path to NFL stardom has been an unlikely one. Sure, there have been a small handful of others—most notably Kurt Warner—who followed a similar course to the big leagues, but the odds against such an ascension are long indeed. While it's true that Jackson is yet to win a Super Bowl or be named league MVP like Warner, the more one looks at his story, the more incredible it seems.

Fred and his twin brother, Patrick, were born in Fort Worth, Texas, to athletically gifted parents Latricia and Fred Jackson Sr. Fred was a semipro football player and Latricia a track star whose Olympic aspirations ended when she became pregnant with the twins. The boys were still very young when the Jacksons moved down the road to nearby Arlington, where Fred grew up a fan of Emmitt Smith and the Dallas Cowboys. (Ironically, the family lived in a house that was razed in 2004 to make room for parking space for the Cowboys' new $1.2 billion stadium.)

The boys played ball at Nichols Junior High School and later Lamar High, but Fred's numbers provided little indication that he would one day be an NFL star. In fact, he entered his senior year as a 5'8", 140-pound third-string halfback. He moved up to the second squad during the year but never started a game. There were, of course, no Division I colleges scouting benchwarmers, but the Jacksons had an advocate in Wayne Phillips, who had coached them at Nichols. Phillips believed so strongly in their potential that he took it upon himself to drive them 850 miles to visit Coe College, an NCAA Division III school in Cedar Rapids, Iowa. Phillips had played football for the Kohawks back in the 1950s and later served as head coach. Both Fred and Patrick made the team, but it was Fred who blossomed into a star, being twice named Iowa Intercollegiate Athletic Conference MVP. His senior year was a tour de force, as he rushed for 1,702 yards, scored 29 touchdowns, and was named to five different All-America teams.

But again, Jackson wasn't seeing scouts beating a path to his door. At 195 pounds, he was told by a representative from the Green Bay Packers that he lacked the size to play in the NFL. Other teams also passed, but Jackson refused to be discouraged. The so-called experts that claimed Jackson was too small had underestimated the size of his heart.

He cast his lot with the Sioux City Bandits of the United Indoor Football League and became the team's standout player. In his second season with the Bandits (2005), Jackson was named the league's MVP and Offensive Player of the Year, gaining 1,770 yards on the ground and scoring 53 touchdowns.

In the spring of 2006, Marv Levy, the Bills' former head coach who had led the team to four straight Super Bowls in the early 1990s, took over as the team's general manager. It just so happened that Levy was a graduate of Coe College and had coached Wayne Phillips when he was playing there. "When I went back to the Bills," Levy recalled, "Wayne called me and said, 'Marv, there's a guy at Coe you should look at. He's probably the best player that ever played there.' I had seen Fred play at Coe, but I asked Wayne to send some film on him."

Levy liked what he saw but felt Jackson could use a little more seasoning. He arranged for Jackson to spend a season with the

Rhein Fire of NFL Europe. Jackson responded by leading the team with 731 rushing yards. He came to the Bills' camp that summer and performed well enough to earn a spot on the practice squad. He didn't get into a regular-season game but paid his dues and made it onto the active roster in 2007, becoming the first refugee from the UIF to make it as a regular on an NFL team.

Jackson spent most of the 2007 season on special teams and backing up top draft pick Marshawn Lynch, but he got his first start on December 2 against the Washington Redskins, picking up 82 yards on the ground and 69 more receiving. One week later, the 26-year-old rookie enjoyed his first 100-yard game, gaining 115 yards on 15 carries in leading the Bills to a 38–17 shellacking of Miami.

Lynch was still the featured back in 2008, but Jackson made the most of his opportunities when he got on the field, gaining 571 yards on 130 carries (a solid 4.4 average) and catching 37 passes for another 317 yards, all the while endearing himself to Bills fans with his rugged, blue-collar style.

The Bills showed their appreciation by signing Jackson to a four-year, $7.5 million contract during the off-season. Lynch entered 2009 as the starter, but a three-game suspension and decreased production opened the door for Jackson, who eventually unseated Lynch as the team's top back. Though he only started 11 games, the man once considered too small to make it in the pros rewarded the Bills' faith by racking up 1,062 yards on the ground and catching 46 passes for an additional 371 yards.

The Bills had two good backs in Jackson and Lynch as they looked forward to the 2010 campaign, so when they chose halfback C.J. Spiller with their first pick in the draft, Jackson and his growing following were left scratching their heads. But the troubled Lynch was eventually traded, and Spiller proved he was not quite ready to step into the starting role, leaving Jackson as the team's featured back. Jackson came through with another solid season, picking up 927 yards on the ground.

So what more did Jackson have to prove? After topping the 1,000-yard plateau in 2009, leading the team in rushing for the second straight season in 2010, supplanting incumbent Marshawn Lynch, and fending off challenger C.J. Spiller, apparently a lot. He came into the 2011 training camp as the nominal starter, but when Spiller saw as much action as Jackson in preseason games, nearly everyone—Jackson, his fans, the media—wondered just how secure his hold on the position was.

Jackson needn't have worried. Head coach Chan Gailey had no intention of replacing his best player, and once the season got under way, there was no question about who was No. 1. Jackson stormed out of the gate, putting up dizzying numbers, including two straight 100-yard games to start the year. By midseason, Jackson's name was on the short list of league MVP candidates. But it all came crashing down in Week 10, when Jackson suffered a fractured fibula in a tough loss to the Miami Dolphins, thus ending his brilliant campaign. At the time of the injury, Jackson was third among NFL rushers with 934 yards (an astounding 5.5 average) and six touchdowns. His 442 receiving yards gave him a total of 1,376 yards from scrimmage, ranking him second overall and accounting for about 40 percent of the Bills' total offense. He appeared to be a lock to make the Pro Bowl, but his name was removed from the ballot after the injury.

It was a huge disappointment for Jackson and the Bills, but anyone paying attention has learned that no matter what obstacle is placed in front of him, it's almost certain Jackson will overcome it. He always has.

16
26

The Buffalo Bills entered the 1991 season as defending AFC champions, having lost the previous year's Super Bowl by a single point when a fateful 47-yard field goal attempt sailed wide of the uprights in the game's dying seconds. The team was determined to return to the Big Game and prove wrong the detractors who labeled them a one-trick pony, a team dependent upon a gimmicky offense and a whole lotta luck.

The squad returning to camp that summer was virtually unchanged, save for the addition of safety Henry Jones, defensive end Phil Hansen, linebacker Mark Maddox (acquired via the draft), and punter Chris Mohr (via free agency). Otherwise, the team was stocked with veteran Pro Bowlers on all three sides of the ball (offense, defense, and special teams). On offense, there was quarterback Jim Kelly, halfback Thurman Thomas, wide receivers Andre Reed and James Lofton, center Kent Hull, guard Jim Ritcher, and tackle Will Wolford. The defense was studded with stars of its own, including All-World defensive end Bruce Smith and linebackers Cornelius Bennett, Shane Conlan, and Darryl Talley. Then there was Steve Tasker, quite possibly the greatest special teams player of all time. Not only were they favored by many experts because of their abundance of talent, they were also the sentimental favorite because of the heartbreaking manner in which they had lost the most recent Super Bowl.

The K-Gun offense was again the team's primary mode of attack, and it again served them well. The Bills led the league in total yards gained with 6,252, and finished second in total points scored with 458 (up 30 points from the year before). Kelly and Thomas had the best campaigns of their careers. Kelly completed

64.1 percent of his passes for 3,844 yards and 33 touchdowns, and Thomas picked up 1,407 yards on the ground and another 631 through the air to lead the league in yards from scrimmage for the third straight year and earn both the NFL's Offensive Player of the Year and Most Valuable Player awards. Both Reed and Lofton surpassed the 1,000-yard mark in receiving.

The season got off to a rollicking start with a 35–31 win at home over the Dolphins, setting the pace for the next four games as the Bills cruised to 5–0. They experienced their usual midseason lull in Week 6, getting steamrolled 33–6 by Kansas City. They rebounded the following Sunday with a 42–6 drubbing of the Colts to begin an impressive 8–1 stretch before the season finale against Detroit. Having clinched home-field advantage throughout the playoffs with the 35–7 defeat of the Colts the week before, coach Marv Levy decided to rest many of the team's starters, and the Bills lost in overtime, 17–14, leaving them with a second straight 13–3 record.

In the AFC Wild Card round, the Chiefs squeaked past the Raiders to advance to the divisional round against the Bills. The Chiefs had embarrassed the Bills when the two clubs met earlier in the year and All-Pro running back Christian Okoye exposed Buffalo's weak run defense by pounding out 122 yards and two touchdowns. But the Bills would be playing in the friendly confines of Rich Stadium, and most of their starters would be well rested after sitting out the season finale and enjoying the first-round bye.

Neither team seemed able to get anything going at the start, trading punts twice before Kelly engineered a beautiful 80-yard drive that culminated with a 25-yard strike to Andre Reed, giving the Bills a 7–0 first-quarter lead. Kelly and Reed hooked up again early in the second, this time from 53 yards out, and Buffalo led 14–0. A Scott Norwood field goal with two seconds left gave his team a 17-point advantage at the half. When Kelly hit Lofton with a 10-yard strike early in the third, the game was essentially over. The Bills coasted to a 37–14 rout, with Kelly completing 23 of 35 passes for 273 yards and three scores, Thurman Thomas picking up 100 yards on 22 carries, and Reed compiling 100 yards and two touchdowns on his four catches.

With the win, the Bills advanced to the AFC Championship Game against the John Elway–led Denver Broncos. What was anticipated to be a shootout between gunslingers Kelly and Elway never materialized. Ultimately, it was a defensive struggle, as the Broncos held the vaunted K-Gun to a season-low 213 total yards (104 rushing, 109 passing), while the Bills defense registered four QB sacks, limited the Broncos' ground game to a mere 81 yards, and produced Buffalo's only touchdown. With the teams deadlocked in a scoreless tie late in the third quarter, nose tackle Jeff Wright tipped an Elway pass into the hands of Carlton Bailey, who returned it 11 yards for the score, to give the Bills a 7–0 lead. A 44-yard Scott Norwood field goal in the fourth provided all the cushion the Bills needed to secure a dramatic 10–7 victory and their second straight trip to the Super Bowl.

Held in Minnesota's Metrodome, Super Bowl XXVI pitted the teams with the best regular-season records in their respective conferences—the Bills at 13–3 and the Washington Redskins at 14–2. They were also the two highest-scoring teams in the NFL. The Redskins defense, however, was much stronger, yielding the third-fewest yards in the league, while Buffalo's ranked second-to-last. The Bills, it appeared, had met their match.

Things started badly for Buffalo when Thomas could not find his helmet and missed his team's first two offensive plays. The teams battled through a scoreless first period before the Redskins seized control in the second, taking a 17–0 lead on a Chip Lohmiller field goal, a 10-yard touchdown pass from Mark Rypien to Earnest Byner, and a one-yard plunge by Gerald Riggs. Riggs went over again early in the third to increase the lead to

24–0 before Buffalo finally cracked the goose egg with a 21-yard field goal from Norwood. The Bills closed the gap to 14 points midway through the period when Thomas scored from one yard out, but that was as close as they would get. The Redskins then put up 13 unanswered points to make it 37–10. The Bills continued to fight, as Kelly connected for two touchdown passes (two yards to Pete Metzelaars and four yards to Don Beebe) in the final stages, making the final score appear more respectable than the game actually was.

It was an ugly and embarrassing loss. As a result, the Bills joined the Broncos and Vikings as the only teams to lose back-to-back Super Bowls. Thurman Thomas, after his ignominious start, gained a grand total of 13 yards on 10 carries. For Kelly, it was the worst game of an otherwise magical season. The Bills signal-caller threw four interceptions and was sacked five times, including one that momentarily knocked him unconscious. His counterpart, Mark Rypien, completed 18 of 33 passes for 292 yards and two scores, earning MVP honors. Redskins coach Joe Gibbs became the third head coach in league history to win three Super Bowls.

17 Tailgate at the Ralph

Tailgaters in every NFL city have at least one thing in common: the fervent belief that their city's pregame parking lot experience is the best in the league. Whether it's because of the food, the atmosphere, the size, or some unique custom in which revelers superstitiously take part before each game, the tailgate party has traditionally been the one area in which football fans (no matter what their team's record is at the time) have never had to feel inferior.

At least not until Joe Cahn came along. "Who is Joe Cahn?" one might ask. Mr. Cahn is the self-proclaimed "Commissioner of Tailgating" who travels across the country in his customized recreational vehicle checking out as many tailgate parties as he possibly can. Cahn at one time operated a cooking school in New Orleans, but in 1996, he sold the business, purchased a motor home, and dedicated himself to visiting every stadium in the league so that he could experience each city's unique traditions firsthand. Since then, he has participated in well over 500 tailgate parties from NFL and NCAA football to NASCAR.

In 2009, the well-traveled commissioner published his top-10 list of NFL tailgating cities, and Ralph Wilson Stadium in Orchard Park ranked third behind only Reliant Stadium in Houston and Arrowhead Stadium in Kansas City.

Third?! Well, that ain't too shabby, considering there are 30 other stadiums competing for the title. And besides, that is just one man's opinion.

"We're better than that," counters superfan Greg Tranter, who has been tailgating at the Ralph since 1973. "When those Reliant Stadium guys sit through a cold, snowy December Sunday afternoon in Orchard Park, then I'll believe. We're out there tailgating whether it's 80 degrees or zero."

Tranter, like most tailgaters, takes his pregame ritual seriously. "We get to the stadium at 9:15 to set everything up—tables, chairs, grill, even a canopy in case it rains. The cooler is stocked with beer, wine, and soda. The food varies from week to week—chicken, steaks, smoked salmon, grilled veggies and potatoes." Tranter's party usually includes between four and 10 people, and sometimes more depending on the week's opponent.

For some, the game is almost an incidental feature of the tailgating experience. The party that began four or five hours before kickoff might continue right on through the game, especially for those fans who couldn't get tickets to get into the stadium. And afterward, the party will pick up right where it left off, as fans return to the same spot to partake in the postgame celebration (or commiseration).

There are even some who arrive at the stadium two days early, in RVs decked out in team colors. There's nothing like having a home-away-from-home to duck into on those cold December afternoons, but then again—for most hard-core tailgaters in Buffalo—being out in the elements is an integral part of the whole experience. "In September, you're in shorts sitting around on lounge chairs," says Tranter. "In December, you're sitting around a bonfire. It's all different, but it's all in the same season."

For veteran tailgater and season-ticket holder Mike Burns of Cheektowaga, New York, the pregame revelry is a family tradition that dates back to the days of War Memorial Stadium. "I learned how to tailgate from my dad at the Rockpile when I was six years old," says Burns. "He always had the grill going, but there was never much room there."

The ritual continued after the Bills moved into Rich Stadium in 1973, said Burns, but it assumed a new dimension of seriousness once he took charge of the festivities. "Probably around 1984 or '85, before Marv came, everything started to excel after that. I bought a tent at Kmart and made a little bench out of wood and cut a hole in it to use as a toilet."

Over the years, Burns' group has grown to include anywhere from 20 to 50 people at any given time and signifies the true spirit of fellowship and camaraderie that unites Bills fans as a community. "We've incorporated a group of younger fans who just kind of blended in."

Even the food has graduated from the standard fare of hot dogs and hamburgers to include chili, bratwurst, and any meat that can be cooked over an open flame. "We've brought smokers in to smoke meat, and we've even deep-fried turkeys."

For novice fans planning their first tailgating event, be aware that the Bills do have some rules regarding lot use and fan behavior.

And be sure to show your team spirit by wearing your Bills paraphernalia—such as T-shirts, jerseys, hats, and jackets—waving your Bills flag, and doing some good-natured ribbing when fans from the opposing team walk by. But most of all—have fun!

"Buffalo and the tailgate are like a big community party," says Tranter. "The game wouldn't be the same without the tailgate. It's part of the ritual."

18 The Hundred-Dollar Man

One-hundred dollars. That's all winning cost. That's what the Buffalo Bills paid to claim quarterback Jack Kemp off waivers from the San Diego Chargers in 1962. In return, the Bills got a franchise quarterback who within a year led the team into its first golden era, which included four postseason appearances, three division crowns, and two AFL championships.

Kemp was in his third year with the Chargers when the Bills acquired him, but he had been playing pro ball as far back as 1957, when he was drafted in the 17th round by the Detroit Lions out of Occidental College. But since the Lions already had Bobby Layne and Tobin Rote, Kemp was released before the start of the regular season. Over the next three years, he spent time with the Pittsburgh Steelers, New York Giants, Calgary Stampeders of the CFL, and San Francisco 49ers before finding a home in 1960 with the then–Los Angeles Chargers of the new American Football League.

"The Chargers had an old friend of mine, Don Klosterman, [who] was the personnel director," Kemp recalled. "I got a phone call from Klosterman and went down and met him and Frank Leahy and Sid Gillman. I had had three years of being around NFL football, and I had a good strong arm and was in good shape, and they signed me to be the first Chargers quarterback."

Kemp guided the bombs-away Chargers to the AFL title games in both 1960 and '61. But early in the 1962 season, Kemp was placed on waivers after injuring the middle finger of his throwing hand against the New York Titans. "I threw a pass to Lance Alworth," Kemp explained. "I hit the helmet of a blitzing linebacker and dislocated my right middle finger, but I stayed in the game because I didn't want John Hadl to play. After the game was over, my finger looked like a baseball, so clearly I wasn't going to be able to play. I couldn't even brush my teeth much less throw the ball."

The doctors decided on a utilitarian solution when it came time to set the finger. "They put my hand on a football," he recalled, "and that's how it was shaped." Kemp's finger was permanently fused at the middle knuckle in the shape of the ball. He'd play the rest of his career unable to bend the middle finger on his throwing hand.

The Chargers placed Kemp on the waivers list on Friday, September 21, in order to make space for another player in their upcoming game. They planned to recall Kemp after the game, but a paperwork snafu left the quarterback vulnerable to being claimed by other teams.

"I got a call from one of the gals in the office [saying] that he was put on waivers," Bills head coach Lou Saban recollected. "I think [Chargers head coach] Sid Gillman was trying to hide him, because if he had gotten through the 48-hour period then he would still have him on his squad. But she called me and said, 'He's going to be available.' He had that bum finger, but I actually saw something in Jack that was special. So I went ahead and claimed him." Denver and Boston also put in claims. Despite Gillman's protestations, AFL commissioner Joe Foss awarded Kemp to Buffalo. The team paid the $100 waiver fee, and Kemp was officially a Buffalo Bill.

"Gillman made a mistake," said Eddie Abramoski, the Bills' longtime trainer. "They thought nobody would notice, so we cut a player and played one guy short so we could get him."

"He had a great arm, and he hit the medium passes beautifully—the 10-, 15- or 20-yard out," said Saban. "He could get rid of the ball very quickly, and I felt that could probably save us while [we were] still in the process of building an offensive line."

Kemp saw his first action with the Bills on November 18 when he came off the bench to throw the game-winning touchdown pass in a 10–6 victory at Oakland. A week later, he supplanted incumbent starter Warren Rabb and finished the year in the role.

For the first time in their history, the Bills had an established No. 1 quarterback as they entered the 1963 season. The position had been a revolving door since the team's inception, with eight different men starting in three years.

"The other teams in the AFL had an advantage over us with guys like George Blanda, Cotton Davidson, Frank Tripucka, Tom Flores, Butch Songin, and Al Dorow," Abramoski observed.

Behind Kemp's leadership, the Bills made their first playoff appearance in 1963. A year later, the team won its first league title with a 20–7 drubbing of the San Diego Chargers—Kemp's former team. In 1965, the Bills again claimed the title by defeating the Chargers even more convincingly—23–0—and Kemp was voted the league's MVP by the Associated Press.

The Bills returned to the title game in 1966 but lost to Kansas City in a game that decided the AFL representative in the first Super Bowl. From that point, the aging Bills found themselves in a free-fall that lasted the rest of the decade. After going 4–10 in 1967, the team registered a pitiful 1–12–1 record in '68 as Kemp missed the entire year with a severe knee injury. He made a full recovery and returned to action in '69, but despite having a healthy Kemp and the league's top draft pick in O.J. Simpson, the aging Bills could do no better than 4–10.

By that time, Kemp was giving serious thought to running for political office. Always politically active—he was president of the AFL Players Association five times—there was little doubt among those who knew him well that he would one day end up serving in a national office. "I was starting to think about running for congress toward the end of the season," he recalled. "I went to the All-Star Game because somebody had gotten hurt, so my last actual ballgame was in January of 1970. My career started in 1957 and ended in 1970, so I played in three decades. I had a four-year, no-cut contract, so if I had lost [the election] in '70 I would have come back and exercised the no-cut clause. I could have played a few more years. I wasn't going to be like Blanda and play 25 years. I had a pretty good contract—I was making around $50,000 [a year], which was good in those days."

Kemp won the race, however, and served nine terms in the U.S. House of Representatives (1971–89), representing the Buffalo, New York, region. In 1988, Kemp sought the nomination of the Republican Party for the presidential candidacy but lost to the eventual office winner George H.W. Bush. President Bush subsequently named Kemp to the post of Secretary of Housing and Urban Development (1989–93). In 1996, Kemp was the Republican Party's vice presidential nominee alongside Senator Bob Dole, but the duo lost to the Democratic team of Bill Clinton and Al Gore.

Kemp was enshrined on the Bills' Wall of Fame in 1984. In 1992, he was inducted into the Greater Buffalo Sports Hall of Fame.

Kemp passed away on May 2, 2009, at the age of 73, after a brief battle with cancer.

Not Again!

In July 1992, for the second year in a row, the Buffalo Bills returned to training camp as the defending AFC champions. This time, however, they did not return as everyone's darlings. After losing a heartbreaker to the Giants in Super Bowl XXV and getting demolished by the Redskins in Super Bowl XXVI, the last thing football fans across the nation wanted to see was the Bills back for a third kick at the can. But Bills die-hards remained optimistic that their team had another, hopefully more successful, run left in its tank.

Most of the players who had been part of the past two Super Bowl runs remained, the main exceptions being linebacker Ray Bentley, who signed a Plan B free agent contract with Cincinnati, and kicker Scott Norwood, who was waived after the Bills signed Steve Christie to a four-year contract. Buffalo's offense, propelled by the no-huddle attack, ranked second in the league, with 5,893 total yards, and first in rushing offense, with 2,436. Thurman Thomas lugged the leather for 1,487 of those yards, while also grabbing 58 aerials for 626 more to lead the league in yards from scrimmage for a record fourth straight season (2,113). Quarterback Jim Kelly enjoyed another big season, throwing for 3,457 yards and 23 touchdowns. Wide receiver Andre Reed led the team with 65 receptions for 913 yards and three touchdowns, and James Lofton contributed 51 receptions for 786 yards and six scores.

The defense was anchored by All-World end Bruce Smith; a linebacking corps that included Darryl Talley, Shane Conlan, and Cornelius Bennett; and a defensive secondary led by safety Henry Jones (who tied for the league lead in interceptions with eight) and cornerback Nate Odomes.

The season got off to a fast start, with the Bills winning their first four games while outscoring their opponents by a combined 153–45. But the Bills lost the next two before rebounding to claim five straight and improve to 9–2 after 11 games. After splitting their next four outings, the Bills entered the season finale against Houston at 11–4 and needed a win to secure the division title. But the Oilers prevailed for a 27–3 win, dealing the Bills' quest for a third straight Super Bowl a major blow. Buffalo's final record of 11–5 caused them to fall to second place in the division behind Miami. It was still good enough for a wild-card berth, but it also meant that after the first round, all of their remaining playoff games would be on the road.

In a strange twist of playoff seeding, the Bills were matched up against the same team—the Houston Oilers—that they had faced a week before in the regular-season finale. Playing without Jim Kelly, who had suffered a serious knee injury in that game, backup quarterback Frank Reich was pressed into action, and engineered the 41–38 come-from-behind victory that would become known simply as "the Comeback."

With Reich still leading the charge, the Bills clobbered the Pittsburgh Steelers 24–3 in the AFC Divisional Playoff Game, earning the right to play in their third conference championship game in as many years. Kelly returned to the lineup for the showdown in Miami against Dan Marino and the Dolphins, showing no ill effects from his injured knee as he completed 17 of his 24 passing attempts in guiding the Bills to a convincing 29–10 triumph. Steve Christie kicked five field goals for the Bills.

The Bills were on their way to their third straight Super Bowl, this time against the NFC champion Dallas Cowboys. Unfortunately for the Bills and their fans, Super Bowl XXVII would prove to be the most painful one yet, with the team's chances obliterated by nine turnovers.

One wouldn't know it by looking at the final score, but Buffalo actually had the first lead of the game. After forcing the Cowboys to punt on their opening possession, special teams ace Steve Tasker broke through and blocked Mike Saxon's kick, giving the Bills the ball at the Dallas 16. Moments later, Thurman Thomas scored from two yards out, and the Bills were up 7–0. But the Cowboys answered right back, scoring two quick touchdowns (23-yard pass from Troy Aikman to Jay Novacek and two-yard return of fumble by Jimmie Jones) off Buffalo turnovers to take a 14–7 lead at the end of the first quarter.

Early in the second quarter, Dallas linebacker Ken Norton Jr. fell on Kelly's knee—the same one that had been injured in the season finale against Houston—forcing the quarterback from the game. Reich stepped in and drove the Bills to a 21-yard Steve Christie field goal to make it 14–10. Dallas quarterback Troy Aikman took command at that point, hitting Michael Irvin for back-to-back touchdown strikes to give the Cowboys a 28–10 lead at the half.

After Lin Elliott extended Dallas' lead with a 20-yard field goal early in the second half, Reich hooked up with Don Beebe for a 40-yard touchdown to make it 31–17 after three quarters. But the Cowboys posted three unanswered touchdowns in the fourth, giving them a 52–17 lead that remained the final tally.

The most memorable moment of this debacle, from the Bills' perspective, came in the game's dying moments. "The win was wrapped up for the Cowboys," recalled coach Marv Levy, "but there was no way the Bills wouldn't keep trying." Reich drove the Bills to the Dallas 31, and on the next play, Dallas lineman Jim Jeffcoat broke through and knocked the ball from his hands. Another Dallas lineman, Leon Lett, scooped up the fumble and headed straight for the Buffalo end zone.

"There was no one between Lett and one more Dallas touch-down," said Levy. "The instant the ball came out of Reich's hands, Don Beebe, 25 yards downfield, began sprinting back in the direction of the line of scrimmage. No one thought he had a chance of catching Lett—no one, that is, except Beebe."

Just as Lett began showboating near the Buffalo 5, Beebe had closed the gap. The speedy Buffalo receiver reached out and slapped the ball from Lett's outstretched hand at the 1. The ball rolled into the end zone and out of bounds for a touchback.

"It really didn't make much difference whether we lost that game by a score of 59–17 or 52–17, did it?" said Levy. "In this instance, the answer is yes, it did make a difference. It sent a message to the entire football world that the Buffalo Bills would never quit. It reaffirmed in the minds of all of our players and coaches that this was the most resilient group of athletes who ever came up the tunnel and onto the playing field. And it set the tone for the season that lay ahead, when our Bills would battle their way back to the Super Bowl for the fourth consecutive year."

20 At Last!

The photo of Joe Cribbs leaping over a pile of bodies to score the game-clinching touchdown in the Bills' historic triumph over the Miami Dolphins on opening day of the 1980 season is almost as memorable to Buffalo fans as Robert Smith's shot of Mike Stratton destroying Keith Lincoln in the 1964 AFL Title Game. And like the Stratton image, the picture of the airborne Cribbs captures one of the greatest moments in the team's existence and represents a collective catharsis surpassed only by the clinching of the Bills' first Super Bowl berth.

The Bills had set a dubious record during the 1970s, losing 20 straight games to the Dolphins during the decade for a standard of

Joe Cribbs goes airborne to put the icing on the cake in the Bills' streak-breaking 17–7 victory over the Dolphins on September 7, 1980. Photo courtesy of Buffalo State College Archive—E.H. Butler Library

futility (or, from the Dolphins' perspective, a benchmark of dominance) against one team that may never be surpassed. But the Bills of 1980 were not only beginning a new decade, they were literally beginning anew—a team on the upswing with several new players and a winning attitude imported along with third-year coach Chuck Knox. And what better way to kick off the new decade than against the team that had completely dominated them throughout the previous one? This was their chance to make a statement, and they did so emphatically.

The sellout crowd of 79,598 watched as the teams battled through a scoreless first quarter, but the Bills gave them something to cheer about late in the second quarter when kicker Nick Mike-Mayer provided the game's first points on a 40-yard field goal. Fans were cautiously optimistic as the teams repaired to the locker rooms for halftime with the Bills ahead—after all, they had seen this before. Just one year earlier, the Bills had taken a 7–0 lead into the locker room, only to see Tom Dempsey shank a 34-yard field goal on the game's last play to send the Bills to their 19th straight loss to the Dolphins. Something, they thought, was bound to happen to spoil the party.

It appeared those fears were realized early in the third period when Miami quarterback Bob Griese hit Tony Nathan with a four-yard scoring pass, lifting the Dolphins into a 7–3 lead. Even the players, as Bills signal-caller Joe Ferguson later confessed, were feeling a bit snakebitten. "I'll admit," he said, "I thought, *Here we go again,* when they scored."

Not this time, though. The score remained unchanged as the Bills traded blows with their bitterest rival late into the fourth quarter. The Bills took possession at their own 32, and Ferguson engineered a seven-play scoring drive that ended with a four-yard toss to Roosevelt Leaks to give Buffalo a 10–7 lead with 3:42 left. The crowd was on its feet, anxiously awaiting the return of the Miami offense and an inevitable Dolphins comeback. The ensuing kickoff was returned to the Miami 33, but when the Dolphins took the field, it was Don Strock calling the signals in place of Griese. Strock's first-down throw was picked off by linebacker Isiah Robertson and returned 33 yards to the Miami 11, giving the Bills a golden opportunity to put the game away. A short pass to Frank Lewis on third-and-6 placed the ball shy of a first down just outside the 1-yard line. Rather than kick the

Dolphins Domination

The Buffalo Bills lost a record 20 straight games to the Miami Dolphins during the 1970s. Here's how the series played out:

October 18, 1970: Dolphins 33, Bills 14 (War Memorial Stadium)
December 20, 1970: Dolphins 45, Bills 7 (Orange Bowl)
September 26, 1971: Dolphins 29, Bills 14 (War Memorial Stadium)
November 7, 1971: Dolphins 34, Bills 0 (Orange Bowl)
October 22, 1972: Dolphins 24, Bills 23 (Orange Bowl)
November 5, 1972: Dolphins 30, Bills 16 (War Memorial Stadium)
October 21, 1973: Dolphins 27, Bills 6 (Orange Bowl)
November 18, 1973: Dolphins 17, Bills 0 (Rich Stadium)
September 22, 1974: Dolphins 24, Bills 16 (Rich Stadium)
November 17, 1974: Dolphins 35, Bills 28 (Orange Bowl)
October 26, 1975: Dolphins 35, Bills 30 (Rich Stadium)
December 7, 1975: Dolphins 31, Bills 21 (Orange Bowl)
September 13, 1976: Dolphins 30, Bills 21 (Rich Stadium)
December 5, 1976: Dolphins 45, Bills 27 (Orange Bowl)
September 18, 1977: Dolphins 13, Bills 0 (Rich Stadium)
December 17, 1977: Dolphins 31, Bills 14 (Orange Bowl)
September 17, 1978: Dolphins 31, Bills 24 (Orange Bowl)
November 12, 1978: Dolphins 25, Bills 24 (Rich Stadium)
September 2, 1979: Dolphins 9, Bills 7 (Rich Stadium)
October 14, 1979: Dolphins 17, Bills 7 (Orange Bowl)

sure field goal that would have extended the lead to six points, Coach Knox made an uncharacteristically bold move and went for the kill, leaving the offense on the field to go for the clincher. Ferguson barked the signals, took the snap from center Will Grant, turned, and handed off to Cribbs, who soared over the mass of humanity into the end zone for the score, giving Buffalo a nine-point bulge that Mike-Mayer extended to 10 with the conversion. The crowd, sensing that it was witnessing Buffalo sports history in the making, erupted into hysteria. When the game ended, literally thousands of fans stormed the field to celebrate the momentous occasion.

"The fans were going crazy," said Fred Smerlas. "We were going crazy. It was an electric atmosphere. When that final gun sounded, there were no problems in the world that day. It was unbelievable."

In the postgame frenzy, overzealous fans attacked the goal posts, eventually tearing both down and carrying a large section of one up the stands toward Ralph Wilson's box to present to the team's owner as a souvenir. "This is the biggest win in the history of the team," Wilson observed. "Bigger than the AFL championships."

Indeed, it was truly a moment of civic pride shared by an entire community.

21 Dre

During his high school days at Louis E. Dieruff High in Allentown, Pennsylvania, Andre Reed was a quarterback. By all accounts, he was pretty good at it, too. In fact, in 1981, his senior season, Reed guided his team to a three-way tie for the East Penn Conference championship.

Reed later attended Kutztown State University in Pennsylvania, where he was converted to wide receiver. While becoming the most heralded football player ever to suit up at the small Division II school, he attracted the attention of several NFL scouts, including Buffalo's Elbert Dubenion, who immediately recognized Reed's pro potential. "Ray Charles could see he was a great player," Dubenion remarked. "He was fast, caught the ball in traffic...he was just great. It didn't matter what level he came from."

Dubenion convinced the Bills to draft Reed in 1985, and they did so with their fourth-round pick (86th overall selection and 13th among wide receivers). But Reed was coming into a bad situation, joining a team that had gone 2–14 the year before and that was not projected to do much better in 1985, despite the arrival of Reed and the top overall pick in that year's draft, defensive end Bruce Smith.

Reed was an immediate starter and one of the few bright spots on a pathetic Bills team that managed just two wins for the second straight year as he led all wide receivers on the team with 48 catches for 637 yards and four scores. Things started to change in 1986, however, with the arrival of quarterback Jim Kelly and head coach Marv Levy. Suddenly the culture of losing was no longer accepted, and the team began its ascent toward the top of the AFC heap. Reed would play an essential role in that ascent.

The Bills doubled their number of victories in '86 while Reed again led the team in receptions, grabbing 53 aerials for 739 yards and seven touchdowns. The Bills improved to 7–8 in '87, and despite missing four games due to a players' strike, Reed's numbers also improved as he racked up 57 catches, 752 yards, and five touchdowns.

Reed's breakout season was 1988. The 6'2" 180 pounder led the Bills in all receiving categories (71 receptions, 968 yards, six touchdowns) and was named to his first Pro Bowl. A year later, Reed topped the 1,000-yard mark for the first time, setting a club record with 1,312 receiving yards on 88 receptions (also a record) and nine touchdowns.

"As time evolved," observed Steve Tasker, "you could see Jim Kelly gaining more and more confidence in Dre. Jim connected with some very good receivers in Buffalo—guys like James Lofton and Don Beebe—but there's no question Dre was his favorite target, the guy he trusted most, especially in crunch time."

The Bills finally reached the AFC pinnacle in 1990, finishing the regular season with a 13–3 record and advancing all the way to their first Super Bowl appearance. It was another fine season for Reed as well, as the sure-handed receiver earned his third straight Pro Bowl selection after leading Buffalo in catches (71), receiving yards (945), and receiving touchdowns (eight). Despite the Super Bowl loss to the Giants, Reed played well, catching eight passes for 62 yards.

Reed topped the 1,000-yard mark (1,113) for the second time in 1991, caught 81 passes, and tied the club mark for touchdowns in a season (10) to earn yet another trip to Honolulu and help the team return to the Super Bowl stage. Uncharacteristically, the normally poised Reed drew an unsportsmanlike-conduct penalty in the second quarter after throwing his helmet. It was a costly call, taking the Bills out of field-goal range. Then again, it probably wouldn't have mattered anyway, since the Redskins steamrolled to a 37–24 win.

Reed's numbers fell off a bit in 1992, as he registered 65 catches for 913 yards and three scores during the regular season. His performance against Houston in that year's AFC Wild Card Game on January 3, 1993, however, was nothing short of spectacular and was by itself worthy of Hall of Fame consideration. Houston had taken a commanding 35–3 lead early in the third quarter, and then Reed hooked up with quarterback Frank Reich for three touchdowns in the second half to lead the Bills to the largest comeback in NFL history. In what is considered by many to be his greatest moment as a Bill, Reed hauled in eight passes for 136 yards and three touchdowns. He continued to be stellar in the loss to the Cowboys in Super Bowl XXVII, catching eight passes for 152 yards.

The Bills returned to the playoffs for the sixth straight year in 1993, and Reed earned his sixth straight Pro Bowl nod despite catching only 52 passes for 854 yards and six touchdowns. Reed's club-record 90 catches (for 1,303 yards) and seventh straight Pro Bowl season in 1994 were not enough to prevent the team from suffering its first losing campaign (7–9) since '87.

Reed's numbers began to dwindle in the next five seasons. He was part of the Bills' last playoff team in 1999, but the playoff loss to the Tennessee Titans was the final Buffalo hurrah for Reed and two other all-time greats—Thurman Thomas and Bruce Smith—all of whom were let go for salary cap reasons during the off-season.

Reed left Buffalo holding every meaningful career receiving record, including receptions (941), yards (13,095), touchdowns (86), and 100-yard receiving games (36). He also holds the mark for most receptions in a single game (15). He holds the record for most games played as a Bill (221) and is tied with Bruce Smith for most seasons (15). He spent one season with the Washington Redskins before retiring from the game. At that time, he ranked sixth on the all-time receiving yardage list with 13,198.

"Those yards," observed coach Marv Levy, "came not just because he made the catch, but because of the talent and courage Reed possessed when called upon to come bursting across the middle to make those difficult catches and then do something about it afterward. His nickname of "Yac" wasn't bestowed upon him because he talked a lot. It was a product of his unique ability and desire to rack up those 'Yards-After-Catch' stats."

Reed has been enshrined in the Kutztown University Athletic Hall of Fame, the NCAA Division II Football Hall of Fame, the Greater Buffalo Sports Hall of Fame, and the Bills' Wall of Fame. He has been a finalist for the Pro Football Hall of Fame six times but has been stuck in a logjam of contemporary wide receivers.

 **Cookie**

Carlton "Cookie" Gilchrist became a Buffalo Bill on August 4, 1962, after six brilliant years in the Canadian Football League. Gilchrist was a bona fide star in Canada, earning a reported $20,000 a year—remarkable money for the CFL at the time—prior to signing with Buffalo. He was as versatile as he was talented, having played fullback on offense and linebacker on defense with equal proficiency, while contributing on special teams as a punt and kickoff returner. Oh, and he handled the place-kicking, too.

Gilchrist played high school ball at Har-Brack High in Brackenridge, Pennsylvania, where he caught the eye of ever-vigilant Paul Brown, the legendary coach of the Cleveland Browns. Brown offered the 18-year-old phenom a chance to forego college and go directly into pro ball, but when the National Football League declared the signing violated league rules, Gilchrist headed north and signed with the Sarnia Imperials of the Ontario Rugby Football Union. Three years later, Gilchrist joined the CFL's Hamilton Tiger-Cats and led them to the 1957 Grey Cup. He enjoyed his best season the following year as a member of the Saskatchewan Roughriders, gaining 1,254 yards on 235 carries and scoring five touchdowns. He then spent three seasons with the Toronto Argonauts and was runner-up for the league's Most Outstanding Player Award in 1960. Remarkably, he was an All-League player in each of his six CFL seasons.

But there was another side of the abundantly gifted Gilchrist that gave coaches and other team officials headaches. Whether it was breaking curfew, missing practice, or some other disciplinary issue, by 1961 he had worn out his welcome in Toronto and was headed back to the States and four-down football.

Gilchrist's signing was a coup for Buffalo, giving them an impact player who was soon recognized as the AFL equivalent of Jim Brown. Gilchrist's reputation for marching to the beat of his own drummer was well known, but coach Lou Saban nevertheless felt the 6'3", 251-pound fullback with halfback speed was just the man to carry the load on the ground for the Bills.

And carry the load he did, becoming the AFL's first 1,000-yard rusher in 1962 by gaining 1,096 yards, setting an all-time AFL record for touchdowns in a season with 13, and being named the league's Most Valuable Player. Gilchrist barely missed the millennium mark in 1963, gaining 979 yards and scoring 12 touchdowns while helping the Bills to their first-ever playoff appearance. He set a single-game rushing record on December 8 against the New York Jets, racking up 243 yards on 36 carries and scoring five touchdowns.

Cookie enjoyed another terrific year in 1964, rushing for 981 yards and recording a career-best 345 yards on 30 pass receptions. He topped it off with a brilliant performance in the AFL title game against the San Diego Chargers, picking up 122 yards on 16 carries in the Bills' 20–7 victory.

The afterglow of the championship was short-lived for Gilchrist, however, as the rebellious streak that strained his CFL career had accompanied him to Buffalo. But missed practices and curfews were aggravating, yet tolerable, misdeeds compared to the events that took place in the Bills' regular-season matchup with the Boston Patriots on November 15, 1964, more than five weeks before the title game was even played.

The Bills, at 9–0, held a two-and-a-half-game lead over the Patriots, but Coach Saban wasn't taking any chances. Buffalo's game plan called for a heavy dose of passing, thus requiring Gilchrist—one of the top ball carriers in all of pro football—to be used primarily as a blocker. That, of course, did not sit well with Gilchrist, whose dissatisfaction boiled over into anger as the first half wore on. Shortly before halftime, he stormed off the field and declared he was through for the day.

The Patriots prevailed, narrowing the gap between themselves and the division-leading Bills. Saban wasn't pleased. In the midst of a heated playoff race, he suspended his best player for "conduct detrimental to the team." Through some effective diplomatic intervention by Jack Kemp and Billy Shaw, Gilchrist was convinced to issue an apology, and Saban agreed to reinstate him. Cookie would be back for the team's next game, but his days in a Buffalo uniform would soon be over.

Not, however, before the embattled fullback put in near-heroic performances in the rematch between the Bills and Patriots in the season finale and a week later in the title game. But Gilchrist's actions in the first Pats game had driven a permanent wedge between him and his coach, and though Saban had agreed to bring him back for the team's title run, it was with the understanding that Cookie would be gone once the season was over. The following February 24, Saban made good on his word and traded Gilchrist to the Denver Broncos in exchange for fullback Billy Joe, the AFL's Rookie of the Year in 1963.

Gilchrist had one more good year left in him, as he led the Broncos in rushing with 954 yards. A salary dispute prompted Gilchrist to retire prior to the 1966 season, but he reemerged later in the year with the Miami Dolphins, appearing in eight games for the expansion franchise before returning to the Broncos in 1967. In a strange turn of events, Cookie was reunited with the very man who had banished him from Buffalo, as Lou Saban had been hired to coach the Broncos. But a knee injury ended Gilchrist's season after a single game. It would be his last.

In his three seasons with the Bills, Gilchrist rushed for 3,056 yards on 676 carries (an average of 4.5 yards per carry) and 31 touchdowns. He also caught 78 passes for an additional 875 yards and four touchdowns. As the team's primary place-kicker in 1962, Gilchrist booted eight field goals and 14 extra points.

Gilchrist spent his last years living in self-imposed seclusion in a tiny apartment in Norfolk, Virginia, estranged from family and friends and those he felt were out to exploit his name. He passed away on January 10, 2011, after a long battle with bladder cancer. An autopsy revealed that Gilchrist had also been suffering from the effects of Chronic Traumatic Encephalopathy, the result of brain damage caused by numerous blows to the head during his playing days. The condition undoubtedly contributed to Gilchrist's erratic behavior in later life.

He was inducted into the Greater Buffalo Sports Hall of Fame in November 2011.

23 The Bermuda Triangle

Longtime observers of the Buffalo Bills can recall just how dismal things were during the late 1970s. After suffering through seasons of 2–12 (1976) and 3–11 (1977), Bills fans, or what was left of them, were ready to revolt. In fact, the crowd of 22,975 who turned out for the 1977 home finale against the Washington Redskins was the smallest crowd for a Bills home game since 1963! But team owner Ralph Wilson brought smiles to the faces of the team's faithful when he hired Chuck Knox, head coach of the five-time defending NFC West–champion Rams, to take over for the Bills in 1978. The results were immediate, as the Bills improved to 5–11 in Knox's first year.

The following year, Knox made the decision to switch from a 4-3 base defense to a 3-4, an alignment that required a huge, dominating nose tackle and a matching set of mobile inside linebackers. He found two of the needed cogs with a pair of second-round selections Buffalo held in the 1979 draft. The Bills chose 6'3", 277-pound defensive tackle Fred Smerlas from Boston College and then grabbed linebacker Jim Haslett from little Indiana (PA) University.

The third member of the trio was linebacker Shane Nelson, who had earned a starting spot after joining the Bills in 1977 as an undrafted free agent out of Baylor. Together, they helped the Bills improve to 7–9 in 1979. In his first game as a pro, Haslett made 17 tackles as Buffalo battled division rival Miami. He started all 16 games that year and was named the NFL's Defensive Rookie of the Year. Smerlas accumulated 57 tackles along with a team-high three fumble recoveries, one of which he returned for a touchdown.

The Bills emerged as a force in 1980. After starting the season at 5–0, the Buffalo defense, with Smerlas, Haslett, and Nelson at its core, was gaining recognition as one of the league's best. "Halfway through the season," Smerlas recalled, "it became clear we had the top defensive unit in the NFL. People noticed that opponents had a hell of a time trying to run on us through the middle. Backs who got between me, Haslett, and Nelson just seemed to disappear into thin air." Mike Dodd, a writer for the *Buffalo Evening News*, took notice of this tendency and christened the trio "the Bermuda Triangle."

The defense ended the season ranked No. 1 overall, paving the way to the team's first playoff appearance since 1974 and first division title since 1966. With Smerlas tying up two or three blockers on nearly every play, Haslett and Nelson were free to seek and destroy enemy runners almost at will. Haslett paced the club with 143 tackles, two interceptions, and a pair of sacks, while Nelson chipped in with 126 tackles. "The Big Greek," as Smerlas liked to call himself, recorded six and a half sacks and earned what would be his first of many trips to the Pro Bowl.

Buffalo's defense continued to dominate in 1981, finishing seventh overall as the Bills made their second straight postseason appearance. But the glory days of the Bermuda Triangle came to a screeching halt in Week 9 against Cleveland. While the Bills were laying down a 22–13 thrashing on the Browns, Nelson tore up his right knee and was ruled out for the rest of the regular season, breaking a string of 71 consecutive starts.

Nelson attempted to come back in 1982 but reinjured the knee in the season opener against Kansas City, forcing a premature end to a promising career.

The dynamic duo of Fred Smerlas and Jim Haslett always knew how to have fun. Photo courtesy of the Buffalo State College Archives—E.H. Butler Library

The fun-loving, practical-joking duo of Haslett and Smerlas soldiered on. They even had their own call-in radio show on WBEN on which, Smerlas told *Sports Illustrated,* "We'd have guess-the-combined-length-of-our-noses contests, guess-the-name-of-Haslett's-dog contests. The callers would get out of control sometimes."

However, finding a suitable replacement for Nelson proved impossible. The Bills defense that finished second overall in 1982 dropped to 24th in 1983 and remained near the bottom of heap for the next three seasons. The Bills fell to 8–8 in 1983 before suffering through back-to-back 2–14 seasons in 1984 and '85.

Haslett broke his leg in the final exhibition game and missed the entire 1986 campaign. He tried to return in '87 but was waived before the season began. He signed on with the New York Jets and played three games as a replacement player before calling it a career. He has since made a name for himself as a head coach with the Saints and Rams and also as a defensive coordinator with the Saints, Steelers, Rams, and Redskins.

Smerlas enjoyed an 11-year career with the Bills, returning to the Pro Bowl for a fifth time in 1988. He was left unprotected by the Bills in 1990 and signed with the San Francisco 49ers. He played one season with the 49ers and two more with the New England Patriots before retiring, having played in 200 regular-season games in 14 NFL seasons. His name was affixed to the facade of Ralph Wilson Stadium in 2001 as a member of the Bills' Wall of Fame. Smerlas was named to the Bills 50th Anniversary Team in 2010.

The Rockpile

From their inception in 1960 until 1972, the Buffalo Bills played their home games at War Memorial Stadium, located at the corner of Jefferson and Best streets (285 Dodge Street) in downtown Buffalo. Constructed as a Works Progress Administration project over three years during the Great Depression, the stadium opened in 1937 with a seating capacity of 35,000. It was originally named Roesch Memorial Stadium in honor of former Buffalo mayor Charles E. Roesch (1930–33) but was renamed Grover Cleveland Stadium later that same year. It was later renamed Civic Stadium and was used mainly as a site for civic celebrations and parades.

The first pro football team to use the facility as its home field was the Buffalo Indians/Tigers in 1940 and '41. It became the home of the Buffalo Bisons of the All-America Football Conference when that league formed in 1946. The following year, the team was renamed the Bills, and that name remained until the AAFC folded after the 1949 season. The National Football League agreed to absorb three AAFC teams into its ranks, but Buffalo, unfortunately, was not one of them. (The senior circuit only wanted the Cleveland Browns, San Francisco 49ers, and Baltimore Colts.) The stadium fell into disrepair during the 1950s, being used mainly as a venue for stock-car racing, along with the occasional high school or college football game. Several NFL exhibition games and one regular-season game (New York Giants vs. Chicago Cardinals, September 28, 1958) were also played there during the decade, but the stadium's decaying state only reinforced the NFL mind-set that Buffalo was not a big-league city.

When Ralph Wilson Jr. was scouting locations in which to place his AFL franchise, he had his choice of several cities. He visited Buffalo and Civic Stadium, but he wasn't impressed; the venue needed a great deal of rehabilitation. The city powers-that-were agreed to make the necessary upgrades, and on November 19, 1959, Wilson signed a two-year lease, agreeing to pay the city $5,000 per year for its use, plus 50 percent of the net proceeds from concession sales.

The facility was officially rededicated as War Memorial Stadium in a ceremony prior to the Bills' exhibition game with the Oakland Raiders on August 24, 1960. A fair-sized crowd of 17,071 came out to be a part of it, only to see the Raiders spoil the day by defeating the Bills 26–21.

For the next 13 seasons, the Bills called War Memorial home. During that time, the team waged many historic battles within its walls, including two AFL title games. The players maintained a love/hate relationship with the building referred to affectionately as "the Rockpile," deriding it for its horrendous conditions yet holding fond memories of the things they experienced and accomplished there.

"War Memorial was—shower situation, our dressing room situation, and our practice situation—probably the worst in the league," linebacker Mike Stratton recalled. "In a way, while we were winning, we took pride in that."

"I loved War Memorial," said Bills Hall of Famer Billy Shaw. "There was a closeness there—[the] fans were close to the field. Behind the bench were season-ticket holders, year after year after year, and you'd look in the stands, and there'd be Bob and Sally and Jim and Joe, and you knew them and you'd wave to them. You got to be friends with the folks behind there. When we started filling it up, it was a great place to play."

Despite upgrades that increased seating capacity to 46,500, the stadium was still considered too small and run-down by NFL standards, and when the historic merger occurred between the two leagues, the Bills were forced to find more suitable accommodations.

The team played its final game at the Rockpile on December 10, 1972, a 21–21 tie with the Detroit Lions. The following fall, the Bills had a new home, an 80,000-seat, state-of-the-art facility called Rich Stadium (today known as Ralph Wilson Stadium), built in the Buffalo suburb of Orchard Park.

War Memorial Stadium sat vacant until 1979, when it was refurbished for the return of the Buffalo Bisons minor league baseball team, who continued to use the building into the 1980s. In 1984, Hollywood put the dilapidated Rockpile to good use as the backdrop for the baseball film *The Natural*, starring Robert Redford, set in the dismal Depression era.

When a new Bisons ballpark (at the time called Pilot Field but today known as Coca-Cola Field) was built in 1988, War Memorial was once again left without a tenant. A year later, the stadium was demolished, leaving only the huge concrete entrances at the north and south ends. The site upon which the stadium sat was transformed into an amateur athletic facility, renamed the Johnnie B. Wiley Amateur Athletic Sports Pavilion in 1997.

25 The Vagabond Coach

Lou Saban was the architect of two golden eras in Buffalo Bills history. The first came when he guided the team to consecutive AFL titles in 1964 and 1965. The second occurred when he came back in the early 1970s, turned around a losing franchise, and helped O.J. Simpson become the greatest running back of his generation. However, both eras were short-circuited by Saban himself. His departures—prompted always by personal reasons—were never fully explained, at least not to the satisfaction of Bills fans who felt that there was so much more to be accomplished. Even so, Saban's overall Buffalo winning percentage of .602 remains second-best among Bills coaches, outpaced only by Marv Levy's .615.

As middle linebacker and captain of the Cleveland Browns' stellar defenses during the team's All-America Football Conference era, Lou served a four-year apprenticeship in the workshop of perhaps the most innovative and successful head football coach of the modern era: Paul Brown. It was Saban's responsibility to learn and understand Brown's systems and to anticipate his every wish, calling the formations that were most likely to—and almost always did—bring about the desired outcomes.

Saban retired before the Browns joined the NFL in 1950, and he spent the next decade paying his dues coaching at the college level before becoming the first head coach of the Boston Patriots of the new American Football League in 1960. His tenure at Boston lasted just a year and a half before he was let go. Bills owner Ralph Wilson hired Saban as the team's personnel director in October 1961 and elevated him to the position of head coach shortly after the season ended. Within two years, Saban guided the Bills to their first-ever postseason appearance, a divisional playoff with the Patriots. Although the Bills lost that game, the success of that season was an indication of things to come, as the Saban-led Bills captured back-to-back AFL titles in 1964 and '65.

But in a move that still has longtime observers wondering, Saban departed abruptly after the '65 season to take the helm at the University of Maryland. Without Saban, the Bills' fortunes declined dramatically, the team suffering five straight losing seasons (1967–71) and numerous coaching changes (Joel Collier, Harvey Johnson, John Rauch, and Harvey Johnson again) before Wilson brought him back in 1972. Saban immediately recognized that he had an underutilized weapon in halfback O.J. Simpson and resolved to make the former Heisman Trophy winner the focal point of the offense. The plan paid immediate dividends, as the team improved from 1–13 in 1971 to 4–9–1 in '72, and Simpson—who didn't come close to 1,000 yards in any of his first three pro seasons—emerged as the NFL's leading rusher with 1,251 yards.

In 1973, the Bills registered their first winning season (9–5) in almost a decade, and Simpson enter the record books by becoming the first back in history to surpass the 2,000-yard mark. Saban's ultimate goal of returning to the playoffs was realized in 1974, as the team secured a wild-card berth with a second consecutive 9–5 campaign. But the dream season ended with a heartbreaking first-round loss to the Pittsburgh Steelers, the eventual Super Bowl champs.

Simpson enjoyed his best season as a pro in 1975, gaining 1,817 yards on 329 carries, plus another 426 yards on 28 catches, and scoring an NFL record 23 touchdowns, but the Bills slipped to 8–6 and missed the playoffs. After beginning the 1976 season at 2–3, the emotionally drained Saban resigned.

"I was close with Lou," recalled defensive back Booker Edgerson, who played for Saban in college and later with the Bills. "He recruited me. His wife used to feed us. We went through good successful seasons at Western Illinois—we went undefeated—and *boom*, he left. But as I found out later, Lou loves a challenge. Once he wins, he needs to move on. He's really into building programs, so he feels like, 'Hey, I've got this program built up, it's successful, it's doing well, so move on.'"

After leaving the Bills for the second time, Saban held numerous jobs, beginning with head coaching stints at the University of Miami (1977–78) and Army (1979). In 1981, he switched over to baseball when his old friend George Steinbrenner named him president of the New York Yankees. He spent two years with the Bronx Bombers before returning to football as head coach at the University of Central Florida, remaining there for two seasons (1983–84). Saban returned to the Yankees as a scout and consultant in 1984, but he was back on the football sideline two years later as the defensive coordinator at Stuart Martin County (Florida) High School. Saban accepted the head coach position at Peru State College in Nebraska in 1991 but resigned after one season. He resurfaced in 1995 with SUNY Canton and remained there until resigning in 2000. In 2001, Saban was named head coach at Division III Chowan College in North Carolina but, true to form, resigned after the 2002 season. He was 81 years old.

Speculation that the man known as "the Vagabond Coach" would eventually make another comeback ended when he passed away on March 29, 2009, at the age of 87.

The First Game

It had been two months since the Buffalo Bills of the newly formed American Football League assembled for their first training camp in early July 1960. It had been a full decade since the city of Buffalo's last professional football team—the original Bills of the All-America Football Conference—last stepped onto a playing field.

Buoyed by anticipation, the team—and the city—were ready.

The new Bills had already played five preseason games, including the very first exhibition game in AFL history when they hosted the Boston Patriots at War Memorial Stadium on July 30, 1960 (a 28–7 loss). During those games, head coach Buster Ramsey experimented with several different quarterbacks—including first-ever draft pick Richie Lucas of Penn State—but, as expected, NFL veteran Tommy O'Connell emerged as the team's starter in name. O'Connell had led the Cleveland Browns to the NFL Championship Game in 1957, and Ramsey was hoping there was still a little magic left in old Tommy's arm. Considering the team's dismal 1–4 record, there was reason for doubt. As if things didn't already look bad enough, the Bills were in an odd scheduling twist, slated to open the regular season against the New York Titans, who had drubbed them 52–31 in the preseason finale.

The Bills gathered for a light workout at War Memorial Stadium the morning before the opener, then boarded a plane bound for New York City. They arrived later that afternoon and took lodgings at the Concourse Plaza Hotel in the Bronx. Many of the players took advantage of their first visit to the Big Apple by taking in some of the city's more popular attractions.

"We ate at Mamma Leone's," defensive lineman Mack Yoho recalled. "We went out—five or six of us. Archie Matsos knew the maitre d', and we got preferential treatment. That's were he got the 'Big City' name. The guys started calling him 'Big City Arch.'"

But while most of the players were turning in early, hoping to get a good night's sleep before the biggest game of their young lives, at least one Bill decided that he was going to make the most of his time in the city that never sleeps. "Chuck Muelhaupt wasn't real loose with the dollars, and he skipped the second bed check that night," remembered guard Don Chelf. "We were staying together down there, and he told me after bed check he was leaving. So they took bed check and he left. And he didn't know it until the next morning just before the game, that they had taken a second bed check. We were at the team meeting just before we were ready to go out, and Buster said, 'It'll cost Chuck Muelhaupt five hundred dollars for missing the second bed check last night.' Chuck just turned white."

The Bills, adorned in their road white, silver, and blue uniforms, became "official" on September 11, 1960, when they took the muddy field against the Titans on a rainy day at the decrepit Polo Grounds before an announced crowd of 9,607. The clouds grew even darker for the Bills when Tommy O'Connell was lost on Buffalo's fifth offensive play after being tackled hard by Titans defenders scrambling to recover a fumble.

"Tommy was the quarterback, and I was supposed to get a reverse," Elbert Dubenion explained. "On the handoff, the guy broke through, and I saw the guy coming and Tommy didn't, so I veered a little wider so the guy wouldn't kill both of us, but he caught Tommy and hurt him. That's the reason why Tommy [was behind] me. I escaped free. He didn't like me after that. That big guy was Sid Youngelman, coming head-on at 250 pounds—I'm 135—so I veered out of the way and I was hoping Tommy would pitch me the ball, but he kept it."

O'Connell was replaced by Bob Brodhead, who directed the Bills down to the New York 28-yard line before the drive stalled. Ramsey then sent Darrell Harper in to attempt a field goal. Harper's successful 35-yarder gave the Bills the first lead of the game and the first official points in their history. Unfortunately, it was all New York after that, as the Titans put up 27 unanswered points, led by quarterback Al Dorow's two touchdown runs, and won 27–3.

"I had three fumbles," Dubenion said. "I dropped five or six balls. It was a rough game."

"Buster was so mad at Dubenion," recalled Buffalo's radio announcer Van Miller. "He said, 'Damn you, when we fly back home and we get over the Finger Lakes, I'm dropping you out of the plane! And if you make it back to Buffalo, I'm sending you back to Ohio where you belong!'"

The facilities at the Polo Grounds were dreadful. Built in 1911 as the home for the New York Baseball Giants, the stadium was last used in 1957, the Giants' last year in New York before moving to San Francisco. For Miller, making his first regular-season broadcast, the Polo Grounds were a far cry from the luxurious accommodations he'd expected for a big-league football game.

"I broadcast the game from the baseball press box behind the goalpost," Miller remembered. "This was a baseball park.... I could

only see out to the 20-yard line, and then I had to try to look and
see how far the chain gang would move after a play. Buffalo lost
the game 27 to 3, and every point was scored at the far end of the
field."

It was not exactly the auspicious beginning the Bills and their
fans were hoping for. And it didn't get any better the following
week as the Bills dropped to 0–2 by losing their home opener to the
Denver Broncos. The team's first victory finally came in Week 3, a
13–0 road win over the Boston Patriots.

# Denied!

On January 1, 1967, the Buffalo Bills found themselves playing in
the AFL title game for the third straight year. This time, however,
the implications were greater than they had ever been. Winning
this one would earn them the honor of representing the AFL in
the first-ever interleague championship game—the very first Super
Bowl—against the winners of the NFL crown.

A crowd of 42,080 turned out on a frigid New Year's Day
afternoon at War Memorial Stadium hoping to see their beloved
Bills make history. The opponent that day was the tough Kansas
City Chiefs (11–2–1), winners of the Western Division crown, with
whom the Bills (9–4–1) had split their regular-season series that year.

The Bills won the coin toss and elected to receive, but that's
pretty much when their luck ran out. It took one play—just one—
to set the tone of the most important game ever played between
two AFL teams up to that point.

The kickoff was high and short, so reserve defensive tackle
Dudley Meredith, one of the up men on the Bills' receiving team,

Not-So-Super Bowl

Watching the Super Bowl from the warmth of their living rooms left many of the Bills players with a cold feeling. Would they have fared better against the Packers than the Chiefs had? Linebacker Mike Stratton believed so, despite the fact that the Chiefs had beaten Buffalo for the right to find out.

"It's never correct to say the better team lost," said Stratton, "but I certainly did feel that was the case. We made some terrible mistakes that allowed Kansas City to win and go on and play a game they were not prepared to play. But we were. Kansas City, from 1963 on, had the best personnel—on paper—in the league, but they did not play well as a team. Buffalo played as a team, and Buffalo would have played better against the Packers."

"We felt we would have played better against Green Bay because of our defense," recalled center Al Bemiller. "Not our offense, but our defense."

"I think that game would have been extremely tight, and I wouldn't have been surprised if we had won the game," added wide receiver Charley Ferguson. "I think our defense would have done extremely well. Green Bay had two good backs between Hornung and Taylor, and they believed in controlling the game, but I think our defense would have been able to compete and stop them."

"With a healthy team, we probably would have beat them," said Booker Edgerson, "or we would have given them a good fight."

Not everyone in blue felt that way, however. As quarterback Jack Kemp saw it, the Chiefs had overtaken the Bills as the dominant team in the league. "They were just too good for us by then. I don't take anything away from Kansas City—I think they beat us pretty squarely. They had a pretty good team."

Guard Joe O'Donnell agreed: "It was a decisive victory on the part of Kansas City. If you sat down and looked at the film, they were a better team than we were. The natural thing to say is, 'Well, they weren't that much better,' but that day they took us to the cleaners."

fielded the ball on the 27-yard line. "I was on the wedge with Dudley," recalled center Bob Schmidt. "There were always four guys on the wedge. I was on the outside, Dudley was one of the inside guys, and it just came right to him." Meredith instinctively started to negotiate a return, but after eight yards he was hit and fumbled.

"He just wasn't a real athletic type of guy," said Schmidt. "When we saw the fumble, we were thinking either jump on the ball or hit somebody so we could recover it." But Jerrel Wilson recovered for the Chiefs at Buffalo's 31-yard line. Three plays later, Len Dawson hooked up with tight end Fred Arbanas for a 29-yard touchdown pass, and before the game was even two minutes old, Kansas City had a 7–0 lead.

The stunned Bills struck back on their next drive, catching a lucky break when defensive back Fred "the Hammer" Williamson fell attempting to cover Elbert Dubenion, leaving "Golden Wheels" wide open to receive Jack Kemp's throw and race 69 yards to tie the score. The Chiefs regained the lead early in the second quarter when Dawson found Otis Taylor for another 29-yard touchdown pass. Kemp then led a drive to the Kansas City 11, but at that point coach Joe Collier made a strategic move that backfired, resulting in a 10-point swing.

"It was 14–7, and we were driving," recalled halfback Bobby Burnett. "Joel took me out and put Jack Spikes in for blocking. I could block. Maybe I wasn't as good as Jack Spikes, but I could block. But when they took me out, they took a weapon away, and they didn't have to worry about Spikes being any weapon."

Kemp dropped back into the pocket, saw wide receiver Bobby Crockett had beaten his man, and fired for what appeared to be a sure touchdown. However, Chiefs safety Johnny Robinson played it perfectly, waiting until just the right moment to step in to pick off Kemp's throw and race 72 yards the other way before being hauled down by a hustling Billy Shaw. Mike Mercer then connected on a 32-yard field goal, and the Chiefs went into the locker room with a double-digit deficit.

"They [went] in at halftime ahead 17–7 instead of tied 14–14," Burnett observed. "It was basically over after that."

The third quarter was scoreless, but the Chiefs dominated in time of possession as Dawson relied on short passes to control the clock. Hank Stram's stout defense took over in the fourth, sacking Kemp twice and not allowing the Bills beyond the Kansas City 40. Mike Garrett extended the Chiefs' lead to 24–7 with a one-yard effort at 6:16, then put and exclamation point on the Chiefs' day with a spectacular 18-yard touchdown run a minute and a half later.

It was all over. The Chiefs coasted to a 31–7 victory and the AFL title. They would have to wait to find out whether they were playing the Dallas Cowboys or the Green Bay Packers, who were facing off later in the afternoon at Dallas' Cotton Bowl. The Packers prevailed 34–27 for their second straight NFL title and would face the Chiefs on January 15 at Los Angeles Coliseum.

The AFL-NFL World Championship Game, as it was officially dubbed, was played on a beautiful West Coast afternoon before a crowd of 61,946. The first half was tight, but the Packers managed to take a 14–10 lead by halftime. They totally dominated the second half, however, and cruised to a convincing 35–10 triumph and the undisputed championship of professional football.

28 Gaze Upon the Wall of Fame

The Buffalo Bills' Wall of Fame was created in 1980 to, in the words of the Bills organization, "honor former players, administrators and coaches who have played significant roles in the team's history." For a player to be eligible for induction, he must have played with the Bills for at least three years (the one exception to this stipulation being Bob Kalsu) and be retired from professional football. Also eligible are nonplayers who have made outstanding contributions to the franchise, including administrators and coaches.

Selections are made by a panel composed of club personnel and media.

The names of the individuals enshrined are affixed to the facade at Ralph Wilson Stadium. As of 2012, 27 players, coaches, and administrators have received the team's highest honor, along with the 12th Man, which represents the team's legion of devoted fans.

1980 O.J. Simpson, Running Back (1969–77)*

1984 Jack Kemp, Quarterback (1962–69)

1985 Patrick J. McGroder, Administrator (1960–86)

1987 Tom Sestak, Defensive Tackle (1962–68)

1988 Billy Shaw, Guard (1961–69)*

1989 Ralph C. Wilson Jr., Owner/President (1959–Present)*

1992 12th Man

1993 Elbert Dubenion, Wide Receiver (1960–68)

1994 Mike Stratton, Linebacker (1962–72)

1995 Joe Ferguson, Quarterback (1973–84)

1996 Marv Levy, Head Coach (1986–97)*

1997 Joe DeLamielleure, Guard (1973–79, 1985)*

1998 Robert James, Cornerback (1969–74)

1999 Eddie Abramoski, Trainer (1960–96)

2000 Bob Kalsu, Guard (1968)

2000 George Saimes, Safety (1963–69)

2001 Fred Smerlas, Nose Tackle (1979–89)

2001 Jim Kelly, Quarterback (1986–96)*

2002 Kent Hull, Center (1986–96)

2003 Darryl Talley, Linebacker (1983–94)

2004 Jim Ritcher, Guard (1980–93)

2005 Thurman Thomas, Running Back (1988–99)*

2006 Andre Reed, Wide Receiver (1985–99)

2007 Steve Tasker, Special Teams/Wide Receiver (1986–97)

2008 Bruce Smith, Defensive End (1985–99)*
2010 Booker Edgerson, Cornerback (1962–69)
2011 Phil Hansen, Defensive End (1991–2001)
2012 Bill Polian, General Manager (1986–93)

*Member of the Pro Football Hall of Fame.

29 No Rodney Dangerfield

The Buffalo Bills locker room was filled with superstars, not to mention a few Hall of Famers. Names such as Bruce Smith, Jim Kelly, Thurman Thomas, and James Lofton resonated with besotted fans who watched their beloved team dominate the AFC during its glory days of the late 1980s and early 1990s. But there was one player who is often cited as being the most respected man on the team who is nowhere near as well known as those aforementioned players. In fact, he was often referred to as the Rodney Dangerfield of football (a guy who "can't get no respect") for the fact that he made just two Pro Bowls in his 12 seasons with the Bills. Still, he was the universally acknowledged leader of the defense that helped the Bills make six playoff and four Super Bowl appearances during his tenure with the team and probably the only one with the gumption to tell Bruce Smith to take a seat. His name was Darryl Talley.

Steve Tasker, himself a seven-time Pro Bowler, said of Talley, "Everybody—and I mean everybody—on the team respected Darryl, and they feared him too. Nobody wanted to mess with him. He was clearly one of our leaders, and he was not afraid to speak his piece when he believed it was necessary. He'd tell Bruce Smith

Dragging down elite rusher Emmitt Smith in Super Bowl XXVII, Darryl Talley shows why he deserves a little respect.

to shut up and sit down, and he'd pull Jim aside and say, 'Jim, you can't do that. You've got to knock it off.' Jim and Bruce and all the other stars would listen to him and take his word to heart."

It's quite obvious that Darryl Talley was—to his teammates anyway—no Rodney Dangerfield.

Talley came to the Bills in 1983 with little fanfare. After all, he was in the same draft class as Jim Kelly, who attracted all of the attention not only for being picked No. 1, but also for announcing shortly afterward that he had no desire to play in Buffalo. Talley, a consensus All-American selection in his senior year at West Virginia, on the other hand, signed his contract and reported on time. Right from the get-go, Talley was the consummate pro, doing whatever was asked of him, even if that meant he wasn't an immediate starter. The coaches loved his hustle and aggressiveness, but Talley did not perform up to expectations once the games started.

"In his rookie year he [struggled] on the field," recalled Eddie Abramoski, the Bills' athletic trainer at the time. "He was a second-round draft pick but not playing like it. [In] one game in particular he was struggling, and at halftime the defensive coaches were getting on him pretty good. We had Talley fitted out for contact lenses when he took his physical after the draft. When the coaches stopped yelling at him, I asked Darryl if he was wearing his contact lenses."

When Talley replied he wasn't, Abramoski ordered him to put them in.

"Things got better for him right after that."

Did they ever! Beginning in 1984, Talley became the starter at left outside linebacker and a permanent fixture on the Bills defense for the next decade. Those first few years were painful, but Talley's tenacity and never-say-die mind-set steadily made him a fan favorite. At the same time, his stature as a leader in the locker room was growing with each passing week. The team may not have been winning many games, but Talley wasn't about to let his team get pushed around.

"If anyone screwed with us," said nose tackle Fred Smerlas, "all I had to do was point to Talley. As always, he'd be standing there with a psychotic look on his face, huffing and puffing and foaming at the mouth."

The lean years eventually paid off, as the Bills garnered several top draft picks by virtue of their losing records. The team was slowly building for its future by selecting the likes of Bruce Smith, Frank Reich, Andre Reed, Ronnie Harmon, Will Wolford, and Mark Pike. Things really began to solidify in 1986, with the arrival of Jim Kelly and Marv Levy.

"It was a real struggle, those first three seasons," Talley recalled. "Things had not been good under Hank Bullough. The attitude on the team was not a good one. And then Marv Levy came to town." Talley flourished under Levy. After being moved to right outside linebacker, which placed him directly behind All-World defensive end Bruce Smith, Talley recorded career highs in tackles (116) and sacks (3).

More key moves came in 1987, as the Bills drafted linebacker Shane Conlan, cornerback Nate Odomes, and defensive end Leon Seals, and then acquired Cornelius Bennett in a blockbuster trade. The team improved to 7–8 and a year later finished with a 12–4 record to take the division title and secure its first postseason appearance since 1981. They made it all the way to the AFC Championship Game.

The era of unprecedented success for the Bills arrived in 1990, as the team claimed four straight AFC championships and won an incredible 49 of 64 regular-season games.

Talley had his best year to date in 1990, registering a team-high 123 tackles and picking off two passes during the regular season, earning his first trip to the Pro Bowl. But he was saving his best performances for the playoffs, and perhaps his greatest game as a pro, for the AFC Championship Game against the Los Angeles Raiders. All Talley did in that game was make five tackles, intercept two passes, and return one 27 yards for a score, leading the Bills to a 51–3 victory. He said afterward: "In order to be rated among the best and receive the accolades, you have to show up in the big game. This was the only game in town this week. The whole nation was watching." Unfortunately, the whole nation was also watching a week later when the Bills' dream season came to a crashing end at the hands of the New York Giants in Super Bowl XXV.

The Bills returned to the Super Bowl the following year, and two more times after that, setting a record of four straight appearances that will, in all likelihood, never be matched. That kind of success is built on strength of character and depended as much on Darryl Talley's leadership on defense as it did on Jim Kelly's on offense.

"The way they dedicated themselves to preparing for an opponent," Levy observed, "to bouncing back from a bad play or even from a devastating team loss, to gutting it out in bad weather situations or in shrugging off some nagging physical discomforts, to inspiring—by virtue of their actions rather than some blather—confidence in what we were all seeking to accomplish, those were some of the ways in which Jim and Darryl stood out as team leaders. Beyond that, they cared about their teammates, and many of those compatriots could tell you how the success they enjoyed in their own careers was enhanced by their association and friendships with Jim and Darryl."

Talley enjoyed his best year in 1991, registering 117 tackles, four sacks, and picking off five enemy aerials en route to a second consecutive Pro Bowl. He registered two more 100-tackle seasons, and although he did not make another Pro Bowl, he did receive All-Pro recognition in 1993 from *Pro Football Weekly* and the *Sporting News*.

But Talley's numbers dropped off dramatically in 1994, and the Bills had to make the very tough decision to not re-sign the then-34-year-old warrior who had served them so nobly for 12 seasons. He wasn't through, though. He played two more years, one with the Atlanta Falcons and his last with the Minnesota Vikings, before calling it a career.

Since then, Talley has seen four of his teammates and one head coach get enshrined in the Pro Football Hall of Fame. While Darryl waits patiently for his call from Canton, he continues to be one of the most honored figures ever to play for the Bills. He was inducted into the West Virginia University Hall of Fame in 1996 and in 2000 received the Ralph C. Wilson Jr. Distinguished Service Award (given to former Bills players for outstanding service to the organization and the community). Talley's name was affixed to the Bills' Wall of Fame in 2003. In 2007, he was enshrined in the Greater Buffalo Sports Hall of Fame. Talley returned to Ralph Wilson Stadium in 2010 to join several of his former teammates in being honored as part of the Bills 50th Anniversary Team. In 2011, he was named to the National College Football Hall of Fame.

30 Southern Comfort

In the early days of the AFL, the league's franchises found themselves in direct competition with the more-established National Football League in their efforts to secure top college talent. Personnel men from both leagues were forced to come up with creative ways to find—and ultimately sign—talented football players before a scout from the other league could beat them to the punch. Sometimes that meant signing a player before he was eligible, or even hiding a player from other suitors until he became eligible.

For many AFL talent scouts, it meant scrounging around small, out-of-the-way colleges where the guys from the NFL weren't looking.

"[Bills personnel man] Harvey Johnson got on an idea," said trainer Eddie Abramoski, "which was to try to get the players from the areas that didn't have pro teams, like the Deep South, so we'd have a chance to sign them."

Johnson had received a bit of intelligence from one of his sources about a tight end named Tom Sestak from McNeese State way down in southwestern Louisiana. McNeese was not exactly a greenhouse for growing football talent—it had only sent four of its football alums to the pros between 1939 and 1962—but Johnson's contact was adamant, so Johnson arranged a visit.

"I was impressed," Johnson later recalled, "but Tom didn't send me out of my mind." That tepid first impression might explain why the Bills waited until the 17th round to pick the 6'4" 235-pounder. The NFL Detroit Lions had apparently been poking around some of the same Southern schools, too, and thought enough of Sestak to draft him with their 16th-round pick. But Sestak, like many other players drafted by both leagues, decided to go with the AFL because his chances of actually making the team were better.

The Bills were just beginning their third AFL season and their first under new coach Lou Saban, who had taken over for Buster Ramsey at the end of 1961. When the prospective tight end from McNeese State showed up at camp weighing 265 pounds, Saban instinctively directed him to where the defensive linemen were working out. Sestak's strength and quickness were a revelation to the new coaching staff and commanded the attention of his new teammates.

"[Tom] didn't think that he was that much of a presence," recalled guard and fellow rookie George Flint, "but the rest of us knew that he was. He was going up against Billy Shaw, which was good training for him. Tom wasn't impressed with himself at all. He was a hell of a ballplayer."

Sestak was the Bills' starting right defensive tackle when the season kicked off, and by year's end, he was already recognized as one of the premier interior linemen in the league. After averaging an impressive seven unassisted tackles per game, Sestak won Rookie of the Year honors from *Pro Football Illustrated* and was chosen to play in the AFL All-Star Game. A year later, he averaged nine unassisted tackles per game, helping the Bills to their first-ever playoff appearance. Sestak was again selected to play in the All-Star Game and was also named First-Team All-AFL.

Sestak's best year might have been 1964. After being named the team's defensive captain, Big Ses went on a tear, being credited with 14.5 sacks (in 14 games!) and helping the Bills win their first AFL championship, a 20–7 win over the favored San Diego Chargers. He was the cornerstone of the Bills' league-leading defense, which set an AFL record by not allowing a rushing touchdown for 16 consecutive regular-season games (17 counting the AFL Title Game) between October 24, 1964, and October 31, 1965. When the Bills faced the Chargers in the 1965 AFL Title Game, Sestak had two sacks to pace a 23–0 whitewash. *Sport Magazine* selected him to its combined NFL-AFL All-Pro team.

But bad knees began to take their toll on Sestak. Despite another strong season and a third straight AFL title game appearance in 1966, he missed the AFL All-Star Game for the first time in his career. He continued to play at a high level in spite of several off-season surgeries and excruciating recoveries. "It was amazing how well he played considering how bad his knees were," said Abramoski. "All he did each day during practice was ride the stationary bike, his knee was so bad."

Unfortunately, those knees forced Sestak into early retirement after the 1968 season. More than 40 years later, he is still considered by many to be the greatest defensive tackle in team history. In seven seasons, he recorded (unofficially) 51 sacks—an incredible number for an interior lineman in the 14-game era. He was the only defensive lineman in the AFL to be a unanimous All-League selection three times and one of only six in all of professional football who were unanimous All-League selections three or more times. The other five (Bob Lilly, Merlin Olsen, Willie Davis, Deacon Jones, and Gino Marchetti) are all Pro Football Hall of Famers.

Despite his relatively short career, Sestak was named to the All-Time AFL Team by the Pro Football Hall of Fame in 1970. McNeese State inducted him into its Athletic Hall of Fame in 1983. He has been named to the Bills Silver Anniversary Team, the team's Wall of Fame, the Greater Buffalo Sports Hall of Fame, and the Bills 50th Anniversary Team (in 2010).

Sadly, Sestak was not able to enjoy many of these accolades. He was just 51 when a heart attack claimed his life on April 3, 1987.

31 The Legend of No. 31

When Bills third-string halfback Preston Ridlehuber trotted onto the War Memorial Stadium turf against the Boston Patriots on October 11, 1969, no one could have known he was about to make team history. It would have been even more unfathomable that his brief appearance in this game was actually going to be memorable for *two* reasons—the first for what he did and the second for what he was wearing.

When Ridlehuber entered the game, the Bills and Pats were tied 16–16, with less than six minutes remaining in the fourth quarter. Halfback Max Anderson, who had started the game in place of the injured O.J. Simpson, had himself been knocked out with an injury, necessitating Ridlehuber's entrance.

Wearing No. 31 and not having been with the club long enough to have a nameplate sewn on his jersey, Ridlehuber's identity was a mystery to all but a few of the 46,201 fans in attendance. With the ball resting at the Patriots' 45-yard line, the right-handed halfback took the handoff from quarterback James Harris and rolled left. The Boston defenders came up to play the run, but Ridlehuber—a quarterback in college—stopped suddenly, turned his body, and heaved the pigskin toward receiver Haven Moses, standing wide open at the Boston 10. Moses hauled in Ridlehuber's floater and sprinted into the end zone to give Buffalo the go-ahead score with 5:02 remaining. The defense did the rest, and the Bills escaped with an unforgettable 23–16 win.

It was a terrific play, indeed, but there was another aspect to Ridlehuber's dramatic play that spawned one of the greatest stories in team lore. When Ridlehuber entered the contest wearing No. 31 on his jersey, he became the first Buffalo Bill ever to wear that particular number in a regular-season game. It was his first game with the team, and since there had not been sufficient time to have a proper jersey with a number and nameplate made, equipment manager Tony Marchitte gave him a spare jersey bearing the number 31 until something permanent could be put together. Ridlehuber wore the shirt for just this single game, switching to No. 36 thereafter.

What makes this part of the story so interesting is the legend behind it. It goes something like this: One of the team's corporate logos from the 1960s featured a football player astride a charging buffalo and wearing a jersey emblazoned with No. 31. According to Denny Lynch, the Bills' longtime archivist, the team had never issued 31 before because, it was assumed, the number was reserved for the official team logo. The tradition was broken momentarily when Ridlehuber wore the number in that one game against the Patriots, but it was placed back into storage where it remained for the next two decades.

"In 1990, I was involved with the No. 31 story," Lynch recalled. "We knew that [first-round draft pick] James Williams wore 31 in college. People kept telling me that 31 could not be used because 'Ralph [Wilson] said so.' I talked to [general manager] Bill Polian, and we asked Ralph, who said, 'I don't know anything about it.' Evidently, the equipment guys had carried on the Tony Marchitte myth that the number couldn't be used. Polian said, 'Give him the number,' and the myth was finally broken."

Since that time, several Bills players have sported the number. It is currently being worn by safety Jairus Byrd.

The King of Comebacks

Frank Reich is considered one of the greatest backup quarterbacks in NFL history. In nine seasons with the Bills, he started only eight regular-season games, but that includes an unforgettable three-game stretch in October 1989 filling in for injured starter Jim Kelly. Reich won all three starts of those starts (23–20 against the Rams, 34–3 against the Jets, and 31–17 against the Dolphins), connecting on 40 of 66 passes for 482 yards and six touchdowns (with only one interception).

He was even better in the playoffs, winning both of the games he started, including, of course, the historic come-from-behind win against Houston in the 1992 AFC Wild Card Game. That incredible game—in which Reich brought his team back from a 35–3 deficit to claim a 41–38 win in overtime—still stands as the greatest comeback in the annals of pro football.

Of course, Reich was already known for architecting the greatest comeback in the history of *college* football.

Reich was in his senior year at the University of Maryland when his Terrapins traveled to Miami to face Jimmy Johnson and the defending 1983 national champion University of Miami Hurricanes on November 10, 1984. Reich was still recovering from a separated shoulder suffered earlier in the season, so backup Stan Gelbaugh—with whom Reich later played on the Buffalo Bills—got the start. Gelbaugh had led the Terrapins to victories in their three previous games, but Miami's quarterback Bernie Kosar was in full control of this one, staking the 'Canes to a 31–0 lead at the half.

Maryland coach Bobby Ross inserted Reich at the start of the second half, and the 6'4", 210-pounder proceeded to slice up the Miami defense with the precision of a surgeon. In the third quarter alone, Reich threw for two touchdowns and ran for a third to cut the lead to 34–21. Early in the fourth, he engineered a nine-play, 55-yard drive that culminated in a 14-yard scoring pass to close the gap to six points. Reich then connected with Greg Hill on a 68-yard touchdown pass that gave Maryland a 35–34 lead. Miami fumbled the ensuing kickoff and Maryland returned it for a score, extending the lead to 42–34. Miami managed to pull within two by scoring a late touchdown, but the two-point conversion failed, preserving the 42–40 score and Maryland's miraculous victory.

Reich had been nearly flawless in the second half, completing 12 of 15 for 260 yards with four touchdown passes and another rushing TD. The 31-point deficit that the Terrapins overcame that day was an NCAA record that stood until it was broken in 2006 when Michigan State rallied from a 38–3 deficit to defeat Northwestern 41–38.

Bills fans like to think of that game as merely a rehearsal for what was to come eight years later. After all, Maryland's deficit was one point less than what the Bills were facing when Reich took destiny in his hands.

He finally got his chance to be a starter when he signed to play for the expansion Carolina Panthers in 1995. Frank threw the team's first touchdown pass to former Bills teammate Pete Metzelaars. He spent one season with the Panthers, one with the New York Jets, and two with Detroit before retiring after the 1998 season.

Reich currently serves as the wide receivers coach for the Arizona Cardinals. He also gives motivational speeches, drawing lessons from his extraordinary experiences to encourage anyone facing adversity.

Four straight Super Bowls. No team had ever done it before. No team has done it since. It's very unlikely that any team will ever do it again. The Buffalo Bills are the only ones who can say that they have accomplished the incredible feat. But in the aftermath of Super Bowl XXVII—the team's third appearance and third straight loss—it seemed more likely that the Bills were preparing to self-destruct than make a run at an unprecedented fourth.

Anyone who thought that way was mistaken, of course, but in the early months of 1993, all indications pointed toward the end of the road for the Bills' Super Bowl run. The first sign came just four days after Super Bowl XXVII when Bill Polian, the man credited with putting together the team, announced that he and owner Ralph Wilson had mutually agreed to part ways. The former general manager was very popular among the players, and perhaps the only thing that prevented a full-scale revolt was the hiring of the equally popular John Butler—formerly the team's director of player personnel—to fill the vacancy.

As the off-season progressed, several key players also left, many of whom had been present for all three of the team's Super Bowls, including tackle Will Wolford and linebackers Carlton Bailey and Shane Conlan, all of whom signed big-money deals with other clubs. Fifteen-year veteran wide receiver James Lofton, who had seen a career resurrection after signing with the Bills in 1989, was given an outright release.

Despite the seemingly insurmountable loss of talent, the Bills proved their core resilience by improving upon their 11–5 finish in 1992 to post a 12–4 mark and claim their third division crown in four years. One of the highlights of 1993 was the sweep of the teams Buffalo had lost to in the three previous Super Bowls (13–10 over Dallas on September 12, 17–14 over the New York Giants on October 3, and 24–10 over the Redskins on November 1). Still, after 12 games, they stood at 8–4, trailing Miami for the division lead by one game. However, the Bills ended with a flourish, winning their last four—including a huge 47–34 victory over the Dolphins at Joe Robbie Stadium—to finish 12–4 and clinch home-field advantage throughout the playoffs.

The Bills hosted the 10–6 Los Angeles Raiders in the AFC Divisional Playoff Game, which was the coldest home game in Bills history (0 degrees at kickoff with wind chills as low as minus-32). The weather conditions, however, offered no advantage to the Bills, who found themselves trailing 23–22 heading into the final quarter. But Jim Kelly engineered a scoring drive that covered 71 yards in nine plays and culminated in a 22-yard strike to James Lofton's replacement, Bill Brooks, giving the Bills the lead and the margin of victory.

A week later, Buffalo played host to Joe Montana and the 11–5 Kansas City Chiefs in the AFC Championship Game. The golden-era Bills made one last emphatic statement by crushing the Chiefs 30–13. Thurman Thomas lugged the leather 33 times for 186 yards and three touchdowns. Montana, whom many consider to be the greatest quarterback of all time, was forced from the contest early in the third quarter after suffering a concussion, having completed just nine of 23 passing attempts. For the fourth straight year, the Buffalo Bills were the champions of the AFC and for the second year in a row would be facing the Dallas Cowboys in Atlanta's Georgia Dome for all the marbles.

The Cowboys took the game's initial lead early in the first quarter on a 41-yard field goal by Eddie Murray, but Buffalo's Steve Christie tied the score two minutes later with a Super Bowl–record 54-yarder. Later in the first, Murray knocked through a chip-shot 24-yarder to give Dallas a 6–3 lead.

The Bills dominated play throughout the second period, taking a 10–6 lead on a four-yard run by Thurman Thomas that capped a beautiful 17-play, 80-yard drive. Christie then extended Buffalo's lead with a 28-yard field goal as the half expired.

But just as quickly as the Bills had seized the game's momentum in the second quarter, the Cowboys snatched it right back less than a minute into the third. On Buffalo's third offensive play to open the half, Leon Lett stripped the ball from Thomas. James Washington, who had forced Thomas to fumble back in the first quarter, scooped up the loose pigskin and raced 46 yards for the score. The Cowboys hadn't merely stolen the ball, they had stolen Buffalo's thunder. It was 13–13, but that single play represented the setup for the knockout punch that was to follow. After forcing the Bills to punt on their next possession, the Cowboys came right back with an eight-play, 64-yard drive that Emmitt Smith capped with a 15-yard run, giving the Cowboys a 20–13 lead. They never looked back.

Smith, who would be crowned the game's Most Valuable Player, scored his second touchdown early in the fourth quarter to extend Dallas' lead to 14 points. Eddie Murray kicked a late 20-yarder—his third field goal—to make the final score 30–13.

Once again, the Bills had come up short in the Super Bowl. This time, however, there would be no next year. Though no one knew it at the time (and, quite frankly, no one dared count them out for a fifth shot), the Buffalo Bills' magical Super Bowl run was finally over.

"Winning four straight AFC titles and going to four straight Super Bowls is something you may never see again," observed Darryl Talley, one of the many warriors who appeared in all four of the Bills' Super Bowls. "If another team does it, it will be awfully tough to accomplish. We would walk out on any football field and know that we could win the game."

34 Kent Hull

August 18, 1986, will be forever remembered by Buffalo sports fans as the day Jim Kelly arrived, for it was on that date that the star quarterback cruised into Western New York in a stretch limousine to assume his preordained position as the Bills' signal-caller. But it should not be forgotten that the same date also marked the arrival of another future great—the man who snapped the ball to Kelly and became the unquestioned leader of the Bills' star-studded offensive line for the next 11 seasons. That other guy was a center by the name of Kent Hull, but his ride was not quite as ostentatious as Kelly's. No, Hull's mode of transportation was more indicative of his lunch-pail approach to the game he loved; he arrived in an equipment van. Despite the contrast, Kelly and Hull would be forever linked as perhaps the two most essential parts of the vaunted no-huddle offense that propelled the Bills to four Super Bowls and numerous postseason appearances in the late 1980s and early 1990s.

Hull played his college ball at Mississippi State but was considered too small by NFL standards and went undrafted. The New Jersey Generals of the newly formed United States Football League didn't agree and tapped the 6'5", 250-pound pivot man with their seventh draft selection in 1983. He was their starting center from day one and turned in three solid seasons with the Generals, opening holes that allowed running back Herschel Walker to become the USFL's all-time leading rusher. By the time the ill-fated league folded in 1986, Kent had caught the eye of Bill Polian, the Bills' general manager, who swooped in to sign Hull (who by that time had bulked up to 280 pounds) before any other NFL teams got wise.

Hull later claimed that he fully expected to be cut before the start of his first regular season with the Bills but instead became the starting center midway through the preseason and did not relinquish his hold on the position for more than a decade, playing in 170 regular-season games, an incredible 19 playoff games, and three Pro Bowls.

Whatever Hull lacked in brawn—and it wasn't much—he made up for with brains, for it was his job to call the offensive line's blocking schemes when the unit got to the line of scrimmage. "He was as bright as can be," observed head coach Marv Levy. "The responsibility of seeing that our difficult-to-run-but-vaunted no-huddle offense ran smoothly rested just as heavily upon the physical and mental abilities of Kent Hull as it did upon those of our quarterbacks." Considering the level of success the Bills offenses enjoyed during their four-year Super Bowl run, Hull did his job quite well.

Teammate Steve Tasker put it simply: "Kent wound up becoming the greatest center in Bills history."

Just as integral to the team's ultimate success was Hull's quiet leadership in the locker room. While other team leaders like the fiery Darryl Talley tended to be very vocal, Hull could utter volumes simply by giving a teammate a knowing glance or maybe a few well-chosen, softly spoken words.

"His leadership was by example," Levy recalled. "He knew when to talk to a guy."

"When he spoke in that thick-as-Mississippi-mud drawl of his, guys listened," Tasker said. "[He was] one of the smartest and most respected guys in the locker room."

But if there was one thing he loved to do more than play football, it was tend his 2,500-acre cattle farm back in northeastern Mississippi. There was still some football left in Hull's 35-year-old body when he retired in 1996, but he couldn't ignore his other calling any longer. He returned to his home state and settled into the life of a gentleman farmer, occasionally coming back to Buffalo to attend some team function or, as he did in 2002, see his name added to the Bills' Wall of Fame at Ralph Wilson Stadium.

The Bills family, as well as the entire Buffalo sports community, was shaken to its core when news broke of Hull's death on October 18, 2011, after a long battle with chronic liver disease. He was just 50 years old.

35 The Best Drafts

In 1974, the Pittsburgh Steelers conducted what most historians consider to be the greatest draft in NFL history. In the first five rounds, the Steelers incredibly selected four men who became integral pieces of four Super Bowl–winning teams and all of whom wound up in the Pro Football Hall of Fame. With their first-round pick (21st overall), they selected wide receiver Lynn Swann from the University of Southern California. Picked second was middle linebacker Jack Lambert out of Kent State. In the fourth round, the Steelers tapped Alabama A&M wide receiver John Stallworth. And in the fifth they took center Mike Webster from Wisconsin.

Simply stunning! What makes it even more so is the fact that no other franchise has ever drafted more than *two* Hall of Famers in a single draft class. The Bills, for what it's worth, are among them. Unfortunately, the year they did so, 1964, was at the height of the draft wars between the AFL and NFL, and the two selected—defensive end Carl Eller and wide receiver Paul Warfield—chose to sign with teams in the better-established senior league (Eller with the Minnesota Vikings and Warfield with the Cleveland Browns).

Since the Bills failed to sign either of them—and one of the keys to a successful draft is signing the players picked—1964's draft does not stand among the Bills' best (although they did draft and sign cornerback Butch Byrd, kicker Pete Gogolak, and guard Joe O'Donnell). So which drafts *do* qualify as the team's best ever? Here are the top five:

5. **1979:** Despite the disappointment of failing to sign linebacker Tom Cousineau, the team's top draft pick that year, the Bills scored in a big way with Jerry Butler as the second of their first-round picks and Fred Smerlas and Jim Haslett in the second round.

4. **1983:** This draft was all about leadership. With their second of two first-round picks (acquired from Cleveland in exchange for the rights to Tom Cousineau), the Bills took future Hall of Fame quarterback Jim Kelly from the University of Miami (Florida). In the second round, the Bills picked West Virginia linebacker Darryl Talley. These two became the leaders on

their respective sides of the ball and were essential to the success the Bills enjoyed in the late 1980s and early '90s.

3. **1985:** Most notable for the selection of Virginia Tech defensive end Bruce Smith, who was taken first overall, Buffalo also selected Maryland quarterback Frank Reich in the third round and then struck gold in the fourth, choosing wide receiver Andre Reed from tiny Kutztown University of Pennsylvania.

2. **1962:** There were no future Hall of Famers in this draft class— in fact, no one selected in the top 10 rounds ever played for the team. (First-round pick Ernie Davis, the Syracuse halfback, famously opted for the NFL but lost his life to leukemia before ever playing a down of pro ball.) What's truly significant about this draft, overseen by general manager Dick Gallagher and head coach Buster Ramsey, is the high value they received from two late-round selections in Tennessee tight end Mike Stratton (13th) and McNeese State tight end/defensive tackle Tom Sestak (17th). Both men were integral parts of Buffalo's dominating defenses of the mid-1960s and were selected to the Bills official 50th Anniversary Team in 2010.

1. **1961:** The nod for best draft in team history has got to go to the one conducted in the team's second year. Gallagher and Ramsey pulled off a masterpiece by drafting three-fifths of the offensive line that would lead the way to the Bills' first golden age. After missing on Auburn tackle Ken Rice in the first round, Buffalo tapped Georgia Tech tackle Billy Shaw in the second. The Bills moved Shaw to guard, where he developed into the best one in the league. In the fourth round, Buffalo picked another tackle—Stew Barber from Penn State. After playing a season at linebacker, Barber was switched back to tackle and became a fixture at AFL All-Star Games. The seventh round brought Syracuse center Al Bemiller, perhaps the most versatile one of the bunch, who played both guard and tackle during his nine-year career.

With Shaw, Barber, and Bemiller running interference, the Bills appeared in three straight AFL championship games in the mid-'60s. For a blue-collar town and team like Buffalo, it is fitting that their most successful draft focused on the grunts in the trenches.

36 Take In a Practice at St. John Fisher

For many Bills fans, a visit to the team's summer training camp at St. John Fisher College just outside of Rochester is tantamount to a pilgrimage. They not only have the opportunity to see their favorite players up close, they also get to view that particular year's crop of prospects and maybe secure an autograph or two. And best of all, it's free!

The Bills have partnered with St. John Fisher since 2000 as part of the team's regionalization strategy. The camp regularly attracts thousands of zealots each year from across New York State, Pennsylvania, Ohio, and Canada and is considered among the finest in the entire league. The team holds daily workouts at the school, and most are open to the public. Evening practices are also free, but tickets are required for admission.

In addition to seeing the team put through its paces, fans have the opportunity to meet their favorite players at daily team autograph sessions. A popular attraction at the camp is the Bills Experience, in which fans of all ages can test their football skills and partake in other interactive games. Fans can also visit the vendor tent to shop for Bills gear or purchase tickets for the upcoming season.

St. John Fisher College is located in Pittsford, about six miles southeast of Rochester. The practice schedule changes from year to year and is also subject to in-season changes, so it is a good idea to visit the team's official website (www.buffalobills.com) for the most accurate and up-to-date information.

Prior to moving their summer operations to St. John Fisher, the Bills held training camps at the Knox Farm and Roycroft Inn in East Aurora (1960–62), the Camelot-Voyager Motor Inn in Blasdell (1963–67), Niagara University (1968–80), and Fredonia State College (1981–99).

37 Putting the *Special* in *Special Teams*

There is an ongoing debate among football historians over whether a player who spent his career on special teams should be considered a legitimate candidate for enshrinement in the Pro Football Hall of Fame. Of course, in order to be considered at all, that player must have been pretty darned good at it. The main argument against the special-teamer, however, is that he participates in a low percentage of the actual plays on the field, so his level of impact in comparison to a regular offensive or defensive player is therefore very small.

Marv Levy disagrees with that assertion. Sure, Levy might be a little biased, due to the fact that he pioneered the science of the kicking game by being the second-ever full-time special teams coach employed by an NFL team, but he offers some interesting insight.

"George Allen had a great belief in the importance of the kicking game," Levy explained, "and that is what motivated him to bring a full-time special teams coach onto his staff. When I did a rather nonscientific study to determine the number of kicking-game plays in a game, I determined that approximately one out of every five plays was a kicking-game play. It certainly would vary from game to game, but when I finally tabulated up all the games and plays that I researched, it came out to close to 20 percent. Both George and I, however, held the deep belief that kicking-game plays impact the outcome of a game a lot more heavily than the 20 percent stat might lead people to believe, and I always stressed that sentiment when talking to our players about that issue.

"To emphasize that point, I always informed them that on every kicking-game play, one of three extremely important scenarios that affect the outcome of the game happens. These are:

1. There is a change of possession (either punt or kickoff).
2. There is a considerable change in field position involved.
3. There is a specific 'yes' or 'no' involved as to whether points will be scored on that play (field goal, PAT, two-point conversion)."

Furthermore, what Levy's list doesn't include is the possible change that can occur as a result of a blocked field goal or punt, an onside kick, bad snap, or kick returned for a score. Any one of these plays can affect the game's outcome, or swing the momentum from one team to another.

Assuming special-teamers belong in the Hall of Fame, who is most deserving of the honor? There have been some great ones over the years, including Mosi Tatupu, Bill Bates, Western New York's own Ron Wolfley, and many more, but the one name that is at or near the top of most experts' lists is Steve Tasker of the Buffalo Bills.

The Houston Oilers made Tasker their ninth-round selection in 1985 after his stellar career at Northwestern University. But Tasker could not crack the starting lineup and spent his first season returning kickoffs and playing on special teams. He was injured early in 1986, and the Oilers were forced to place him on waivers before they could reactivate him. It just so happened that the week

Tasker was waived was the same week Levy took over as coach of the Bills. His first personnel move, after being convinced by assistant coach Joe Faragalli that the 5'9", 175-pound receiver could help the Bills' special teams, was to put in the waiver claim.

In Tasker's first full season with the Bills, he was named to the Pro Bowl. He returned again in 1990 and five more times after that. In 1993, he was the game's MVP after making four special teams tackles, forcing a fumble, and blocking a field goal. Bills highlight films of the era are peppered with shots of the diminutive Tasker slamming into kick returners a split second after the ball reaches their hands, of Tasker blocking punts or even occasionally making a spectacular return of a kickoff or punt. Along the way, he became recognized as the best special-teamer in the game and, many argue, the greatest of all time.

"There has never been a special teams player like Steve Tasker," said Levy. "I was once told by a renowned head coach from another team that the man on our team for whom they had to prepare most specifically, despite all the many stars we had on offense and defense, was Steve."

Tasker's importance to the team went beyond the kicking game and disproved another common assertion that a player relegated to special teams is not as good an athlete as an every-down player, otherwise he'd also be an every-down player.

Quarterback Jim Kelly lobbied to have Tasker used more on offense, but Levy and special teams coach Bruce DeHaven wouldn't hear of it. Whereas most coaching staffs refused to allow every-down players to be used on special teams for fear they might be injured and unavailable for their regular positions, it was the other way around with Tasker. Yet when called upon to fill in after the Bills receiving corps was riddled with injuries in 1995 and '96, Tasker caught 41 passes for 627 yards and six touchdowns. In a 35–10 victory over the Jets in 1996, he caught six balls for 160 yards and two scores!

"He wasn't just an okay, nice, try-hard guy," observed renowned football writer Vic Carucci. "Steve Tasker [was] a world-class athlete."

So the argument rages on—is there space in the Pro Football Hall of Fame for special teams players and, if so, should a spot be reserved for Steve Tasker? In a poll conducted by the NFL Network in 2008, he was ranked ninth among players who should be in the Hall but are not. In a recent hypothetical all-time team selected by members of the Pro Football Hall of Fame Selection Committee, Tasker was picked as the only special teams player on the squad.

That same committee ultimately holds the key that would open the door for Tasker's induction. He has been a semifinalist four times but never seems to get enough support among committee members to make it in. Perhaps one day soon they will come to see things the way Tasker's many fans do and make him the first special teams player to be enshrined in the hallowed halls of Canton.

Call him "Multi-Tasker"—Steve Tasker could do it all on the field.

38 A True American Hero

People tend to use the word "hero" very loosely—especially in sports. The word is sometimes given to a football player who scores a dramatic, last-minute, game-winning touchdown, or a baseball player who hits a grand-slam home run in the bottom of the ninth inning to propel his team to victory.

But there are times when the term is appropriately applied to sports figures, and one of those is former Buffalo Bill James Robert "Bob" Kalsu. Kalsu, however, is not a hero for anything he did on the gridiron. No, Kalsu earned the title by making the ultimate sacrifice while serving his country in Vietnam, becoming the only active professional football player to lose his life in the conflict.

Bob Kalsu played his college ball at the University of Oklahoma, where he was team captain and an All-American at tackle in his senior year. The Bills selected him with their eighth-round pick in the 1968 draft, and the 6'3" 235-pounder—converted to guard in camp—made a positive impression right from the start.

"The thing that I remember about Bob was his speed," remarked guard Billy Shaw. "He had really good speed. Most rookies that came in were bigger than Joe O'Donnell and me, and mine and Joe's main attribute was our foot speed. Bob fit right into that pattern. I remember making the comment early on that he was about [our] size—Joe and I were almost identical in size and Bob was close to us. Bob played both guards, so he spelled me in practice. Bob was somewhat quiet—he was all business. He stood out as a rookie. I liked him because he gave it everything that he had."

Kalsu was expected to back up Shaw and O'Donnell, but when O'Donnell—the starting right guard—went down with a season-ending injury, the Oklahoma City native took over and filled in admirably. He was one of six rookies to start for the injury-addled Bills on opening day against the Boston Patriots. In all, Kalsu started nine games during the year and was one of the few—very few—bright spots on the 1–12–1 Bills and was named the team's Rookie of the Year.

The following March, Kalsu—an Army ROTC cadet while in college—reported for basic training at Fort Sill in Oklahoma. Friends and family begged Bob—a married man with a baby daughter—to seek a deferment, but he wouldn't hear of it. He had made a commitment and was intent on honoring it. In September 1969, the 24-year-old Kalsu received orders sending him to Vietnam. He shipped out two months later, becoming one of only six pro football players to serve in the war. He found out shortly after reaching Vietnam that his wife, Jan, was pregnant with their second child—a son he would never see. On July 21, 1970, First Lieutenant Kalsu was killed by mortar fire defending Ripcord Base on an isolated jungle mountaintop near Vietnam's Ashua Valley. On the 23rd, Jan gave birth to Robert James Kalsu, not knowing that her husband had died two days earlier. Hours later, still in bed recovering from the birth of their son, she learned of Bob's death. She had the name on the birth certificate changed immediately to James Robert Kalsu Jr.

In 1999, NFL Films produced a feature on Kalsu that was nominated for an Emmy Award. The Buffalo Bills honored Kalsu's memory in 2000 by placing his name on the Wall of Fame at Ralph Wilson Stadium. The army honored Kalsu in 2005 by redesignating the Fort Campbell Replacement Company in Kentucky to the 1st Lt. James Robert Kalsu Replacement Company.

A plaque memorializing Kalsu hangs in the Bills' administrative offices at Ralph Wilson Stadium. Its last line says it best: "No one will ever know how great a football player Bob might have been, but we do know how great a man he was to give up his life for his country."

39 James Lofton

James Lofton's credentials prior to coming to Buffalo might very well have been good enough to qualify him for induction into the Pro Football Hall of Fame, but if they weren't, his four years in Buffalo certainly put him over the top. By the time he signed with the Bills in September 1989, Lofton had already played 11 NFL seasons, caught 599 passes for 11,085 yards and 54 touchdowns, and been named First-Team All-Pro four times. The Bills were looking to shore up the receiver spot opposite Andre Reed and were hoping that the 33-year-old receiver had a little gas remaining in the tank.

They weren't disappointed.

The Green Bay Packers had selected Lofton with their first pick (sixth overall) in 1978 after a brilliant career at Stanford, where he was also a standout track-and-field performer as well as an academic All-American. Lofton was a starter from his first regular-season game with the Pack. Combining soft hands with blazing speed, Lofton was a threat to go the distance whenever he was on the field and was named NFC Rookie of the Year. In nine seasons with the Packers, Lofton was one of the most feared deep threats in the league, averaging better than 1,000 yards and nearly 60 receptions per season, and was voted to seven Pro Bowls.

But after a down year in 1986 in which he averaged a career-low 13.1 yards per catch, Lofton was dealt to the Raiders in exchange for draft choices. The Raiders, however, were already stacked at receiver with Mervyn Fernandez, Willie Gault, and later Tim Brown—there simply weren't enough balls to go around. After two years, Lofton, the elder statesman of the group, was deemed expendable and was unceremoniously released.

The Buffalo Bills, by this time, were an up-and-coming team but were still a player or two away from the league's upper echelon. The Raiders' poor judgment would turn out to be the Bills' good fortune.

"Our director of pro personnel, Bob Ferguson, suggested that we bring in James Lofton, who had just been cut by the Los Angeles Raiders," recalled coach Marv Levy. "While I thought that James' release meant that he no longer possessed the outstanding talents he had displayed for so many years, I saw no harm in taking a look, so I said, 'Okay.'"

Good thing! "On tryout day he stunned us all!" Levy continued. "He was as fast as ever, he ran great routes, and his receiving skills were all that we could have asked for. I couldn't believe or understand why the Raiders had cut him."

Lofton became an integral part of the Bills' explosive attack, and his career experienced a rebirth. In 1990, when the no-huddle became the team's primary offense, Lofton caught 35 passes for 712 yards (an average of 20.3 per catch) and played a crucial role in helping the team to its first-ever Super Bowl.

"James turned out to be the perfect complement to Andre Reed," Levy observed. "Their being on the field together at the same time made both of them more of a threat than they would have been had not the other one been there, too. His arrival helped to add so much balance to our attack."

But it was in the playoffs that the veteran really sparkled. In the Bills' 44–34 defeat of Miami in the 1990 divisional playoff game, Lofton caught seven balls for 149 yards and a touchdown. In the next week's 51–3 destruction of the Los Angeles Raiders in the AFC Championship Game, Lofton smoked his old team with five catches for 113 yards and two scores.

As good as Lofton was in 1990, he was even better in '91, catching 57 passes for 1,072 yards and eight touchdowns in helping the Bills reach a second straight Super Bowl. At age 35, he became the oldest player in NFL history to record 1,000 receiving yards in a single season and earned his first trip to the Pro Bowl since 1985.

But by 1992, Lofton was finally beginning to show signs of slowing down. He caught 51 passes for 786 yards, but his average of 15.4 yards per catch was more than three yards off his career standard. The Bills had made the decision to begin rebuilding for the future and informed Lofton that he was not in their plans for 1993. At the time of his release, Lofton was the league's all-time leader in receiving yardage with 13,821.

Lofton spent one last season splitting time between the Philadelphia Eagles and the Los Angeles Rams before announcing his retirement. Even before that inevitable day, fans and media were speculating about his Hall of Fame chances. After being a finalist in 2000 and 2002, Lofton was selected for enshrinement in 2003, the same year as another former Bill, Joe DeLamielleure.

Since retiring, Lofton has served as wide receivers coach for the San Diego Chargers (2002–07) and Oakland Raiders (2008) and is considered a prime candidate to be an NFL head coach. He is currently the color commentator for Westwood One radio's *Sunday Night Football* broadcasts.

 **Upset!**

The Buffalo Bills were a team in disarray when they met the New York Jets at War Memorial Stadium on September 29, 1968. After losing their first two games that year—including an embarrassing 48–6 pasting at the hands of the Oakland Raiders in Week 2—owner Ralph Wilson fired coach Joe Collier and replaced him with Harvey Johnson, the team's chief scout. By all accounts, Johnson

Great Returns

Tom Janik's 100-yard return against the Jets eclipsed the old Bills record of 91 yards set by Booker Edgerson against Houston in 1964 and stood untouched until October 3, 1976, when Tony Greene went 101 yards with an interception against the Kansas City Chiefs. Janik's single-game total of 137 interception-return yards also set a new club record that still stands, as does the record three interceptions the team returned for touchdowns that day.

In all, the Bills intercepted Joe Namath five times in the game. That mark, however impressive, was not a record, though. The club mark was actually six, and they had reached that number on four occasions prior to 1968 (November 20, 1960, at the Los Angeles Chargers, November 19, 1961, at the Denver Broncos, September 9, 1962, against the Houston Oilers, and December 9, 1967, at the Boston Patriots).

was an astute judge of football talent, but by no means was he prepared to lead a team as head coach.

"Harvey was just in there to manage it until the season was over, until they could hire somebody else," said defensive end Ron McDole. "He didn't have the background to be the head coach, and he'd be the first to tell you that. He didn't want the job. He knew enough ball, and so, like anything else, the boss comes in and tells you, 'You're the new head coach.' Harvey was probably the only guy they could get at that point in time, and so Harvey took the job."

The team's first game under Johnson was played at Nippert Stadium in Cincinnati, and the change in leadership saw the same result, as the expansion Bengals handed Buffalo its third straight loss. It didn't appear that things were going to be any different when the Bills returned home to face the undefeated Jets in Week 4. The Jets featured a high-flying offense, led by the most glamorous player in the game—quarterback Joe Namath. They were the odds-on favorite to take the AFL crown and represent the league in Super Bowl III. But the Bills were a proud bunch, with several veterans remaining from the team that just a few years earlier won back-to-back AFL championships. They might not have been playing for any titles, but they certainly weren't rolling over for anyone.

That's not how it looked, however, when New York marched down the field to score on a four-yard Namath-to–George Sauer touchdown pass only two minutes into the action. But the Jets' next possession was spoiled by safety Tom Janik, who picked off a Namath pass and returned it 37 yards, setting up a 35-yard field goal by Bruce Alford. Buffalo took the lead at 14:56 of the first quarter when Ben Gregory bulled over the goal line from the 2. The Jets defense rose up late in the second quarter, forcing Bills quarterback Dan Darragh to fumble at his own 10. After throwing two straight incompletions, Namath attempted to hit Curley Johnson in the right flat. But Janik intervened to make his second theft of the half, snatching Namath's pass before it could reach Johnson in the end zone.

"I was covering Johnson all the way," Janik explained. "The ball was perfectly thrown. I hesitated a split second, then stepped inside my man. All I saw was daylight."

Janik turned upfield and headed straight for the New York end zone, sprinting past the riotous Buffalo bench as he streaked down the left sideline. "Namath came up on the play downfield, and I was getting tired," he continued, "but I knew he was, too, and that knee had to be bothering him, so I just kept going."

There was no way the Jets' gimpy quarterback was going to catch the speedy Texan, who cruised untouched the rest of the way for a 100-yard touchdown run. Just like that, the Bills were on top, 17–7.

The Jets were able to bounce back and take a 21–20 lead before intermission, but Janik's play had given his team a much-needed infusion of confidence. The Bills reestablished the momentum midway through the third quarter, reclaiming the lead when Alford nailed his third field goal. The Buffalo defense stepped up in the fourth, with veteran cornerbacks Butch Byrd and Booker Edgerson returning two more of Namath's passes for touchdowns (53 and 45 yards, respectively) within a span of 62 seconds to give the Bills a commanding 37–21 lead. The Jets scored twice more, but the damage was done. The Bills—19-point underdogs at game time—claimed the biggest upset of the AFL season, defeating the eventual Super Bowl champions 37–35.

This was the only victory the Bills would record in 1968, as the team went 0–9–1 the rest of the way to finish 1–12–1—the worst record in the AFL *and* NFL—and earn the first overall pick in the upcoming college draft. They used that pick to great effect, selecting O.J. Simpson.

The Man Who Made the Hit Heard 'Round the World

Robert Smith's iconic photograph of Mike Stratton crashing into Keith Lincoln of the San Diego Chargers in the 1964 AFL Title Game is arguably the most famous action shot in the league's history and captured the defining moment of the Bills' AFL era. Stratton's tackle not only forced the Chargers star from the game with cracked ribs, it turned the tide in favor of the Bills, who went on to win the game and their first of two American Football League championships.

But if things had gone differently during Stratton's rookie campaign, it's quite possible that he would have ended up as a backup to starting tight end Ernie Warlick instead of one of the greatest linebackers in Bills history. He had been a two-way player at the University of Tennessee, playing tight end on offense and defensive end on the other side of the ball. The Bills, under the direction of head coach Buster Ramsey, selected Stratton in the 13th round of the 1962 college draft, but by the time training camp rolled around, Ramsey was gone and no one, including Stratton, knew where he was supposed to fit in.

"When the coach called everybody's name when we were going out, he didn't call my name," Stratton later recalled of his first day at practice. "I said, 'Where do you want me to go?' He said, 'What is your name again?' I figured I was in a little bit of trouble at that time. He said, 'Why don't you go with the defensive ends?' So I went out with the defensive ends. Then apparently they got several linebackers hurt, and they switched me to linebacker, and I couldn't have been happier."

Nor could the Bills. Stratton possessed great speed and instincts and quickly developed into one of the premier outside linebackers in the game, picking off six passes in his rookie year despite missing the first two games with an ankle injury. In 1963, he helped lead the Bills to their first playoff appearance and was selected to play in his first AFL All-Star Game. Stratton's defining moment came the following season, when his tackle of Lincoln, forever after known as "the Hit Heard 'Round the World," propelled the Bills to victory in the title game. With Stratton leading the way, the Bills formidable defense set an AFL record by not allowing a rushing touchdown for 16 consecutive regular-season games between 1964 and 1965 and carried the team to a second straight league title in 1965.

In all, Stratton played in six AFL All-Star Games and three title games, winning two. Buffalo's superb linebacking corps of Stratton, John Tracey, and Harry Jacobs started 62 consecutive games as a unit from 1962 through 1967. In 11 years with the team, Stratton chalked up 18 interceptions. He was the last remaining link to the Bills' title teams when he was traded to the Chargers before the 1973 season.

"Fortunately, I got to play 11 seasons with Buffalo, which was, at that time, longer than anyone else had played there," Stratton said proudly. "It didn't turn out like I would have wanted. I would have much preferred to end up with Buffalo, but they knew that they were going to have to trade me for some other things. They needed other people, and if they could get a draft choice or they could get something for me, better to trade me now and get something for me than to let me retire and not get anything."

He played just one season in San Diego but enjoyed a final hurrah when he intercepted two passes in the Chargers' 34–7 destruction of the Bills on September 23, 1973.

Stratton was named to the All-Time AFL Team as an outside linebacker (second squad) by the Pro Football Hall of Fame Selection Committee in 1970. He has since been named to the Bills' Wall of Fame, the Greater Buffalo Sports Hall of Fame, and the Bills 50th Anniversary Team.

# The Giver

Perhaps you've seen—or more fittingly, heard—them coming through your town. Thousands of motorcycles roaring by every summer, on their way across the country with a singular purpose. No, they aren't some nefarious biker gang bent on pillaging your neighborhood. The bikers in question are riding for a noble cause as partakers in Ruben Brown's annual Run for Kids fund-raiser, an eight-city, 7,000-mile cross-country event created in 2001 by the former Buffalo Bill to raise money and awareness for Salvation Army programs focused on improving the lives of children. It is a massive undertaking, requiring a man with a massive heart to organize it. Ruben Brown is just that man.

Most Bills fans are more familiar with Brown for what he accomplished on the football field, but they should also know that community service is as much—if not more—a part of him as the game itself. It was instilled in Ruben at a young age, when he spent his days participating in Salvation Army–sponsored programs.

Brown was a standout athlete at E.C. Glass High School in Lynchburg, Virginia, where he made a name for himself on the wrestling and football teams. He was good enough to earn an athletic scholarship to the University of Pittsburgh, where he became an All–Big East choice as a tackle for three consecutive seasons (1992–94). The Bills were looking to fill some holes in their offensive line and picked Brown with their first selection (14th overall) in the 1995 draft.

"He was ranked high on our board," said coach Marv Levy. "You knew he had talent."

Did he ever! Brown impressed coaches from his first reps and became an immediate starter, unseating incumbent Corbin Lacina at the left guard position before the end of the exhibition season. But Brown was a victim of bad timing, as his rookie campaign came a year after the last of the Bills' four straight Super Bowl trips. It was an aging team that had missed the playoffs in the previous season for the first time in six years. But with Brown reenergizing the offensive line, the club was back in the postseason in 1995. They defeated Miami in the wild-card round but lost to Pittsburgh in the divisional round. For his role in the Bills' success, Brown was rewarded with selection to the Pro Football Writers of America's All-Rookie Team.

The Bills returned to the playoffs in Brown's sophomore year, and despite the fact that they were eliminated in the first round, Brown was selected to his first Pro Bowl. He had rapidly developed into not just one of the game's premier offensive linemen, but also an inspirational leader on the team.

Ruben Brown gets hyped in game action against the Miami Dolphins in 1999.

"He had that infectious personality," Levy recalled. "He had one of those personalities that when he walked on the field he was smiling."

Brown would appear in eight consecutive Pro Bowls between 1996 and 2003 and was foreman of the offensive line that helped the team to reach the postseason four times. But after nine stellar seasons in Buffalo, Brown signed a free-agent contract with the Chicago Bears in 2004. He enjoyed four productive years in the Windy City, adding a ninth Pro Bowl to his résumé in 2006. That same year, Ruben finally got his chance to play in a Super Bowl when the Bears faced the Indianapolis Colts in the Big Game. He played one more season with the Bears but missed eight games due to injuries. After failing to hook on with a team in 2008, Brown announced his retirement.

But retirement from the gridiron didn't slow Brown's charity work. If anything, it allowed him more time to concentrate on the projects in which he had been involved since first coming to Buffalo. Being a professional athlete had provided Ruben with the forum and wherewithal to give back to his community, and he became one of the most charitably active players in the entire league. His football résumé is undoubtedly one that would make any player proud, but Brown's greatest accomplishments have occurred away from the gridiron, where his ongoing efforts on behalf of those less fortunate—such as Ruben's Run for Kids—continue to benefit and inspire so many. The "run" has raised more than a half-million dollars since its debut as the primary fund-raising event of the Ruben Brown Foundation in 2001.

In recognition of his efforts, Brown received the Bills' Walter Payton Man of the Year Award in 1999, 2001, and 2002. In 2003, he won *Pro Football Weekly*'s Arthur S. Arkush Humanitarian of the Year Award. The Common Council of the City of Buffalo honored Brown for his charity work in 2008.

Ruben has settled down in Western New York and remains one of the area's most visible and beloved sports figures. He was inducted into the Greater Buffalo Sports Hall of Fame in 2011, and is currently cohosting a popular cable sports program—*The Enforcers*—with former Buffalo Sabre Rob Ray.

Jerry Butler

On the afternoon of November 16, 1986, the Buffalo Bills were hosting the Miami Dolphins at Rich Stadium in Orchard Park. Already up by a touchdown in the second quarter, the Bills were threatening to extend their lead with the ball resting on Miami's 25. Quarterback Jim Kelly marched his team to the line of scrimmage, placed his hands under center Kent Hull, and barked out the signals. The ball was snapped, and 22 players sprang into motion. Jerry Butler, Buffalo's sure-handed but oft-injured receiver, made his way into the Miami secondary and headed toward the end zone. Kelly saw that Butler had a step on his man and threw the ball on a trajectory that in a matter of nanoseconds would intersect with his streaking wide receiver. As Butler crossed the goal line, he leapt up to snatch Kelly's aerial with two Dolphins defenders draped on his back. He hauled the ball in and held on tight as he braced for impact with the Rich Stadium turf. When he finally hit the ground, the ball was still in his grasp. The officials raised their hands to signal a touchdown. The stadium crowd leapt to their feet, electrified by Butler's spectacular catch and the two-touchdown advantage it had given their team. But what most did not see was that when Butler hit the ground, the two Dolphins had landed on top of him, the force of the collision shattering his right ankle in the process.

It was more than just another setback for the star-crossed Butler, who in his seven seasons with the Bills had never been able to live up to expectations as a result of numerous injuries. This one was different. Butler's heroic reception had extended the Bills' lead, but the resulting injury was so severe that it proved to be the death knell to a career that had begun so promisingly.

The 6'0", 170-pound speedster had come to Buffalo in 1979 as the team's No. 1 draft choice (fifth overall) after a stellar college career at Clemson. He made an immediate impact, finishing second on the team in catches with 48 and yards with 834 and setting a team record for receiving yardage in a single game when he picked up 255 yards on 10 catches against the New York Jets on September 23, 1979. Oh yeah—he also scored four touchdowns that day to lead the Bills to victory. Butler's outstanding debut earned him selection as UPI's AFC Rookie of the Year.

Now with a season under his belt, Butler blossomed in 1980, pacing the Bills in both catches (57) and yardage (832) and tying Frank Lewis for the club lead in touchdown receptions with six. With Butler leading the way, the Bills earned their first postseason appearance in six years, and the lanky receiver was rewarded with selection to the Pro Bowl. His numbers in 1981 were nearly identical—55 catches for 842 yards—with a team-best eight touchdown receptions as the Bills made the playoffs for the second straight year.

Given a choice, it's a sure bet Butler would prefer to forget his next three seasons, as he wound up missing parts of two and all of one to injuries. His 1982 campaign was cut short by a shoulder injury and the protracted players' strike. The following year, Butler suffered a knee injury and missed the last seven games. That injury was so severe that it caused him to miss the entire 1984 season as well. Through sheer hard work and painstaking determination,

Butler returned to the field in 1985 and performed at a high level—catching 41 balls for 770 yards and two touchdowns—on an otherwise dreadful Buffalo team that won only two games for the second year in a row.

But as the 1986 season began, the Bills had a boatload of young talent, including quarterback Jim Kelly, wide receiver Andre Reed, center Kent Hull, defensive end Bruce Smith, and linebacker Darryl Talley, interspersed with some key veterans like Butler, defensive tackle Fred Smerlas, and safety Steve Freeman. And the team appeared to be on the cusp of turning things around. Still, under the watch of unpopular head coach Hank Bullough, the team got off to a dismal 2–7 start. Things began to look up, however, when Marv Levy took over as coach in Week 10. The mood in the locker room was more relaxed, and the players responded immediately by defeating the Pittsburgh Steelers in Levy's first game. At last, the Bills and their fans had reason to believe.

Unfortunately for Butler, who, as one of the longest-tenured players on the squad, had seen his share of disappointment, the good feeling was short-lived, for up next on the Bills schedule was the Miami Dolphins and No. 80's date with destiny.

"Hopes were high that he would be a part of our return to respectability when I took over the team," Levy recalled, "but it wasn't meant to be. Throughout a long coaching career there are events that remain indelibly etched in one's memory—some joyful and some devastating. I will always remember the jubilation we shared in the locker room after defeating Pittsburgh in my first game with the Bills. On the other hand, I will never forget the sadness I felt when I learned, just a week later, that Jerry Butler's playing days were over."

Butler officially retired from the field in October 1988. He returned to the Bills in 1993 in an administrative capacity. He accepted the position of wide receivers coach with the Cleveland Browns in 1999 and two years later became the Browns' director of player personnel development, where he helped develop programs that assisted players to transition successfully into life after football. In 2011, Butler joined the front office of the Denver Broncos.

Always one of the most active Bills when it came to public service, Butler was voted the team's Man of the Year in both 1981 and 1982. In 1983, Butler was given the Jackie Robinson Award by the Buffalo and Erie County YMCA. In 1989, he was presented with the Ralph C. Wilson Jr. Distinguished Service Award, given to former Bills players for outstanding service to the organization and the community.

Clemson University honored Butler in 1986 with enshrinement in its Athletic Hall of Fame and paid Butler its highest tribute by inducting him into the school's prestigious Ring of Honor in 1999. In 1997, he was inducted into the South Carolina Athletic Hall of Fame.

44 Revolutionary

Pete Gogolak revolutionized the art of place-kicking when he became the first soccer-style kicker in professional football upon joining the Buffalo Bills in 1964. Up to that point, every kicker at the pro level—AFL, NFL, and CFL—had approached the ball straight-on. Gogolak approached the ball from a 45-degree angle, and though many scoffed at his unorthodox method, the so-called soccer-style kick caught on, eventually became the norm, and ultimately led to the total extinction of the conventional straight-on kicker.

Gogolak played soccer growing up in his native Hungary, but after his family emigrated to the United States when he was 14 years old, Peter discovered his high school did not have a soccer team. He decided to try his hand at the North American version of football, initially playing tight end. When his coach asked if anyone on the team could kick extra points, Gogolak figured he'd give it a shot.

"I said, 'Hey, Coach, let me try it. I used to kick [in] soccer.'" But he discovered that kicking a round soccer ball was far different from kicking an oblong football. "I lined up in this 45-degree angle, and before the ball was snapped—I've never forgotten the frightened look on my holder's face—he said, 'Coach! Geez, this guy's gonna kick me right in the ass!' I said, 'Hey, let me just try it.' So the ball was snapped, and I kicked the ball, and it was a long, low drive, maybe about 40 yards, under the crossbar, and it was going in different directions, and it was a big joke. 'Send this kid back to Hungary, Coach!' It looked funny, but suddenly I realized that this was something I could work on. I said, 'Geez, I should be able to do this.'"

He continued to work on his technique and eventually convinced the coach to let him try again. This time, Gogolak kicked well enough to win the job. "The first high school game, I kicked off, and the two kickoff return guys, they were on the 25. I hit the ball and it just went way over their heads, into the end zone, and nobody could believe it. It was like a rocket."

Gogolak later attended Cornell University, and despite playing on a poor team and receiving little, if any, publicity, he was discovered by Harvey Johnson, the Buffalo Bills' chief scout. "We had a bad team at Cornell, but Harvey came down to Ithaca—he heard from a friend, 'You've got to look at this guy.' So I kicked a few field goals for Harvey, and they drafted me in round 12. Nobody in the NFL drafted me. I was totally disappointed—I just couldn't believe it. I knew I could do it, but Harvey took a chance [on me], and I came to the Bills."

Gogolak spent two very productive seasons with the Bills, leading the AFL in kicking points both years and helping the team

It may look normal now, but at the time, Pete Gogolak's kicking form was literally a game changer.

win back-to-back league titles in 1964 and '65. He left the Bills in a contract dispute after the '65 season, and his signing with the NFL New York Giants is recognized as the precipitating event leading to the historic merger between the two leagues. Until that time, there was an unwritten understanding that the leagues would not raid each other for players. It was one thing to battle over college players, sure, but quite another to target established veterans such as Gogolak. "That enraged us," said Bills owner Ralph Wilson, "because we did not raid the NFL for their veteran players. It was a gentleman's agreement, so to speak. We fought each other for the college guys but not the veterans. When they signed Gogolak, that enraged our league. It certainly did enrage me."

While Gogolak's audacious move made good financial sense to him at the time, looking back he admits to some regret over the decision. "I would have stayed in Buffalo forever, but I'm a businessman, and business is business."

Gogolak went on to play another nine seasons with the Giants, but he never enjoyed the same level of success he had achieved with the Bills. "It's the best team I played for," he remarked. "We won two AFL championships. Every time we went on we knew we were going to win."

45 Magic Man

Doug Flutie was thrust into the national spotlight when he threw the famous last-minute Hail Mary pass that vaulted Boston College to a sensational 47–45 victory over the Miami Hurricanes at the Orange Bowl in 1984. Despite winning the Heisman Trophy as the top college player that year, NFL teams had serious concerns about Flutie's height (he is listed at 5'10"). Determined to prove he should be a starter, Flutie signed with the New Jersey Generals of the United States Football League and led the team in passing in his one and only season (1985) before the league folded. He finally entered the NFL in 1986 and endured brief stints with the Chicago Bears and then the New England Patriots, who unceremoniously released the hometown hero despite a respectable 8–5 record as a starter in three seasons with the club.

Undaunted, Flutie signed with the British Columbia Lions of the CFL, where he was united with his brother Darren, a wide receiver for the team. Over the next eight seasons, Flutie forged a CFL career that some consider the greatest in the history of the league, winning a record six Most Outstanding Player Awards (1991–94, 1996–97). Flutie's teams won three Grey Cups (the CFL equivalent of the NFL's Super Bowl), and he was named Most Valuable Player in each of those wins (1992 with the Calgary Stampeders and 1996 and '97 with the Toronto Argonauts).

Flutie returned to the NFL with something to prove in 1998 after signing a free-agent contract with the Buffalo Bills. In his first year back in four-down ball, Flutie earned Pro Bowl honors by completing 202 of 354 passes for 2,711 yards and 20 touchdowns and guiding the Bills to the playoffs. However, a 24–17 loss to Miami in the AFC Wild Card Game ended an otherwise terrific campaign. He became a fan favorite for his fiery leadership style, feats of derring-do, and his uncanny knack for eluding pass rushers and scrambling for first downs. By sheer force of will and—some believed—a little "Flutie Magic," he was able to overcome the perceived height disadvantage and befuddle the defenses stacked against him.

Flutie's popularity inspired the creation of a breakfast cereal called "Flutie Flakes." A large portion of the profits from sales of the cereal were donated to the Doug Flutie Jr. Foundation for Autism, created in honor of Flutie's autistic son. The foundation's goal is to promote awareness and support families affected by autism spectrum disorders.

To the Buffalo faithful, who saw the diminutive signal-caller as the very reflection of the city's hardworking, blue-collar image, Flutie was the answer to the quarterback quandary that had plagued the team since Jim Kelly's retirement. But a quarterback controversy developed anyway, as coach Wade Phillips flip-flopped between Flutie and his other quarterback, Rob Johnson. An icy feud developed between the two and divided the team. It came to a head in 1999 when, after Flutie again led the team to the playoffs, Johnson was given the start in the AFC Wild Card Game against the Tennessee Titans. Although Johnson played fairly well, the Titans stole the game out from under the Bills in the final seconds. Would the Bills have won with Flutie at the helm? There are literally thousands of Flutie fanatics who will go to their graves believing the team would have.

Phillips threw fuel on the fire by giving Johnson the starting job at the beginning of the 2000 season. Flutie fans flooded radio talk shows with phone calls and wrote letters demanding that their man be the starter. The complaints appeared justified when the team failed to make the playoffs for the first time since Flutie's arrival.

Flutie became an unrestricted free agent in 2001 and signed with the San Diego Chargers, where he played four years before returning to New England in 2005 to play one last season for the Patriots. He saw spot duty as Tom Brady's backup but made history in the season finale against Miami when he became the first player since 1941 to successfully execute a drop kick in a regular-season game. The play turned out to be the last in a legendary career, as Flutie announced his retirement in May 2006.

Flutie was elected to the College Football Hall of Fame in 2007 and the Canadian Football Hall of Fame a year later. He is currently a college football commentator for NBC.

46 Sideline Acrobat

Wide receiver Bob Chandler joined the Buffalo Bills in 1971 as a seventh-round draft choice out of the University of Southern California. Chandler was a three-year starter with the Trojans and served as team captain in 1970. He was named Most Valuable Player in USC's victory over the Michigan Wolverines in that year's

Rose Bowl and received such a strong recommendation from fellow USC alum O.J. Simpson that the Bills drafted the Long Beach, California, native.

Chandler's rookie season was spent in apprenticeship, watching from the sideline as starting wideouts Marlin Briscoe and Haven Moses, along with top draft pick J.D. Hill, handled the brunt of the receiving duties. Hill and Chandler graduated into starting roles in 1972 and responded to the call by combining for 85 catches—compared to the 67 delivered in 1971 by the previous starters—and soon fans forgot the names of those other guys. Chandler's 33 catches and five touchdowns were merely a glimpse of what was in store, as the lanky player (6'1", 180 pounds) developed into one of the top receivers in the league. An insatiable student of the game, he studied film of other great receivers, especially Oakland Raiders Hall of Famer Fred Biletnikoff, with whose style Chandler's was most frequently compared. Over the next seven seasons, the sure-handed Chandler became the quintessential possession receiver and the favorite target of quarterback Joe Ferguson. His trademark fingertip grabs as he tiptoed the sideline became staples of Bills highlight reels.

Despite the fact that his 176 catches between 1975 and 1977 topped all NFL receivers, Chandler was denied the chance to play in a Pro Bowl. He was, however, named to UPI's All-Pro teams in 1975 and '77 but—strange as it seems—not in '76, which was his finest season, with 61 receptions for 824 yards and 10 touchdowns.

Unfortunately for Chandler, the Bills made just one playoff appearance in his nine years with the club. His fortunes changed dramatically in 1980, however, after being traded to the Raiders, who were looking for a possession receiver to replace the recently retired Biletnikoff. They found just the man. The Raiders went all the way to Super Bowl XV that year, with Chandler contributing 49 receptions and 10 touchdowns during the regular season, plus four catches for 77 yards in Oakland's 27–10 drubbing of the Philadelphia Eagles in the big game.

Being back in his home state of California brought other opportunities for the matinee-idol-handsome Chandler, who raised a few eyebrows—as well as some good-natured ribbing from teammates, no doubt—in January 1982 when he appeared au naturel in the pages of *Playgirl* magazine!

Chandler played three seasons with the Raiders before hanging up his cleats and, like former teammates O.J. Simpson and Ahmad Rashad before him, moving effortlessly from the playing field into the broadcast booth. From 1984 to 1987, Chandler hosted *2 On the Town* for CBS. In 1989, he became the host of ESPN's *Amazing Games*, a show that focused on various sports from around the world. He also served as a radio analyst for the Los Angeles Raiders.

Though he never smoked, Chandler was diagnosed with lung cancer in the summer of 1994. He remained positive and upbeat throughout his battle, serving as an inspiration to those who knew him, as well as his countless fans. Chandler was just 45 when the disease claimed his life in January 1995.

Head Games

The helmet was one of the last pieces of protective equipment to be adopted in the game of football, but it is probably the most important. It seems somehow fitting, then, that when the Bills held their first training camp in July 1960, the last pieces of equipment assembled were the helmets. Since then, the helmet has become emblematic of the team's rich heritage and a source of some very interesting anecdotes.

The Helmet Stretcher

In 1961, Bills head coach Buster Ramsey hired an irascible bartender named Tony Marchitte as the team's equipment manager. Marchitte had no previous experience with football equipment, but his years behind the bar had turned him into a bit of an amateur psychologist. In his first camp with the Bills, Marchitte was able to put those skills to good use.

"Chuck McMurtry, a defensive lineman, complained that his new helmet was too tight," recalled Eddie Abramoski. "Marchitte thought it fit right and kept putting McMurtry off. Finally, Tony agreed to send the helmet back to the manufacturer to get it stretched, telling McMurtry it would be back in a couple of days. Instead, he just hid the helmet in the back of a shelf in the equipment room. McMurtry came in a few days later and tried on the helmet and was satisfied with how it fit. 'See, Tony,' he said. 'This is the way it was supposed to fit in the beginning.'"

The Helmet Stretcher, Part Two

When O.J. Simpson arrived in 1969, the team did not have a helmet big enough to accommodate the Heisman winner's over-sized cranium.

"O.J. had a big head," remembered Abramoski. "They used to call him 'Big Head' or 'Water Head'—that was only his close friends who could do that."

Marchitte might have considered playing the same trick on Simpson that he had on McMurtry eight years earlier, but this was the team's No. 1 draft pick, and the Bills wanted him on the field as quickly as possible.

The solution? "We had to get his helmet from USC," said Abramoski, "because we couldn't get one fast enough from Riddell."

Changes

The Bills helmets in 1960 and '61 were silver with blue numbers on the sides, styled after those worn by the NFL Detroit Lions—for whom original coach Buster Ramsey had previously toiled as an assistant coach and of whom Ralph Wilson had owned a minority share. In 1962, Lou Saban took over and changed the Bills color scheme to the red, white, and blue the team wears to this day. The helmets were changed to white with a single red stripe and the classic red buffalo logo on each side.

The standing buffalo logo was put out to pasture in 1974 and replaced with the sleeker, more modern-looking "vaulting buffalo." In 1984, the helmet's base color was changed from white to red. This change was made when the team's quarterback commented on the difficulty of distinguishing between his receivers' helmets and those worn by three of Buffalo's Eastern Division rivals.

Hall of Famer Joe DeLamielleure explains: "The crown [in the Rich Stadium playing surface] was one reason that the Bills got the red helmets. Joe Ferguson said he couldn't see the shorter receivers like Lou Piccone when he was on one side of the crown and the receiver was on the other. The only thing he could see was the top of their helmets. Since the Colts, Dolphins, and Patriots all had white helmets too, Ferguson thought it would be easier if we changed to red. I know helmet color seems simple, but he was the only one who figured it out. It was a good thing that Ferguson's opinion was so respected, because it made a huge difference."

Sure enough, Ferguson went from throwing 25 interceptions in 1983 to 17 a year later. In 2011, the Bills returned to white helmets, and Ryan Fitzpatrick's interceptions went from 15 to 23. Coincidence?

The Case of the Missing Helmet

Poor Thurman Thomas. As if losing the Super Bowl for the second straight year wasn't bad enough, he had to face wisecracks from fans and media after losing his helmet in the game and missing the first few plays.

"If we had beaten the Redskins," Steve Tasker surmised, "this incident probably would have wound up as a footnote. But because we lost, the media made a huge deal out of Thurman missing the first two plays of the game. The Redskins had a great team that year. Even if Thurman had been in for those two plays, we still would have lost handily."

Thomas superstitiously would place his helmet on the Bills bench at the 34-yard line before games. Tasker believes someone—probably an equipment man—moved it for safekeeping. When Thomas went back to find it, it was gone. Because he couldn't take the field in another helmet, Kenneth Davis started in his place.

The incident had no bearing on the game's outcome, of course, but commentators saw it as symbolic of the team's Super Bowl failures. Thomas' Hall of Fame career deserves a better memory.

Gazoo

Safety Mark Kelso played eight seasons with the Bills between 1986 and 1993. He intercepted 30 passes in his career but is probably best remembered for wearing an extra layer of padding on the outside of his helmet that made him look like the Great Gazoo from the old *Flintstones* cartoon.

"I had my first concussion in 1988," Kelso told the *Philadelphia Inquirer*. "I had subsequent concussions, and I was diagnosed with migraine syndrome—the symptoms of a migraine as opposed to the severity of a concussion. I started wearing that extra pad in 1989, and I definitely credit it with extending my career the additional five years that I wore it. After a few games, there was no way I would have played without it."

Kelso wore the shell-like accessory for the rest of his career. He later gave the set to avid memorabilia collector and former teammate Jim Kelly, who subsequently donated it to the Hall of Fame.

48 Buster

When the AFL was formed in 1959, the eight charter franchises had to build their teams from the ground up. Ralph Wilson, owner of the Buffalo franchise, was inundated with letters from candidates for his team's head coaching job but ultimately settled on Garrard "Buster" Ramsey, the Detroit Lions' assistant coach who was considered to be a defensive genius for coordinating the dominating defenses that led the Lions to three NFL championships over the previous eight seasons.

"You've heard plenty about the Giants' Tom Landry and Al Sherman," said Wilson in comparing Buster to some of the better-known assistants at the time, "but in Ramsey, we have at least their equal or perhaps their better."

Ramsey was a Tennessee man, born and raised in the eastern Tennessee city of Maryville, in the foothills of the Great Smoky Mountains. He played his college ball at the College of William & Mary in Virginia and was the school's first-ever All-America selection in his senior year. He was drafted by the Chicago Cardinals in the 14th round of the 1943 draft. In six years with Chicago, Ramsey was named First-Team All-Pro twice (1948 and 1949) and helped them win the NFL championship in 1947.

In 1951, his final season with the Cards, Ramsey served as a player/assistant coach. A year later, Ramsey was hired to coach the lines on Buddy Parker's staff in Detroit but soon was given full charge of the defense, becoming, in essence, the Lion's defensive coordinator. Under Buster's guidance, the Lions defense developed into one of the most dominant units in the league and led the way to Detroit's three titles during the decade (1952, '53, and '57). He is often credited with the development of the 4-3 defense, for pioneering the practice of blitzing linebackers, and also for shaping the careers of Hall of Famers Joe Schmidt, Yale Lary, and Jack Christiansen.

Wilson had been a longtime minority stockholder in the Lions, and though he had never met Buster, he was certainly familiar with the man's accomplishments. He hired Ramsey on December 16, 1959. "I didn't know Buster Ramsey," said Wilson. "I just called him on the phone. I didn't research all of [the candidates] at all. We had to get going."

Ramsey approached coaching much the same way he approached playing. He was tough and aggressive and intolerant of players who weren't. "He was a tough guy, but I don't mind those kind of people," said fullback Wray Carlton. "He reminded me of [former Ohio State coach] Woody Hayes—very passionate, full of fire. He felt football was a rough and tough game, and you had to be rough and tough to play it. X's and O's were not his [strong] suit. He was a football player, and he'd look out there, and if you weren't hitting somebody, [he'd say] 'I don't want you on my team.'"

"He was showing an offensive lineman how to make a block on the defensive lineman that was going to the gap," recalled halfback Willmer Fowler. "Jim Sorey was the defensive guy, and Buster told him, 'Come down the crease like you're going for the quarterback.' He was showing this guy how to make that block to keep that defensive guy from disrupting everything in the backfield. He told Jim, 'Okay, Jim, come now.' Sorey got down and they called the signal and he came at half speed. Buster stood up and he looked at him and said, 'What was that?' Sorey said, 'Well, Coach, you said—' 'I want you to charge like you're going after the guy!' Sorey got down, full pads. Buster? No pads, nothing. Sorey got down and made his charge, fully padded, helmet, everything. Buster hit him so hard it was unbelievable. Here's a guy out there with nothing on—he hit Sorey so hard it straightened him right up. He told the offensive lineman, 'That's the way you're supposed to block a guy!'"

That rough and gruff exterior contrasted the soft spot Ramsey held for his players, a side that few ever saw. "In camp, some guys have to go," said Fowler. "You can't keep everybody. Any time Buster had to make a cut it was like somebody was tearing his guts out. He was that sensitive about the players. I think that was the toughest part of the game for Buster—letting guys go and ending their prospects of a career."

Ramsey also carried a soft spot for his beloved home state, as his players learned very early on. "Whenever we were in training camp eating or something like that," recalled Jim Wagstaff, "we always had to sing the 'Tennessee Waltz,' with our hands on our hearts, and we all had to stand up at the training table."

Given Ramsey's background, it's not surprising that his Bills teams enjoyed their greatest success on the defensive side of the ball, finishing third in AFL rankings in 1960 and fourth in '61. However, the team's overall record of 11–16–1 during his tenure was the third-worst in the entire league. Immediately following the 1961 season, Wilson decided to take the team in another direction. Ramsey was let go and replaced by Lou Saban.

Ramsey eventually reunited with old friend Buddy Parker on the staff of the Pittsburgh Steelers. He retired from football in 1965 and embarked on a career as a cattle farmer.

Despite being fired after just two seasons, Ramsey remained steadfastly loyal to Ralph Wilson for the rest of his life. "My father won every place he was," explained Gary Ramsey, Buster's son. "Three championships in Detroit, two in Chicago, and when he went to Pittsburgh after he lost the job in Buffalo, they had the best year they had ever had up until that time. But he [thought] Ralph Wilson [was] the greatest owner in the history of the game. He loved living in Buffalo. He loved the area because it has rolling hills like east Tennessee—except for all the darned snow. It was just the greatest experience of his life. And that was the only place where he wasn't successful."

Buster passed away in 2007 at the age of 87. He was inducted into the Virginia Sports Hall of Fame in 1974 and the National College Football Hall of Fame in 1978. He also was named to the NFL's 1940s All-Decade Team by the Pro Football Hall of Fame.

49 What Might Have Been

Had things gone a bit differently during his time with the Bills, there's little doubt that running back Joe Cribbs would be considered one of the team's all-time greats. In fact, it appeared that Cribbs was well on his way to a Hall of Fame career after reaching the 1,000-yard mark in three of his first four pro seasons. Unfortunately for everyone involved, a protracted contract dispute and a two-year defection to the USFL short-circuited Cribbs' otherwise brilliant tenure in Buffalo, where he still ranks third on the team's all-time list with 4,445 rushing yards, behind Hall of Famers Thurman Thomas (11,938) and O.J. Simpson (10,183).

Cribbs played his college ball at Auburn University, where his backfield mates included future NFL standouts James Brooks and William Andrews. The Bills tagged him in the second round of the 1980 draft, using one of the picks obtained in 1978 when the team traded O.J. Simpson to the San Francisco 49ers. Cribbs became an immediate starter, gaining 1,185 yards (a Bills rookie record) and scoring 11 touchdowns while catching 52 passes for 415 yards and helping the team make the playoffs for the first time since 1974. His efforts earned him a trip to the Pro Bowl and selection as UPI's AFC Rookie of the Year.

The 5'11" 190-pounder enjoyed another outstanding season in 1981, gaining 1,097 yards and catching 40 passes for 603 yards and seven scores and making his second straight trip to the Pro Bowl. However, things began to unravel in 1982, when Cribbs demanded to have his contract renegotiated from his current salary of $120,000 to $400,000 per year. But despite his incessant off-the-field grumbling, a two-game holdout, and a strike-shortened season, Cribbs still managed to put up impressive numbers, gaining 633 yards on 134 carries for a career-best average of 4.7 yards per carry.

Cribbs topped the millennium mark for the third time in 1983, gaining 1,131 yards while also leading the Bills with 57 receptions, good for a third Pro Bowl nod. However, Cribbs' unhappiness with his contract was a distraction throughout the campaign, and the team's failure to placate their star back led to his signing with the Birmingham Stallions of the then-new United States Football League. He played two seasons with the Stallions and led the USFL in rushing in 1984.

Cribbs returned to Buffalo midway through the 1985 season but found that his role as the feature back had been filled more than adequately by Greg Bell. Once again, Cribbs became unhappy and lobbied for a trade, going so far as to hang strips of athletic tape across the front of his locker and mounting a sign reading BUFFALO PRISON. The Bills finally worked things out just prior to the 1986 season and granted Cribbs' wish, trading the disgruntled halfback to the San Francisco 49ers for a pair of draft choices. He played three more years in the NFL, including stints with the 49ers, Indianapolis Colts, and Miami Dolphins, but never again approached his once-lofty status as one of the top running backs in the league.

Cribbs' NFL legacy lives on through his nephew, Josh Cribbs, the star receiver and kick returner of the Cleveland Browns. Josh is the current league record-holder for most kickoffs returned for touchdowns in a career (eight).

50 Rise of the Moormanators

It's pretty sad when the punter is one of the most popular players on a football team, but that's exactly what the Bills' Brian Moorman was during the first decade of the 2000s. Granted, the team gave its fans little to shout about during that time frame, but Moorman performed at a consistently high level that attracted a passionate legion of followers—self-proclaimed "Moormanators"—who argue that he was, and still is, the team's best player.

A native of Wichita, Kansas, Moorman attended Pittsburg State University, where he was a two-time All-America selection in football. He also competed in PSU's indoor and outdoor track teams and was a three-time national champion in the 400-meter hurdles, earning the NCAA's Division II Outdoor Track and Field Athlete of the Year Award in 1999.

Moorman came to the Bills as a free agent in 2001 after having spent two unsuccessful training camps in the Seattle Seahawks organization and two years with the Berlin Thunder of NFL Europe, where he led the league in punting both seasons. It didn't take long for No. 8 to establish himself as a fan favorite in Buffalo, where followers of the team are quick to identify with gritty, lunch-pail types. Moorman proved himself to be just that, demonstrating his willingness to mix it up by recording three special teams tackles in his first season. In addition to handling the punting duties, Moorman doubled as the team's kickoff specialist, which allowed him even greater opportunities to get in on the action.

His 84-yard boot against the Green Bay Packers on December 22, 2002, bested the previous club record of 80 yards set by Chris Mohr back in 1996. By 2003, Moorman was beginning to attract notice as one of the top punters in the league after finishing second in the AFC with a 44.6-yards-per-punt average. That broke the club mark once held by Paul Maguire, whose 44.5 yard average had stood as the standard for 34 years. He shattered his own record in 2005 with an average of 45.7 and eclipsed that figure in 2009 when a mark of 46.6 yards per punt.

After being chosen as a Pro Bowl alternate in 2002 and 2003, Moorman finally got his due with trips to Hawaii after the 2005 and 2006 seasons. In 2010, he kicked his 770th punt for the team, surpassing the old career mark of 769 (Chris Mohr, 1991–2000). Moorman now holds nearly every significant Bills punting record and was voted to the Bills 50th Anniversary Team in 2010. One of the most durable players in franchise history, he has not missed a game in 11 seasons.

But perhaps more impressive than Moorman's accomplishments on the field are the contributions he has made off of it. When it comes to community service, Moorman has been one of the most active players in the history of the franchise, always making himself available to help a charitable cause, especially when it comes to children. Moorman has twice been awarded the Buffalo Bills/Walter Payton Man of the Year Award (2003 and 2009) for community service combined with a high standard of play. In 2005, he received *Pro Football Weekly*'s Arthur S. Arkush Humanitarian of the Year Award for his charitable efforts in the community. Together with his wife, Amber, Moorman founded the PUNT (Perseverance, Understanding, eNcouragement, Triumph) Foundation in 2004, which is dedicated to making a difference in the lives of Western New York children facing threatening illnesses. PUNT's mission is to provide children afflicted with cancer and their families with opportunities to enjoy the life they fight so hard for by supporting pediatric cancer research, treatment, and support groups. He is also active with the Buffalo City Mission, the Food Bank of Western

New York, and Roswell Park Cancer Institute, which he and Amber visit every Tuesday throughout the season to spend time with young patients and their families.

51 Watch *Buffalo '66*

Next time you, gentle reader, find yourself in the mood to see a good movie but can't decide which title to rent—and if you haven't seen it already—consider the 1998 dark comedy *Buffalo '66*. If you're a fan of the Buffalo Bills and possess thick skin and a hearty sense of humor, you'll be glad you did.

This independent film marked the directorial and feature screenwriting debut of Vincent Gallo, the Buffalo-born model-artist-actor who rose to fame modeling for Calvin Klein and for his appearances in such films as *Goodfellas*, *The Funeral*, and *Palookaville*. Gallo plays Billy, the film's lead character, who has spent the last five years in prison for a crime he didn't commit. He had placed a $10,000 wager with a bookie that Buffalo would win the Super Bowl, but after the Bills lost on a missed field goal (sound familiar?), he could not pay his debt. He instead took a fall for the bookie, leading to his unfortunate incarceration. After his release, he meets up with a young tap dancer named Layla, played by Christina Ricci. Billy "kidnaps" Layla and forces her to pretend to be his wife when he visits his parents (portrayed by Angelica Huston and Ben Gazzara), who are blissfully unaware of their son's recent indisposition. Billy's mother is obsessed with the Buffalo Bills and held Billy responsible for her having to miss the game the last time the Bills played for a championship (1966) because she had gone into labor with him.

Buffalonian Vincent Gallo and Christina Ricci in Buffalo '66.

The subplot of the movie involves Billy's scheme to exact revenge on the kicker (not-so-subtly named Scott Wood) who missed the field goal that would have won the Super Bowl for the Bills as well as Billy's bet. Layla has apparently fallen in love with Billy and seems willing to go along with his plans.

Another aspect of this movie Buffalonians will enjoy is its backdrop, which includes several scenes shot in and around Western New York. In an inspired move, Gallo invited Terry Licata-Braunstein to play Ricci's tap-dance instructor. Licata-Braunstein, who had been Gallo's dance teacher in real life, is best remembered as "Talkin' Proud Terry," the energetic young lady who high-stepped her way through Buffalo's streets in the city's "Talkin' Proud" promos of the early 1980s.

The world premiere of *Buffalo '66* was held in June 1998 at Buffalo's historic North Park Theatre. Gallo, Ricci, and Licata-Braunstein were all on hand for the event. The gritty film received acclaim from critics in Buffalo and across the world.

52 Eric Moulds

Eric Moulds was part of the bountiful draft class of 1996 that included such other outstanding wide receivers as Marvin Harrison, Terrell Owens, Keyshawn Johnson, Joe Horn, and Amani Toomer. The Bills chose the 6'2" 225-pounder with the 24th overall pick based on his stellar career at Mississippi State, where he caught 117 passes for 2,022 yards. But some observers raised concerns regarding Moulds' character, pointing to one incident in particular in which Moulds had a pizza delivered to the sideline in the middle of a practice. Moulds responded publicly to the questions on the eve of the Bills' May minicamp, reassuring fans and teammates they had no reason for concern.

And Moulds need not have worried about his teammates, either. In fact, veteran running back Thurman Thomas made light of Moulds' travails by having three pizzas delivered to the rookie on the minicamp's third day. "It made me feel accepted," said Moulds. "There were a lot of negative things happening, and all the guys were telling me, 'It's going to be all right. Just play ball. We're behind you.' That's all you really need."

Moulds spent his first two years in apprenticeship behind veteran receivers Andre Reed and Quinn Early. He finally got his chance in 1998 and made the most of it by leading the Bills in receptions with 67 and setting a club record for receiving yards with 1,368 for an average of 20.4 yards per catch. As if putting an exclamation point on his coming-out season, Moulds caught nine Doug Flutie passes for an NFL-record 240 yards and one touchdown in the Bills' wild-card playoff loss to the Dolphins on January 2, 1999. Just like that, Moulds was on the map—and off to the Pro Bowl.

Moulds' numbers trailed off a bit in 1999 as a result of missing two games due to injury, but he still managed to snag 65 passes for 994 yards and help the Bills to their second straight playoff appearance. Unfortunately, the Bills' 22–16 playoff loss to the Tennessee Titans would prove to be the team's last foray into the postseason as of this writing.

He rebounded with another spectacular campaign in 2000 in which he caught 94 balls for 1,326 yards (giving him the top two receiving yardage spots in Bills history) and a return trip to the Pro Bowl.

Moulds Bills lost Flutie to free agency after the 2000 season, and Moulds saw his number of catches deflate dramatically as a result, as he pulled in just 67 catches for 904 yards and five touchdowns in 2001. But things would change in a big way in 2002.

The Bills, seeking to find some stability at the quarterback position, acquired star signal-caller Drew Bledsoe from the New England Patriots. With the strong-armed Bledsoe behind center and Peerless Price manning the receiver slot opposite Moulds, the Bills offense exploded. Moulds became the first Bill to hit the 100-reception plateau in a single season by catching exactly that amount for 1,292 yards and 10 touchdowns. Price added 94 catches for 1,252, but the team fell short of its playoff goal with a late-season slump. Still, Moulds' outstanding season earned him a third invitation to the Pro Bowl.

Continuing the pattern of being up one year and down the next, Moulds' catch total fell to 64 in 2003 (his lowest number since becoming a full-time starter in 1998), while his yardage fell to 780 (also a low), which was due partially to his missing three games due to injury. Moulds came back fully recovered for another terrific season in 2004 in which he caught 88 passes for 1,043 yards.

The 2005 season, Moulds' 10th, proved to be his last in Buffalo. He again put up decent numbers (81 catches for 816 yards and four scores), but the Bills limped to a 5–11 record and missed the playoffs for the sixth straight year.

A late-season incident in 2005 marred what had been an otherwise glorious tenure in Buffalo. As the Bills trailed 24–23 at Miami on December 4, a clearly frustrated Moulds came off the field and refused to reenter the game. A heated argument with receivers coach Tyke Tolbert ensued, and Moulds was benched for the remainder of the afternoon. Moulds insisted that he was hurt, but the team's training staff denied knowledge of any injury. The incident prompted head coach Mike Mularkey to suspend the receiver for the Bills' upcoming game against New England. After serving his one-game penalty, Moulds returned with a vengeance, making a statement by catching 27 passes for 305 yards in the team's final three games.

The writing was on the wall by this time, however. Moulds would be turning 33 in the off-season, and the incident in Miami had driven a permanent wedge between the team and its stud receiver. In April 2006, the team dealt Moulds to the Houston Texans for a midround draft choice. He signed a four-year, $14 million deal with the Texans and wound up performing tepidly as the No. 2 receiver behind All-Pro Andre Johnson. The Texans released Moulds at the end of the season, however, and he subsequently signed on with the Tennessee Titans for one last campaign.

Moulds finished his career with the Bills with 675 receptions for 9,096 yards and 48 touchdowns, good for second all-time behind Andre Reed in each of those categories. One can't help but wonder, however, just how much better his numbers would look if he'd had a stable quarterback situation for any significant length of time. In 10 years with Buffalo, Moulds played with eight different starting QBs (Jim Kelly, Todd Collins, Alex Van Pelt, Doug Flutie, Rob Johnson, Drew Bledsoe, J.P. Losman, and Kelly Holcomb), plus three more (Travis Brown, Shane Matthews, and Billy Joe Hobert) who came in off the bench—not to mention four different head coaches and six offensive coordinators. All that considered, Moulds' numbers appear all the more impressive.

He was recognized for his outstanding career by being selected to the Bills 50th Anniversary Team in 2010. A year later, Moulds was honored with selection to the SEC Football Legends.

53 The Pride of Frewsburg

Shane Conlan was a local gridiron star long before he became a Buffalo Bill. Born and raised in the Chautauqua County community of Frewsburg, Conlan enjoyed a standout career at Frewsburg High School, where he also excelled at baseball and basketball. In 1981, his senior year, Conlan was voted Western New York High School Football Player of the Year. He then headed off to play for Joe Paterno at Penn State, developing into one of the greatest linebackers ever to suit up at so-called "Linebacker U." He garnered All-America honors in both his junior and senior seasons, becoming only the sixth two-time All-American in the school's history. As defensive captain, Conlan helped the Nittany Lions win the 1986 national championship by registering eight tackles and two interceptions against the University of Miami in the Fiesta Bowl. He ended his career at Penn State as the second-ranked tackler in school history.

The Bills tapped the Pride of Frewsburg with the their first-round pick (eighth overall) in 1987, and Conlan could not have been happier. "That was the team I wanted to go to all along," said the 6'3", 235-pound run-stuffer. "I grew up watching the Bills. It's close to my home and my family and friends."

He earned the starting spot at left outside linebacker in the Bills' 3-4 scheme and immediately began to attract notice for his aggressive, hard-hitting style. But five games into the season, Conlan was asked to move to the left inside spot after the Bills acquired pass-rushing specialist Cornelius Bennett in a blockbuster trade. The move seemed to suit Conlan just fine. He turned in a brilliant freshman campaign, leading the team with 114 tackles (33 more than his next-closest teammate) during the strike-shortened season and receiving NFL Rookie of the Year honors from the Associated Press.

On a defense stacked with All-Pro talent, Conlan emerged as one of its most recognizable figures, and not just because of the way he punished running backs. As teammate Steve Tasker explained, "Conlan boasted one of the most disproportionate bodies I've ever seen on a football player. He had a huge head, a huge torso, and legs skinnier than a pelican's. Guys in the locker room would joke that the Buffalo Jills cheerleaders had more meat on their gams than Shane did. But those toothpick legs didn't prevent Shane

Hometown Heroes

Conlan isn't the only local boy who went on to play for the hometown franchise. Following is a list of Buffalo Bills players who attended high school or college in Western New York, as well as their tenure with the Bills.

Player	Pos	High School	College	Years
Bernie Buzyniski	LB	DeSales (Lockport, NY)	Holy Cross	1960
Chuck Leo	G	Bishop Duffy (Niagara Falls, NY)	Indiana	1963
Gary Bugenhagen	T	Clarence	Syracuse	1967
Bill Hurley	DB	St. Joseph's Collegiate (Kenmore, NY)	Syracuse	1983
Ron Pitts	DB	Orchard Park	UCLA	1986–87
Shane Conlan	LB	Frewsburg (Carroll, NY)	Penn State	1987–92
Todd Schlopy	K	Orchard Park	Michigan	1987
Mike Panepinto	RB	Kenmore West	Canisius	1987
Drew Haddad	WR	St. Ignatius High (Cleveland, OH)	Buffalo	2004
Naaman Roosevelt	WR	St. Joseph's Collegiate (Kenmore, NY)	Buffalo	2010–11
Jehuu Caulcrick	RB	Clymer (Clymer, NY)	Michigan State	2010
Jon Corto	DB	Orchard Park	Sacred Heart	2008–10

from delivering some of the most hellacious hits you'd ever want to see. He was your classic run-stuffing linebacker. He had kind of an old-school style. He would have fit in nicely with guys like Butkus and Nitschke."

Conlan was again outstanding in his sophomore season, helping Buffalo's defense rank first in the AFC and the team reach the postseason for the first time since 1981. Despite missing three games with foot and leg injuries, Shane finished third on the team in tackles with 84. By then recognized as one of the elite inside linebackers in the league, Conlan earned several postseason honors, including a selection to his first Pro Bowl.

In 1989, Conlan suffered a left knee injury against Denver in Week 2 that sidelined him for the next six games. Shane still managed to make 50 tackles and earn another Pro Bowl invitation. He was outstanding in the AFC Divisional Playoff Game against Cleveland, leading the team with 11 tackles in the Bills' 34–30 loss.

Further proof of Conlan's growing status as one of the game's best came when he was invited to represent Diet Coke in a national commercial that also featured such NFL superstars as Warren Moon, Boomer Esiason, Eric Dickerson, and Ronnie Lott, among others.

Conlan's first injury-free season since his rookie campaign finally arrived in 1990, and the result was a 93-tackle year that earned him a third straight trip to the Pro Bowl. In what might have been his signature game as a pro, Conlan recorded 13 stops in the Bills' 20–19 Super Bowl XXV loss to the New York Giants.

Oddly enough, 1991 might have been Conlan's best statistical year—despite the fact that he did not make the Pro Bowl. He led the team with 122 tackles and also recovered two fumbles. But the nagging injuries returned the following season, forcing Conlan to miss three games. Still, he managed to finish fourth on the Bills in tackles with 82, and also appeared in his third straight Super Bowl with the team.

Conlan became an unrestricted free agent after the 1992 season, however, and jumped at a huge three-year, $5.2 million offer from the Los Angeles Rams, making him their highest-paid player (and almost doubling his Bills salary). He played three injury-marred seasons with the Rams before hanging up his spikes. Although he led the Rams in tackles in 1994, he never again made the Pro Bowl, nor did he ever play on another winning team.

Shane was still an active NFL player when he received his first hall of fame enshrinement in 1992 from the Chautauqua Sports Hall of Fame. He was enshrined in the Greater Buffalo Sports Hall of Fame in 2005. When the Bills 50th Anniversary Team was selected in 2010, he was one of four linebackers to make the squad.

He lives in Swickley, Pennsylvania, with his wife and four children.

54 77 Seconds That May Have Saved a Season

It was going to be the Bills' year. After coming up short against the Cleveland Browns in the Wild Card Playoff Game the year before, the Bills returned with a renewed sense of purpose in 1990. Fueled by their high-octane no-huddle offense and a cadre of superstars that included the likes of Jim Kelly, Thurman Thomas, Bruce Smith, Cornelius Bennett, Andre Reed, and James Lofton, the Bills were favored by most experts to be the AFC representative in Super Bowl XXV.

The season, however, did not get off to the rollicking start the team and its fans were hoping for. After defeating the Colts in the opener, the Bills were crushed 30–7 the next week in Miami. They rebounded to beat the Jets the following Monday night, but the inconsistent start did not bode well with the defending AFC-champion Denver Broncos due to visit Rich Stadium in Week 4.

Unfortunately for the more than 74,000 fans present, the Bills looked more like the team from 1985 than 1989 in the game's first half, falling behind early and seeing the John Elway–led Broncos build a 14–3 lead by the time the teams headed to the locker rooms at intermission.

It didn't look any rosier as the second half got under way. After a couple of possession changes, however, the Bills finally started to show signs of life, courtesy of All-World defensive end Bruce Smith, who forced Elway to fumble deep in his own territory. Darryl Talley recovered at the Denver 10, and three plays later, Don Smith took Kelly's handoff 12 yards for Buffalo's first touchdown of the day. But the conversion attempt failed as a result of a bad snap, leaving the Bills trailing by five.

Buffalo's offense continued to sputter on its next possession, as the usually reliable Thurman Thomas fumbled, giving the Broncos possession at the Bills 19. Two plays later, Sammy Winder bulled over the goal line from three yards out, and Denver had a commanding 21–9 lead.

It looked as if the Broncos were going to put the game away early in the fourth after Elway engineered another impressive drive that finally stalled at Buffalo's 6. However, what transpired next might very well be the most exciting one-minute-and–17-second sequence in the history of the Bills franchise—and is credited by many for saving a season that seemed moments away from going down the tubes.

On fourth-and-1, the Broncos lined up for what should have been a chip-shot field goal for David Treadwell. But cornerback Nate Odomes skirted around left end and blocked the kick. Cornelius Bennett scooped up the bouncing ball and sprinted 80 yards to a touchdown. The extra-point attempt was good, and just like that, the Bills were back in it, trailing 21–16.

On the second play of Denver's next possession, defensive end Leon Seals deflected an Elway pass that came to rest in safety Leonard Smith's bosom at the Denver 39. Smith then weaved his way through the Broncos offense and into the end zone to give the Bills their first lead of the game, 22–21. But Norwood's extra-point attempt caromed off the left upright—his second missed kick and the Bills' third botch of the day—and the lead held at one.

With the frenzied Buffalo faithful taking an active part in the proceedings, the Broncos began their next possession from their own 5. The first-down snap got away from Elway, causing a fumble that Bennett recovered at the 2. Kenneth Davis bulled in from there, giving the Bills a 28–21 lead.

The ensuing conversion attempt was critical, as it would extend the Bills' lead to eight points, meaning the Broncos would then have to score at least a touchdown and a field goal to reclaim the lead (the two-point conversion had not yet been adopted by the league). The crowd was anxious after the previous botches, but Norwood's kick sailed true. In an unbelievable span of 77 seconds, the Bills had gone from being down 21–9 to ahead 29–21.

But as long as the Broncos had John Elway calling the signals, no lead was safe. (When Elway retired after the 1998 season, he was the reputed all-time leader in fourth-quarter comeback wins with 42.) Like clockwork, Elway promptly drove his team 70 yards in 11 plays to score on a seven-yard pass to Ricky Nattiel. With the extra point, the Broncos trailed by one. But that was as close as they would get. The Bills held on to win one of the most dramatic regular-season games in franchise history.

It was indeed a strange day for the Bills, who succeeded not on the strength of their offense, but rather their defense and special teams. The offense couldn't seem to get out of its own way, as Thurman Thomas rushed for only 36 yards on 13 carries while Jim Kelly completed 18 out of 34 passes for a mere 167 yards. The Broncos had outgained the Bills in total yards, 410 to 197, and outrushed them 208 to 64.

The outcome of this game was crucial, since the Bills had been facing the prospect of falling to 2–2 until that breathtaking fourth-quarter flourish. "That win, ugly as it was, served as a tremendous confidence builder for our team," recalled coach Marv Levy. "We kept on winning, getting better and better in every aspect of play—defense, offense, and special teams."

The Bills remained undefeated at home the rest of the way and finished with an overall record of 13–3. At season's end, as predicted, they were the AFC representative in Super Bowl XXV.

55 The First Draft

On November 22, 1959, the owners of the embryonic American Football League gathered in Minneapolis, Minnesota, to conduct the circuit's first college draft. Like most of the other teams, Buffalo's entry (not yet officially named the Bills) did not yet have a scouting or personnel department—just owner Ralph Wilson. And like the other member's of the so-called "Foolish Club," Wilson never claimed to be an astute evaluator of football material. But the teams had to have players in order to have a league, and hoping to get a jump on the established National Football League, the owners decided not to wait until they had front offices.

"We had to draft players," said Wilson. "Here's how we researched: I didn't have any football men on my payroll. We had a hat, and we put the names on little pieces of paper and dropped them in. Each of the eight teams took one piece of paper out. If you wanted a quarterback, you reached in the quarterback hat and drew out a name. That was how we scouted."

Prior to the formal draft, each franchise was allowed one territorial pick to be used in selecting a recognizable regional star who could help sell tickets and, hopefully, ensure financial stability. With Buffalo's pick, Wilson tapped Richie Lucas, the Penn State quarterback who had finished second to LSU's Billy Cannon for the 1959 Heisman Trophy. Among the other Buffalo draftees were tackles Harold Olsen (Clemson), Chuck McMurtry (Whittier), and Joe Schaffer (Tennessee); guards Birtho Arnold (Ohio State) and Vince Promuto (Holy Cross); and backs Larry Wilson (Utah) and Charlie Bevins (Morris Brown). Wilson also drafted a local product in Willie Evans, the star halfback at the University of

Buffalo. In all, 33 selections—or three full offensive squads—were made by each club.

A second draft was held on December 2 after owners decided the pool of draftees was too small. Another 20 choices were made by each club. Among Buffalo's picks were guard Tom Day (North Carolina A&T), halfback Darrell Harper (Michigan), and tackle Jim Sorey (Texas Southern).

"Now we had to go out and sign these guys," said Wilson. Joe Schaffer, a versatile 6'0", 210-pound lineman from the University of Tennessee, holds the distinction of being the first player ever signed by the Bills, inking his contract on December 5. Five days later, the team signed Birtho Arnold, a huge presence at 6'2" and 310 pounds. Darrell Harper made it official on December 11.

One that got away was Utah's Larry Wilson, who instead opted for the NFL's St. Louis Cardinals. Wilson became the Cards' starting free safety and went on to a stellar 13-year career that culminated with induction into the Pro Football Hall of Fame.

56 The Voice of the Bills

For 37 years, he was the voice of the Buffalo Bills. And except for a brief period between 1972 and 1978, Van Miller provided the radio play-by-play of every Bills game from the team's inception in 1960 through the end of the 2003 season. Along the way, Miller called nearly every important play of every important game, from the Bills' AFL titles of 1964 and '65 to the team's resurgence in the late 1970s under Chuck Knox to the four consecutive Super Bowls of the early 1990s. His dynamic style and his famous signature calls of "Do you believe it?!" and "It's *fan*-demonium!" made him a local cultural icon.

Back in the summer of 1960, the Bills were a new franchise in a new league, and with all that goes into putting a professional football team on the field, no one had given much thought to who was going to be the Bills' radio announcer. The job could very easily have gone to another suitor, but someone within the Bills organization had caught the 23-year-old Dunkirk native calling college games and liked what he heard.

"I had been doing college football and basketball for the University of Buffalo," Miller recalled, "so I had a lot of experience doing play-by-play. Bill Mazur was the sports director at Channel 2, and he wanted to do the Bills in the worst way. He absolutely insisted on being the Bills' play-by-play guy. He said, 'WBEN doesn't have anybody that can do football.' Hey, I learned the hard way—in high school—which is much harder [to commentate] than college or the pros. I used to sit on my back porch and talk into a hose or a funnel or an eggbeater and do Notre Dame football. They won 104 and lost none when I was doing Notre Dame games because I was a good Catholic boy. [Bills general manager] Dick Gallagher had heard me do college football, and he said, 'Hey, this guy is good.' So I got the job."

Those first few years were tough, especially on those long road trips when Van did everything by himself. "We used to play three games in a row out West," he explained. "We'd play Oakland, the Los Angeles Chargers, and the Denver Broncos, and I'd stay out there for all three games. I did the pregame show, the play-by-play, the halftime show, and I did the postgame show."

Back then, Miller would ride on the same plane as the players, and they found creative ways to kill time, often involving his all-time favorite player. "We flew DC-6Bs and DC-7s, so we're talking about a seven-hour ride to the coast," Miller recalled. "Cookie Gilchrist was probably the worst card player in the history of

Van Miller was a part of Buffalo fans' game days for nearly four decades.

professional football. We played seven-card stud. He tried to fill that inside straight, and I'd say, 'Cookie, if you don't have any opening cards, toss it in.' But he would never do that. By the time we were over Chicago, Cookie was borrowing money, and I loaned it to him a couple of times, but he always paid it back."

Miller was a very busy man over the years, maintaining his regular gig as the sports director at Channel 4 (WIVB-TV) and at various times calling games for Buffalo's Bisons (baseball), Braves (basketball), and Stallions (soccer), among others. His calls became almost as memorable to Buffalo sports fans as the plays themselves.

Miller called his last game on December 27, 2003, a 31–0 loss to the New England Patriots. John Murphy, his on-air partner since 1994, took over in 2004 and has called the Bills' play-by-play ever since.

Miller has been honored several times for his work, beginning in 1998 with his induction into the Buffalo Broadcast Pioneers Hall of Fame and the Greater Buffalo Sports Hall of Fame a year later. In 2002, Van was voted into the Chautauqua Sports Hall of Fame. He was honored by the Pro Football Hall of Fame in 2004, receiving the Pete Rozelle Radio-Television Award for "longtime exceptional contributions to radio and television in professional football."

Van and his wife, Gloria, have chosen to remain in Western New York, and he never misses a Bills home game. He continues to work when the mood strikes him, lending his voice to the occasional local radio or television commercial.

57 Not the Next Bruce Smith

Bills fans might not know it, but they are very fortunate. As of this writing, defensive lineman Marcell Dareus is entering just his second season in Buffalo, but if his rookie campaign was any indication, the 6'3½" 319-pounder is just beginning what appears to be a long and prosperous NFL career.

The Bills went into the 2011 college draft looking to bolster their defensive front and felt they had identified just the man to help them in Dareus, the University of Alabama defensive end. Dareus had flourished during his three-year career with the Crimson Tide. In 2009, his sophomore year, Dareus was the defensive MVP of the BCS National Championship Game after spearheading the Crimson Tide's 37–21 defeat of Texas by knocking Colt McCoy, the Longhorns' star quarterback, out of the game with a hard hit on their first possession and later returning an interception 28 yards for a score. A year later, Dareus was a First-Team All-Southeastern Conference selection.

Following his junior year, Dareus declared his eligibility for the upcoming draft, and most experts projected him as a high first-rounder. Sure enough, the Buffalo Bills selected him with their initial pick in the draft (third overall) held on April 28, 2011.

By virtue of being the third overall pick, Dareus became the Bills' highest-drafted player since Bruce Smith was taken first overall in 1985, and observers immediately began making comparisons. But comparing anyone to Smith, perhaps the greatest pass-rushing defensive end of all time, is patently unfair. Smith recorded 200 sacks in his NFL career, while Dareus registered just 11 sacks in three seasons at Alabama. Rushing the passer was not his primary role in Nick Saban's defense.

"I'm not Bruce Smith," Dareus told reporters. "I never will be Bruce Smith. I'm Marcell Dareus, and I'm going to be the best player that I can be. We're two types of players with different styles. Me, I'm a power D-lineman."

Bills fans took an instant liking to Dareus' fun-loving, positive approach to the game. He drew hearty chuckles when he hugged NFL commissioner Roger Goodell after being introduced as the Bills' top pick on draft day. When asked how he felt about playing in the chillier climes of Western New York, the Birmingham, Alabama, native knew just what to say.

"I'm a warm-handed guy," he remarked. "The fan base is crazy. I'm going to put a little light up under everybody and warm it up up there. I can't wait to get there so I can really get the feel of everything."

Dareus signed his contract on July 29, a four-year deal worth $20.4 million. The Bills envisioned him lined up at left defensive end in the 3-4 alignment they planned to use as their basic formation in 2011, but fate intervened. He started the first four games at that position, but when Kyle Williams, the team's Pro Bowl nose tackle, went down with a season-ending injury in Week 4, Dareus was moved into the middle of the line and didn't miss a step. He enjoyed his best game against the Redskins in Week 8, recording 2.5 sacks in the Bills' 23–0 victory.

Dareus admitted to slowing down toward the end of the year, but then the NFL season is longer than in college and the nose tackle position is perhaps the most punishing in the sport. He even got a little dinged up along the way, suffering minor injuries to his shoulder and hand, but did not miss a game all year. In fact, 4.5 of his 5.5 sacks on the year came after being moved to nose tackle. That sack total was the most by a Bills rookie since Aaron Schobel's 6.5 in 2001. With the Bills switching to a 4-3 defense in 2012, Dareus is likely to remain inside.

All things considered, it was a solid debut season for Dareus, and though he did not make the Pro Bowl, there is little doubt among the Bills faithful that he will one day line up with the league's best in Honolulu. "Of course, there'll be a Pro Bowl in my future," Dareus boldly stated. "Hopefully, next year."

It might be worth noting that Bruce Smith didn't play in a Pro Bowl until his *third* year; today, Smith is in the Pro Football Hall of Fame.

58 Completing the Puzzle

They came in like pieces of a puzzle. Darryl Talley, 1983...Bruce Smith and Andre Reed, 1985...Jim Kelly, Kent Hull, and Steve Tasker, 1986...Shane Conlan, 1987. Slowly but surely the Buffalo Bills were building toward what would be the greatest era in their history. There were still a couple of pieces missing, but on October 31, 1987, a huge one—perhaps the final piece of the defensive puzzle—was found. That piece was University of Alabama linebacker Cornelius Bennett, whom the Bills acquired in what has gone down as the greatest trade in team history.

Bennett, a three-time All-America selection and 1986 Lombardi Trophy winner, was the top linebacker in the 1987 college draft class. The Tampa Bay Buccaneers held the first pick in the draft and chose Miami quarterback Vinny Testaverde. The Indianapolis Colts picked next and wasted no time in selecting the 6'2", 237-pound defender, who they saw as the future of the franchise. But that vision was never realized, as the two sides failed to come to terms on a contract.

Flash forward to October 31. Bills general manager Bill Polian, the man responsible for masterminding the acquisition of most of the team's star players, casually walked into coach Marv Levy's office and asked him if he wouldn't mind having Cornelius Bennett on the team.

"You're kidding," responded Levy, not taking Polian all too seriously.

He wasn't kidding. Polian had been on the phone with the Los Angeles Rams discussing a possible three-way deal between them, the Bills, and Indianapolis that would send star running back Eric Dickerson to the Colts and bring Bennett to Buffalo.

"Sounds great," said Levy suspiciously. "What do we have to give up?"

Polian laid out the terms: The Bills would send disgruntled halfback Greg Bell, their first-round draft choice in 1988, and their first and second choices in 1989 for the rights to Bennett. The Colts would send Bell and the draft picks they had acquired from Buffalo, along with their own first and second picks in 1988, a second-round pick in '89, and running back Owen Gill to the Rams for Dickerson.

Levy was dead-set against it at first, believing the Bills were giving up too much for a player who had never experienced a down of professional football. "Six hours later," he recalled, "after being subjected to the rationale of Polian, the most persuasive individual to sit in an NFL office, I succumbed to his logic. Boy, am I glad I did."

Polian pulled the trigger on the deal, and Bennett was on the field for his first practice the following Monday. He suited up for his first game with the team on Sunday, November 8, when the Bills hosted John Elway and the Denver Broncos. Bennett did not start but made his presence felt from the moment he stepped onto the field at the left outside linebacker spot late in the first quarter with no score. Denver had the ball at their own 24, and Elway dropped back to pass. Bennett came streaking in practically untouched. Elway got rid of the ball in the nick of time but was knocked down hard. When he got up, Levy observed, he had that "Who is this guy?" look on his face. Bennett's rush had forced the Broncos to punt and led directly to a scoring drive capped off by a nine-yard Jim Kelly–to–Andre Reed strike and a 7–0 Bills lead. Bennett continued to harass Elway throughout the game, and the Bills won 21–14.

All it took was that one game for the Bills and their fans to recognize the lethal bookend combination they had with Bruce Smith on one side and Bennett on the other. It was an exciting time to be a Bills fan.

With Smith and Bennett leading the defensive charge, the Bills made the playoffs in 1988, the first time in seven years. It would be the first in the string of six consecutive seasons that the Bills would make the playoffs, which included the record four straight Super Bowls between 1991 and 1994. During that stretch, Bennett was elected to five Pro Bowls and was a First-Team All-Pro in 1988.

After nine seasons in Buffalo, Bennett signed with Atlanta in 1996 and enjoyed three years with the Falcons—including a return trip to the Super Bowl in '99—before ending his career with, ironically enough, the Indianapolis Colts (1999–2000). He finished with 71.5 sacks, seven interceptions, 31 forced fumbles, and 27 fumble recoveries.

Despite the impressive stats and accolades, Bennett never really seemed to live up to the lofty expectations placed upon him by fans and media. Many felt there should have been more sacks, more tackles, a Super Bowl victory or two. Yes, he was not the next Lawrence Taylor, but the fact is that Bennett was outstanding throughout most of his career with the Bills, averaging 83 tackles and six sacks per season, despite missing most of his rookie campaign and a good chunk of 1989 with an injury. He should also be given credit for taking a little heat off Bruce Smith by giving opposing offenses another excellent pass rusher to worry about.

But hindsight has been kind to Bennett, as his name comes up frequently in Pro Football Hall of Fame discussions among football historians. He has been voted into several other halls of fame, including the College Football Hall of Fame in 2005.

59 Start Your Own Buffalo Bills Library

Over the years, literally hundreds of books have been written about the Buffalo Bills. Some very talented writers, such as Sal Maiorana,

Scott Pitoniak, Jim Gehman, Randy Schultz, and many others have tackled the subject. A complete bibliography of Bills-related books is simply too large to include here, so this list will focus solely on books written by former players, coaches, and staff members that touch upon their experiences with the team. It provides a good starting point for any fan wishing to put together his or her own Buffalo Bills library.

Tale of the Tape: A History of the Buffalo Bills from the Inside. Eddie Abramoski with Milt Northrup. Abramoski saw it all as the Bills' athletic trainer from the team's inception until his retirement in 1997.

The First Black Quarterback: Marlin Briscoe's Journey to Break the Color Barrier and Start in the NFL. Marlin Briscoe with Bob Schaller. Briscoe spent three years with the Bills (1969–71). While a member of the Denver Broncos in 1968, he was the first African American to start a game at quarterback in the modern era.

Violent Sundays. Bob Chandler and Norm Chandler Fox. Bob Chandler recalls his days with the Bills and the Raiders.

Joe D's Tales from the Buffalo Bills. Joe DeLamielleure with Michael Benson. One of the Bills' all-time greats provides a no-holds-barred, behind-the-scenes look at his time in Buffalo.

They Call Me Dirty. Conrad Dobler and Vic Carucci. An unvarnished look at the man known as the NFL's dirtiest player.

Pride and Perseverance: A Story of Courage, Hope, and Redemption. Conrad Dobler. Dobler's second book provides more stories of his playing days as well as his life after football.

Flutie. Doug Flutie with Perry Lefko. An autobiography tracing his unusual path to the NFL, this book takes the reader up to Flutie's first year in Buffalo.

The Cookie That Did Not Crumble. Cookie Gilchrist with Chris Garbarino. As described by the publisher, Cookie Gilchrist's unfinished memoir, lovingly completed and presented by his friend Chris Garbarino, including a foreword by Booker Edgerson.

Nothing to Kick About: The Autobiography of a Modern Immigrant. Pete Gogolak with Joseph Carter. The life story of Pete Gogolak, who became pro football's first soccer-style kicker when he joined the Bills in 1964.

Armed & Dangerous. Jim Kelly with Vic Carucci. Bills quarterback from 1986 to 1996, Kelly recalls his first years in Buffalo in this autobiography.

Hard Knox: The Life of an NFL Coach. Chuck Knox with Bill Plaschke. The Bills' head coach from 1978 to 1982, Knox shares stories from his legendary career.

Where Else Would You Rather Be?. Marv Levy. The autobiography of the most successful coach in Bills history.

Game Changers: The Greatest Plays in Buffalo Bills Football History. Marv Levy with Jeffrey J. Miller. Levy, along with this writer, digs deep into the annals of Buffalo Bills football and extracts critical moments, bringing them back to life with an enthusiasm that will delight every fan who thinks of Orchard Park as a home away from home.

Kick Rejection...and WIN!! G. Booth Lusteg. The autobiography of Booth Lusteg, the controversial kicker who replaced Pete Gogolak in 1966.

O.J.: The Education of a Rich Rookie. O.J. Simpson with Pete Axthelm. The Juice's first biography, written after his first year with the Bills.

By a Nose: The Off-Center Life of Football's Funniest Lineman. Fred Smerlas and Vic Carucci. The honest and often hysterical behind-the-scenes life story of one of the Bills' most beloved characters.

A View Through the Lens of Robert L. Smith: The Buffalo Bills Photos: 1960–1995. Robert L. Smith. By the Bills' official photographer from 1960 through the 2002 season, this book is a compendium of the franchise's most memorable moments, as seen through Smith's lens.

Steve Tasker's Tales from the Buffalo Bills. Steve Tasker with Scott Pitoniak. Buffalo's greatest special teams player shares stories about his amazing career and the colorful cast of characters with whom he played.

60 The *Other* Stevie Wonder

Stevie Johnson is entering just his fifth season in Buffalo, and he has already accomplished something no other Bills receiver ever has. No one in the history of the Bills—not Eric Moulds, not Elbert Dubenion, not Lee Evans, not even Andre Reed—has ever recorded back-to-back 1,000-yard receiving seasons. Stevie Johnson is the only one; and with any luck, he will be adding to the streak for years to come.

Johnson was drafted by the Bills in the seventh round (224th overall) in 2008 after a spectacular 1,000-yard, 13-touchdown senior season at the University of Kentucky. He played sparingly as a rookie, catching just 10 balls, but two of them went for touchdowns. He was expected to compete for more playing time in his sophomore season, but the signing of Terrell Owens and a serious rib injury suffered during training camp limited Johnson to five games in 2009.

The Bills, however, opted not to re-sign Owens for the 2010 season, clearing the way for a healthy Johnson to compete for and win the starting wideout spot opposite veteran Lee Evans. He lost the spot after getting off to a slow start but promptly reemerged with a string of big games, beginning with the first 100-yard outing of his career in the Bills' loss to the Baltimore Ravens in the sixth game of the season. Two weeks later, Johnson had a career-high

11 catches for 145 yards against Chicago. In Game 10 versus Cincinnati, he caught eight passes for 137 yards and three scores.

Johnson finished the season as the franchise leader in receptions (82), receiving yards (1,073), and touchdowns (10), but while he was developing into one of the top young receivers in the league, he sometimes allowed his playful nature to detract from his game. There were times when his lack of focus cost him or his team dearly. After scoring a touchdown against the Patriots in Week 3, Johnson simulated firing a rifle and fell to the ground pretending to be shot, drawing a $10,000 fine from the league. After his first touchdown in the Cincinnati game, Johnson lifted his jersey to reveal the question "Why so serious?" scrawled on his undershirt. The quote was in reference to a line uttered by the Joker in the Batman movie *The Dark Knight*, and was directed at Bengals wide receivers Terrell Owens (the former Bill) and Chad Ochocinco, who referred to themselves as Batman and Robin. It was intended in good humor, but the joke cost Stevie another $5,000.

But while Johnson's antics began to attract criticism from fans and media, teammates were quick to come to his defense, extolling him as the ultimate team player and dedicated family man who never got into trouble off the field. His behavior, they insisted, was not the me-first, attention-seeking type displayed by the likes of Owens and Ochocinco, but rather that of a finely tuned athlete celebrating the ultimate payoff for his hard work.

Even bigger things were expected from Johnson in 2011, and though his numbers were off slightly from the year before, he still managed to grab a team-high 76 balls for 1,004 yards (also a team high), thus becoming the first Buffalo receiver to hit the 1,000-yard milestone in consecutive years. The slight reduction in production can be partially attributed to the fact that Johnson played much of the year with a torn groin and a broken hand.

One statistic that went unaffected, though, was his number of run-ins with officials. The first came in Game 12 against the Jets, when Johnson pretended to shoot himself in the leg (an obvious reference to New York receiver Plaxico Burress) and then wave his arms in the air to mimic a jet crash-landing. The second occurred in the season finale against New England when Johnson lifted his jersey after scoring a touchdown to reveal that he had "Happy New Year" written on his undershirt. This time, however, Bills coach Chan Gailey had had enough. In a bold move, Johnson was benched for the rest of the game.

Again, Johnson's teammates came to his defense. It was just Stevie being Stevie, they chimed.

Despite the distractions, Johnson had been one of the Bills' top producers over the past two seasons, as well as one of their most recognizable characters. But longtime Bills fans had grown accustomed to what had become almost a tradition of seeing the team's top players sign free-agent contracts for big money with other teams. They had cause for concern when the Bills allowed the 2011 season to end without having signed Johnson to a new deal. But management came through on March 5, 2012, rewarding Johnson with a five-year, $36.25 million contract, ensuring fans that this vastly talented, entertaining wideout would be with the club for a long time to come.

"This is where I started, in Buffalo," said Johnson after signing his contract. "They took a chance on me. They did me a favor by picking me. I want to remain loyal to them like they did with me because there could have been times where they could have let me go. This group is the only group I've known since I've been in the NFL. There's a lot of promise here, and I love working with these guys. Just waking up in the morning, even on the cold days out here, and just coming to Buffalo and being around my teammates. That's what it's about. I've always wanted to be here."

61 The Worst Year

Bills fans who suffered through the frustration and embarrassment of the team's dreadful 1968 season found solace in the belief that things couldn't get any worse than that. Unfortunately, those fans were wrong—and they only had to wait three years to find that out.

The Bills' first year as an NFL franchise after joining the senior circuit in the historic merger between the two leagues was in 1970. It was also the team's second season under head coach John Rauch, who had thus far led them to a less-than-stellar aggregate record of 7–20–1.

Just a few days before the 1971 training camp was scheduled to begin, Rauch appeared on a local television program and made some disparaging remarks about former Bills Paul Maguire and Ron McDole. A week later, when owner Ralph Wilson informed Rauch that he planned to issue a statement in support of the players, Rauch threatened to resign. Wilson called his bluff, and on July 20, five days into camp, Rauch tendered his resignation.

So with the start of the regular season a mere two months away, the Bills were without a head coach. Wilson couldn't very well expect the team to continue without someone calling the shots, but who could he get to take over at the 11th hour? Any qualified candidates were either already occupied or simply not interested in getting caught up in the league's ugliest soap opera.

Into the breach again fell poor Harvey Johnson, the Bills' director of personnel who was as unprepared to lead a team on the field in 1971 as he had been in 1968, when Wilson elevated him to the post for the first time after firing Joe Collier. Mr. Wilson had apparently forgotten that the team managed to win just one of the

12 games Johnson coached that season. And what's worse, Johnson didn't want the job any more now than he had back then.

"When Rauch was fired," said Eddie Abramoski, "Harvey knew he was going to get the call again. He tried hiding from Ralph in the training room, trying to avoid the call, but he couldn't get away with it."

On paper, it looked like Johnson had at least a few guys who could play, starting with former Heisman Trophy–winning half-back O.J. Simpson. But Simpson had missed much of 1970 with a knee injury, and after two mediocre seasons, he was dangerously close to being labeled a bust. Quarterback Dennis Shaw, despite throwing 10 touchdowns and 20 interceptions in 1970, had been named NFL Rookie of the Year. The team also boasted a very good receiving corps that included Marlin Briscoe (a Pro Bowler in 1970), budding star Haven Moses, and J.D. Hill, the team's No. 1 draft pick.

Hill, however, wound up missing the first 10 games after injuring a knee in the preseason. Simpson, although delighted that Rauch was gone, had another disappointing year, picking up just 742 yards on the ground behind an offensive line that could be described as porous at best. When the line actually managed to give Shaw time to throw, he was woefully erratic, tossing 11 touchdown passes and 26 interceptions. It was no surprise that they ended the season dead last in the league in points scored and were shut out four times.

As bad as the offense was, the defense was even worse. The unit was a veritable mishmash of has-beens, cast-offs, and never-weres that surrendered a league-worst 394 points, allowing fewer than 20 points just once. The lone bright spot was third-year cornerback Robert James, who was destined to become one of the top cover men in the league. That distinction, however, was still at least a year away.

All that said, the Bills actually got off to a promising start, falling short in a 49–37 thriller against the Dallas Cowboys, the eventual Super Bowl champs. It was all downhill after that, as the Bills lost their next nine outings (a string of 15 straight losses going back to 1970), including a thoroughly embarrassing 43–0 loss to the Colts in Week 4 that saw Simpson rush for an all-time low of minus-10 yards on seven carries. They finally got off the schneid in Week 11 by outlasting the New England Patriots 27–20 at War Memorial Stadium. That proved to be the only win the Bills would muster all year, as they went 0–3 down the stretch to finish 1–13.

At season's end, Johnson happily resigned as coach and returned to his office in the personnel department. Wilson then rehired Lou Saban, the man who had led the team to back-to-back AFL titles in 1964 and '65. Within a couple of seasons Saban would restore respectability to the once-proud franchise and transform Simpson into the greatest running back in the game. No one associated with the Bills in 1971—players, fans, media—would have believed it was possible.

Join the Club

Established in 1961 by first president Vincent Griffin and 50 other Buffalo supporters, the Buffalo Bills Booster Club is a collective of dyed-in-the-wool fans who simply can't get enough of their favorite NFL team. They gather for monthly meetings throughout the year to discuss the latest happenings, share memories, and plan club events. Guest speakers include current and former Bills players and coaches, broadcasters, writers, and fellow Bills fans.

The Booster Club also participates in community activities and provides support to several local charities, such as Veteran's Hospital in Buffalo. Each year the boosters hand out the Bob Kalsu

Memorial Scholarship to an area high school senior for demonstrating courage on and off the field.

The club meets on the fourth Tuesday of every month, except in January and February. They are always looking for new members. Dues are $15 per person, or $35 for the whole family. Dress is casual, but all are encouraged to wear team colors, of course. For more information, send inquires to billsboosterclub@yahoo.com, attn: membership, or visit their website at www.billsboosters.wordpress.com. Sharon Jackson is the current president.

63 The Quarterback War

Many longtime observers regard the trade of quarterback Daryle Lamonica as the worst transaction in franchise history. When the Bills sent Lamonica and wide receiver Glenn Bass to the Oakland Raiders after the 1966 season in exchange for wide receiver Art Powell and quarterback Tom Flores, fans were shocked. Jack Kemp, the team's starting quarterback since 1962, had led them to three straight AFL title games, but he was getting older and was prone to slumps. Lamonica was only 25 and always seemed to play spectacularly in relief of Kemp. Lamonica had, until then, provided the Bills with the best insurance policy they could have hoped for. The team, many felt, was trading away its future.

The 6'3", 215-pound Lamonica was drafted by the Buffalo Bills in the 24th round in 1963 after a stellar collegiate career at Notre Dame. He was impressive throughout his first training camp and eventually unseated Warren Rabb as Kemp's understudy. As Lamonica recalled, "[Coach] Lou Saban said, 'You've got a lot of ability. I want you to work hard. You won't be starting, but learn as much as you can. If something happens to Jack, I want you to be able to step right in and lead us.' With that in mind, I worked extra hard so if he called on me, I wouldn't let him down or the team down."

With Kemp as the primary starter, the Bills made the playoffs for the first time in 1963. But Lamonica's play when called upon was essential to the team's success. On November 3 against Denver, he came off the bench in the second half and threw for 211 yards and two touchdowns to lead Buffalo to a dramatic 30–28 come-from-behind victory. He started the final two games of the season, winning both and helping the team tie for the division lead and a playoff matchup with Boston. The Bills lost 26–8, but Lamonica set a team playoff record for longest touchdown pass when he connected with Elbert Dubenion on a 94-yard strike.

The Bills' fortunes soared over the next three seasons, but there were occasions when Kemp could be erratic. In those instances, Saban did not hesitate to turn to his relief pitcher. Lamonica was often brilliant and occasionally pulled the Bills out of the jaws of defeat with second-half rallies. It wasn't long before Lamonica became a fan favorite, and thus the Bills' first serious quarterback controversy was born, with fans divided into either the Kemp camp or the Lamonica camp.

"They had We Want Lamonica and We Want Kemp buttons passed around," Lamonica recalled, "but that controversy was more through the press and some of the fans. Jack and I were good friends, and there was never any animosity. Sure, I wanted to be a starter—that's what every athlete wants. I knew what my role was because Lou called me in and sat me down and told me. He said, 'Your day will come.' So that's a role I accepted."

Unlike later quarterback controversies, such as the Flutie-Johnson debacle in the late 1990s, the players on the '60s team saw the competition between their QBs as a good thing. "It wasn't divisive at all," said Billy Shaw, the team's offensive captain. "In fact, it was a help. Daryle was an exceptional quarterback. He made Jack a better player. It took Jack to another level."

Judging by the team's success, the arrangement worked. The Bills repeated as AFL champs in '65 and returned for a third straight AFL title game appearance in '66. But the following spring, the Bills made the deal that sent Lamonica to the Raiders. It was a surprise move, and to no one more than Lamonica himself.

"I talked to Ralph Wilson Jr. and his father the night before [the trade]," Lamonica recalled. "They said, 'You're going to come back and be our starting quarterback.' Eight hours later I was traded. I didn't have any clue I was going to be traded. I was ready to compete with Jack and have an opportunity to be the starting quarterback. No one has ever called me from the Bills to let me know why. I had to call the *Fresno Bee*, my hometown paper, to find out if it was true."

Though trading Lamonica put the quarterback controversy to rest once and for all, it was a move the team came to regret several times during the next few seasons. But Lamonica's exit was inevitable. The immensely talented quarterback deserved a chance to start—if not in Buffalo, then somewhere else. He'd have that chance in Oakland.

And he made the most of it! In his first year out West, Lamonica threw for 3,228 yards and 30 touchdowns, led the Raiders to a 13–1 record and a trip to the Super Bowl (which they lost to Green Bay), and was named league MVP. In his first three seasons as a Raider, Lamonica threw for more than 9,000 yards and 89 touchdowns, and claimed a second MVP award in 1969. Those gaudy statistics earned him the moniker "the Mad Bomber."

The Bills, on the other hand, won just four games in 1967 and only one in 1968. Lamonica's supporters argue, probably correctly, that the team would have won more games had he remained with the Bills and been healthy when the team suffered so many injuries at quarterback in '68. But something fans should consider is that if

At peace in 1964, Jack Kemp (left) and Daryle Lamonica would become the central figures in a bitter quarterback conflict.

Lamonica was still a Bill that year and had been able to engineer a win or two, the team would not have finished dead last and would not have been able to draft O.J. Simpson. The history of the franchise would look very different, and much bleaker, if that chapter had never been written.

Lamonica went on to play eight years with the Raiders, retiring after the 1974 season. His aggregate record of 66–16–4 as a starting quarterback gave him an astonishing overall winning percentage of 78.4, second-best in NFL history behind just Otto Graham (81.0).

64 Bryce Paup

Linebacker Bryce Paup's tenure with the Bills was short but oh so memorable. In three spectacular seasons in Buffalo, Paup was voted to three Pro Bowls and earned NFL Defensive Player of the Year honors. He was unquestionably one of the best—if not *the* best—free-agent signings in club history.

The 6'5", 247-pound pass-rushing specialist had already played five seasons with the Green Bay Packers before signing on with Buffalo in 1995. He had previously enjoyed an outstanding collegiate career as a defensive end at the University of Northern Iowa, earning All-Conference honors three times and a Third-Team All-America selection in his senior season. The Packers selected Paup with their sixth-round pick (159th overall) in 1990. After spending much of his first three seasons watching from the sideline and coming in on obvious passing downs, Paup became the permanent starter at left outside linebacker, finishing second on the team in sacks in 1993 with 11. After being named to

1994's Pro Bowl squad, Paup's market value soared. Enticed by a three-year, $7.6 million offer, he inked a contract with the Bills on March 8, 1995.

Paup's signing was a major shot in the arm for a defensive unit that had recorded just 25 sacks the year before—10 of those by Bruce Smith alone—and a team that had missed the postseason for the first time since 1987. In his first campaign with the Bills, Paup earned First-Team All-Pro and was named NFL Defensive Player of the Year after leading the league in quarterback sacks with 17.5, helping the team nearly double its sack total (49) and win the East Division crown. Paup's best game came against the Colts in Week 3, when he recorded three sacks, 14 tackles, and forced a pair of fumbles to earn AFC Defensive Player of the Week honors (his first of two such honors that year).

Hampered by injuries that limited him to 12 games in 1996, Paup managed just six total sacks. He was still one of the most feared pass rushers in the game, however, and was named to his third consecutive Pro Bowl. Paup's sack numbers rebounded to 9.5 in 1997, earning him a fourth trip to Honolulu, but the Bills opted not to pursue re-signing him. He jumped at a five-year, $21.75 million offer from the Jacksonville Jaguars during the off-season, ending a three-year stint in Buffalo that included 33 sacks in 43 regular-season games.

Paup played two years with the Jags and one injury-plagued season in Minnesota before retiring, having recorded 75 sacks and six interceptions in 148 career regular-season games.

Today, Paup lives in De Pere, Wisconsin, where he coaches at Green Bay Southwest High School. He also serves on the Packers Board of Directors.

65 T.O.'s Shining Moment

Terrell Owens was one of the most dominant players of his era. In his 13-year NFL career, the man known simply as "T.O." earned six Pro Bowl trips and five First-Team All-Pro selections. He was feared to go the distance whenever he was on the field, scoring 139 touchdowns during his career. But controversy followed Owens wherever he went, and by the end, there were no teams left willing to take on the baggage that came with his vast talent.

Owens was originally drafted by the San Francisco 49ers in the third round in 1996 and was given the golden opportunity of playing alongside his idol, Jerry Rice. Despite eight productive seasons, five of which saw him surpass the 1,000-yard mark, Owens openly clashed with teammates and coaches and by 2004 had worn out his welcome. That off-season, T.O. signed a seven-year, $49 million contract with the Philadelphia Eagles. He was again productive, making the Pro Bowl and helping the Eagles get to the Super Bowl in his first year with the club, but public criticism of management and quarterback Donovan McNabb (as well as a locker-room fight with teammate Hugh Douglas) led to Owens being suspended in midseason and eventually released after just two seasons. He moved on to Dallas in 2006, signing a three-year deal with the Cowboys worth a reported $25 million. Owens spent three productive years in Dallas, eclipsing the 1,000-yard mark each season, but again wore out his welcome and was released on March 4, 2009.

The Bills, looking to inject some life into an anemic offense that finished 25th and failed to have a 300-yard passing game in 2008, decided to take a flier on the immensely talented but equally troublesome wideout. Four days after his release from the

Cowboys, the Bills made headlines by signing Owens to a one-year, $6.5 million contract.

"I'm leaving America's Team for North America's team," said Owens at the time. "It's another beginning for me. If I can be that extra, added piece to get them to the playoffs, then that's what I'm here for. I looked at the defensive side of the ball and offensive side of the ball, and these guys have all the pieces."

"We all know of his tremendous ability and look forward to what he will bring to our offense," added Bills owner Ralph Wilson. "This is a very exciting day for the Buffalo Bills."

Was it ever! It had been quite some time since the Bills had made such a big splash in free agency, and there were very few bigger—or more controversial—names than Terrell Owens. Fans couldn't wait to see what kinds of fireworks Owens would set off in Buffalo.

Instead, Owens seemed content to be the Bills' No. 2 receiver behind veteran Lee Evans despite a couple of sideline moments that aroused fears that the old Owens was about to emerge. Through the first nine games, Owens had a very un-T.O.-like 26 catches (an average of less than three per game) for 366 yards and one touchdown.

His shining moment as a Buffalo Bill came against the Jacksonville Jaguars in Week 11. The Bills, playing their first game under interim head coach Perry Fewell, were trailing 10–9 early in the third quarter when they took possession at their own 2. Quarterback Ryan Fitzpatrick positioned himself under center, while Owens lined up wide to the right, matched up man-for-man against Jacksonville cornerback Tyron Brackenridge. At the snap, Owens bolted from the line and, after making a slight move to the inside, gained a step on his man. Fitzpatrick, standing in his own end zone, saw Owens streaking past Brackenridge and heaved the ball in his direction. T.O. snagged Fitzpatrick's pass in stride at midfield. Brackenridge made a desperate lunge in an effort to trip

Owens from behind but only caused Owens to stumble slightly before regaining his stride. In the clear, Owens jogged into the end zone for a spectacular 98-yard touchdown reception, giving the Bills a 15–10 lead.

The play eclipsed the old Bills mark for longest touchdown pass (95 yards), set in 1996 by Todd Collins and Quinn Early. It was not a league record, however. There have been 13 touchdown receptions of 99 yards in league history.

Owens finished the game with nine receptions for 197 yards and the touchdown, but it was all for naught as the Jags came back in the fourth quarter to win 18–15 and drop the Bills to 3–7 for the season.

Owens finished the season with 55 catches for 829 yards and five touchdowns, decent numbers for a typical NFL receiver but well off the numbers people expected from him. The Bills, with Lee Evans, Roscoe Parrish, and a young star-in-the-making named Stevie Johnson waiting in the wings, decided not to re-sign the 36-year-old receiver.

T.O. signed with the Cincinnati Bengals and enjoyed one solid season playing opposite Chad Ochocinco before being released.

66 Swing by Jimmy's Old Town Tavern

If you're a Buffalo Bills fan and find yourself near the nation's capital and are feeling a little homesick or craving some good old-fashioned Buffalo cuisine, stop by Jimmy's Old Town Tavern in Herndon, Virginia. You won't be sorry.

Opened for business in 1997, Jimmy's Old Town Tavern is the brainchild of former Western New Yorker and restaurateur Jimmy

Cirrito. Cirrito grew up in the small town of Arcade, New York, about 40 miles southeast of Buffalo, and has been a fan of the Bills and Sabres for as long as he can remember. "I was brainwashed young," he recalled, "and I never lost my love for the Bills."

When he moved to the northern Virginia town of Herndon in the 1990s, he found a large community of like-minded people—Buffalo sports fans in search of a place where they could gather to honor, celebrate, and commiserate the ups and downs of their hometown teams.

In 1996, Cirrito assumed proprietorship of a century-old building—located at 697 Spring Street, in the heart of Old Town Herndon—and after countless hours of planning and renovating, transformed it into the Old Town Tavern. Jimmy opened the doors the following May, and his Buffalo sports–themed enterprise has proven wildly successful.

Jimmy's menu features authentic Buffalo fare, including Anchor Bar–style chicken wings made with Frank & Teressa's Original Wing Sauce (shipped in from Buffalo!) and the heartiest Beef-on-Weck sandwiches south of the New York–Pennsylvania border. Also highly recommended by loyal patrons are the *poutine* (French fries smothered in gravy and cheese), the chili, and, of course, the Friday night fish fries. The bar offers such Buffalo favorites as Molson, Labatt's, and homegrown Genesee beer, as well as wine and cocktails.

The walls are a veritable mini-museum of Buffalo sports, with genuine Bills and Sabres artifacts and signed photos of Jim Kelly, Doug Flutie, Scott Norwood, and other greats covering every square inch. It's all designed to make traveling Buffalonians feel as if they never left Western New York.

Every Bills game since 1997 has been shown on the tavern's big-screens. Visitors interested in the game-day experience, however, should be sure to get there early—say, 11:00 AM. "Sundays are crazy," says Cirrito. "We have an occupancy limit of 150, but sometimes as many as 700 people show up to watch the games here. We open the alley next to the building and put giant screens outside." Bills victories are proclaimed throughout the neighborhood by patrons running up and down Spring Street waving huge Bills flags.

Even during the off-season, Jimmy's is the place to be for Western New Yorkers passing through the DC area. It's not uncommon for visitors to bump into people they know from back home, or maybe even a Buffalo Bill or Sabre. "We're not just a Buffalo bar during the season," says Cirrito. "We feature Buffalo themes all year long, including fund-raisers for charities like Hunter's Hope. It has become a destination for people from back home who are coming to the DC area or heading south. We're only 20 miles from the White House."

67 The Timely Emergence of Carlton Bailey

In 1991, linebacker Carlton Bailey was in his fourth year with the Buffalo Bills but only his first year as a starter. He had supplanted incumbent starting right inside linebacker Ray Bentley near the end of 1990 but remained "that other guy" in a corps that included All-Pro performers Cornelius Bennett, Shane Conlan, and Darryl Talley. But with one memorable play in the 1991 AFC Championship Game, Bailey was lifted from anonymity and became, however briefly, just as famous as his better-known teammates.

The championship game had largely been a defensive contest, with both high-octane offenses sputtering. By the time the teams trudged off to their respective locker rooms at intermission, the

Bills offense had managed a mere 58 yards of total offense and had converted just one of seven third downs.

The offensive futility continued unabated well into the third quarter. The Bills appeared to be on the brink of breaking the stalemate until a promising drive was snuffed out when Kelly was picked off by Tyrone Braxton at the Denver 19. With another misfire from the heralded K-Gun, it looked as if it was going to be up to the defense to make a game-changing play.

And make it they did. On Denver's second play after the interception, Elway dropped back to pass. Buffalo nose tackle Jeff Wright immediately recognized that a screen was coming and broke off his rush. He shot his hands up and deflected the pass into the air. The ball came to rest in Bailey's arms, and the crowd of 80,272 went crazy as the 27-year-old linebacker raced past Elway into the end zone.

"We had an inside blitz called," said Bailey. "It was supposed to be Shane's blitz, then we switched it up. But hey, Jeff Wright made the play by tipping the pass."

Suddenly, the Bills held a tenuous 7–0 lead with still more than five minutes left in the third. But the Bills held on for the victory and the right to take on the Washington Redskins in Super Bowl XXVI.

Suddenly, Carlton Bailey's name was known to all.

He had come to the Bills as an obscure ninth-round pick in 1988 out of the University of North Carolina after being scouted by Linda Bogdan, the daughter of owner Ralph Wilson. He had been a nose tackle in college and won the Lawrence Taylor Award as UNC's top defensive player in his senior year, but Bogdan astutely projected the 6'3" 242-pounder as a linebacker. He spent his first three seasons cutting his teeth on special teams, playing a key role on what was at the time the best squad in the league. After finding his way into the starting lineup late in the 1990 season, Bailey became one of the team's most reliable run-stuffers. But the Bills lost Bailey's services after the 1992 season when he signed a three-year, $5.25 million contract with the New York Giants, making him their highest-paid linebacker, exceeding even the salaries of All-Pro Carl Banks and future Hall of Famer Lawrence Taylor.

When Bill Polian—the man given much of the credit for assembling the talented Bills of the early 1990s—was named general manager of the expansion Carolina Panthers in 1994, he began assembling a roster that looked remarkably similar to the one he had put together in Buffalo. Polian signed several Bills, including quarterback Frank Reich, wide receiver Don Beebe, and tight end Pete Metzelaars. He also signed Bailey, who had been released by the Giants after two seasons. Bailey's signing proved the most important of all, for when the Panthers went to the playoffs in just their second year in existence, he was the only ex-Bill still on their roster. He spent three seasons with the Panthers before retiring after the 1997 season.

 **Butch**

The Buffalo Bills selected George "Butch" Byrd of Boston University in the fourth round of the 1964 college draft. A two-way star at BU, Byrd led the Terriers in rushing in both his junior and senior years and was an All-East selection in 1963. The Dallas Cowboys showed interest, but Byrd signed with Buffalo because the Cowboys had already chosen Mel Renfro in the first round, and, as Byrd explained, "It didn't take a genius to understand that my chances of making the team wouldn't be easy, simply because their No. 1 draft choice was the same position that they drafted me. And politics being what they are, they're going to keep a No. 1."

It didn't hurt that Byrd's offensive coach at BU, John Mazur, was now on the Bills staff. "He was the one who initially called me and told me the Bills drafted me," Byrd recalled. "Being familiar with him, and based on his advice, I decided to go with Buffalo."

It turned out to be a good move for both Byrd and the Bills, as the 6'0" 211-pounder made an immediate impact, winning the starting right corner position in his first training camp and holding it down for the next seven seasons as the final piece of the Bills' championship puzzle. He recorded his first interception in just his third game as a pro, picking off Tobin Rote of the Chargers and racing 75 yards for a score. In all, Byrd intercepted seven passes during his rookie season, setting a Bills record and earning an invitation to the AFL All-Star Game, the first of five in his career. Along the way he gained a reputation as one of the best and most aggressive defensive backs in the league. And he was durable, never failing to suit up in his entire time in Buffalo, a streak of 101 consecutive games (regular and postseason). He went on to record a team-record 40 career interceptions (five of which he returned for scores, also a club record) and appear in three AFL title games with the Bills (1964, '65, and '66). His 74-yard punt return in the 1965 title game set an AFL postseason mark that stood until the AFL-NFL merger.

He was also a pioneer in race relations among AFL players. "My roommate was Mike Stratton," he recalled. "Mike and I were the first mixed[-race pair]. That honor usually goes to Gale Sayers and Brian Piccolo, but I believe we were ahead of them. I think Mike and I were the first white and black ballplayers to room together, and that was controversial. There were some ballplayers on our team that didn't like it. Ballplayers came from all parts of the country, and they brought with them their own baggage. I really can't tell you why or how it happened—he thought it was a good idea or I thought it was a good idea—I can't even remember who raised the subject. Maybe we just found ourselves in the same room by accident and decided to keep it that way." The two have remained close friends ever since.

The Bills traded Byrd to the Denver Broncos prior to the 1971 season, but he played just one season in the Mile High City before calling it a career.

Byrd has gone on to become one of the most decorated members of the AFL-era Bills, beginning with being named to the All-Time AFL Team (second squad) by the Pro Football Hall of Fame Selection Committee, Boston University's Athletic Hall of Fame, and the Greater Buffalo Sports Hall of Fame. He has also won the Ralph C. Wilson Jr. Distinguished Service Award for "service to the Bills organization and the Western New York community during his career" as well as the Kent Hull Hard Working Man Award (along with Booker Edgerson).

69 The First Camp

The Bills' first training camp was held in the Buffalo suburb of East Aurora in the summer of 1960. Since it was a new franchise playing in a new league, there were numerous wrinkles to iron out before a team could be put on the field, beginning with the equipment. "When [head coach] Buster Ramsey and I got to Buffalo," remembered Eddie Abramoski, the team's athletic trainer, "we were starting from scratch. We had no uniforms, no equipment, no players, nothing. Between [equipment manager] Ed Dingman and me we had to order all of the equipment—the shoulder pads, helmets, et cetera. When we went to East Aurora, the stuff was all brand new, so they didn't put the face masks on the helmets. We had to stay up until 4:00 in the morning the night before practice putting all of the face masks on, me and Ed."

The mass of humanity that descended upon the Knox Farm for the team's first workouts included bartenders, truck drivers, former high school players, and seemingly every other frustrated athlete hoping for a chance to live out his childhood fantasy of playing professional football. But with literally hundreds of souls running in and out of East Aurora on a daily basis, that first camp more closely resembled a three-ring circus than a professional football operation.

"Training camp was not well organized because they were just starting," Abramoski remembered. "Everybody was trying out, basically—even the coaches. There would be three or four guys coming in every day and three or four guys leaving every day. We had guys that came in, ran a couple wind sprints, and that was it. In fact, the guy that took people to the airport was the busiest guy on the team. The driver that took them out had a full-time job—every day he was back and forth, back and forth."

"There were people coming and going all of the time," said guard Don Chelf. "They would say they had a team on the field, and one coming and one going."

"Anybody who got cut by the National Football League probably got a chance to play in the AFL," said LaVerne Torczon. "That's where a lot of people came from—people that were cut from the NFL came to the AFL."

One recruit had written a letter to Ramsey requesting a tryout. "He identified himself as 'Ruby Legs' Robinson, 'because I am so fast,'" recalled public-relations director Chuck Burr. "Well, Buster didn't turn anybody down—hell, if I applied, I could [have tried] out. So Robinson came in and lasted one day. Buster said, 'If he had ruby legs, for cryin' out loud, I have no legs at all!'"

According to Abramoski, camp routine went something like this: "I taped 100 guys. I would start taping at 6:30 to be on the field at 10:30. They would get done, and I would eat from 12:00 to 12:15, and I would start taping again at 12:30 to get them on the field by 4:30. A lot of guys would help me out—they would wear their tape from the morning for the afternoon practice, although it would loosen up a lot."

The lockers were a crude fabrication, but Abramoski and Dingman managed to provide accommodations for every player on the squad. "We'd put up a furring strip around the outside and put nails in it," Abramoski explained. "We didn't have enough stools for everybody to sit down; a lot of guys had to sit on the floor. And it was only so big, it could only hold 80, and sometimes we'd bring in 20 more, we'd just make the locker from 36 inches to 18 inches. One guy would be dressing and then would go out to the middle of the floor, out of the way."

The historic Roycroft Inn, located on South Grove Street in downtown East Aurora, served as the team's headquarters and dormitory. "That first year we stayed at the Roycroft," recalled halfback Joe Kulbacki. "It was Richie Lucas, me, Jack Laraway, Dan McGrew, and LaVerne Torzcon. We had one big room—we stayed there the entire season as roommates. We enjoyed the area and the people of East Aurora. Almost every night we were invited to someone's home for dinner, at least once or twice a week."

"We had breakfast at the Roycroft," said Chelf, "then went over to the high school and got dressed, then got on school buses and went out to the polo field. [We practiced] there for a couple of hours and then came back on the buses, went and got undressed, showered, went and had lunch, then laid down for a while, and went out and practiced again in the afternoon."

The players were driven from the school to the practice field in a rented bus. "We supplied the driver," said Abramoski, "usually one of the players. A player who could drive a stick shift and steer the bus became valuable. Buster used to keep the players who could drive the bus until training camp was over. He couldn't drive them because in New York State you have to have a certain class of license as opposed to just an ordinary driver's license, and I couldn't drive it. I remember we had John Scott, a big defensive tackle from Ohio State, and another kid, they lasted the whole season—they weren't really good football players, but we couldn't cut them."

The field at the Knox Estate was, most agreed, simply atrocious. Since the grounds were also used for polo matches, the players had to be careful not to destroy the sod with their spikes and blocking sleds. "We moved around a lot because we didn't want to wear out the field," said Abramoski. "We didn't want to get them upset by wrecking their fields for polo."

"I don't think there was anyone [there who] didn't have leg problems," said Mack Yoho. "It was just like playing on a road. The problem I had all through training camp was shin splints. It was like running on concrete."

To Elbert Dubenion, however, the playing surface at the Knox Estate was actually a step up from what he played on at college. "I didn't think it was awful," he said. "You had to see the field I played on at Bluffton. Just the hard polo ground, but I didn't see anything wrong with it." He was clearly in the minority.

In spite of its shortcomings, the Bills continued to use the Knox Farm and Roycroft Inn until 1962. The following year the Bills moved their camp to the Camelot Hotel in Blasdell.

The Main Man

O.J. Simpson made countless breathtaking runs during his Hall of Fame career. The majority of those runs came between 1973 and 1977 behind the blocking of a legendary offensive line. That line, nicknamed the "Electric Company," might have been better named the "No-Name Line" since very few outside of Buffalo could have named each of the individual players. The two exceptions, however, were the guards—perennial All-Pro guard Joe DeLamielleure and the one whom Simpson referred to as his "Main Man." That man was Reggie McKenzie.

The Bills were in yet another rebuilding mode in 1972, having finished dead last in the entire league the previous year. Owner Ralph Wilson had made the bold step of bringing back Lou Saban, the man who had coached the Bills to back-to-back AFL championships in the mid-'60s, in an effort to turn things around. Saban's first order of business was to build a forward wall to block for the Bills' theretofore underachieving halfback who in three pro seasons hadn't even come close to gaining 1,000 yards.

McKenzie had been an All-America selection in his senior season under Bo Schembechler at the University of Michigan. The Detroit native had been blessed with outstanding foot speed, and Saban, an astute evaluator of football talent, envisioned the 6'4" 255-pounder pulling from the left guard position to lead Simpson on power sweeps around right end. After taking defensive end Walt Patulski with the first-overall pick in the draft, the Bills snagged McKenzie with their second-round selection (27th overall).

McKenzie's impact was immediate. He played with a maturity that belied his inexperience and wound up starting in every game as Simpson led the league in rushing and the Bills improved to 4–9–1. But Reggie sensed that it was only the beginning. When the Bills returned to training camp the following summer, he made a bold prediction—that Simpson was going to be the first back in NFL history to rush for more than 2,000 yards in a single season.

With the Electric Company opening huge holes in enemy defenses, Simpson was putting up astounding numbers. When the Juice reached the 1,000-yard plateau at the season's midway point, the entire league began taking McKenzie's prediction seriously.

Entering the season finale against the Jets, Simpson needed 197 yards to reach the milestone. Late in the game's final stanza, Simpson stood at 193. A seven-yard burst behind McKenzie gave Simpson the yardage he needed and secured his place in sports immortality.

Between 1972 and 1977, Simpson surpassed 1,000 yards five times and won four rushing titles. But the Bills could never find the right balance and made just one trip to the playoffs (1974) with the standout.

McKenzie lost his best friend on the team when Simpson was traded to San Francisco after the 1977 season. He soldiered on as the Bills' elder statesman and was an inspirational leader during the team's resurgence under coach Chuck Knox in the late '70s and early '80s, when the Bills enjoyed back-to-back postseason appearances (1980 and '81). When Knox left to join the Seattle Seahawks after the 1982 season, he worked out a deal with the Bills to bring McKenzie out to the West Coast. With McKenzie anchoring the offensive line, the Seahawks made the playoffs for the first time as a wild-card team in 1983 and repeated the feat again the following year.

After two seasons with the Seahawks, however, the 34-year-old McKenzie decided it was time to retire but remained with the Seahawks front office for the next 11 seasons. He now lives in his hometown of Detroit and oversees the Reggie McKenzie Foundation, which touches the lives of more than 1,500 Detroit-area youth each year through various programs designed to promote academic, athletic, vocational, and life-skill achievement.

Despite being overshadowed by fellow guard and future Hall of Famer Joe DeLamielleure during his years in Buffalo, McKenzie was named to several All-Pro teams between 1973 and 1976 and again in 1980. He is a member of the Michigan Hall of Fame and the College Football Hall of Fame. In 1999, he received the Ralph C. Wilson Jr. Distinguished Service Award.

71 Leadership On and Off the Field

When Booker Edgerson signed with the Bills as a free agent in 1962, he felt an immediate sense of belonging. After all, Edgerson had played at Western Illinois University under head coach Lou Saban and assistants Joel Collier and Red Miller, who made up three-fifths of the Buffalo coaching staff. But despite their presence, Edgerson wasn't sure at first that he was going to make the final cut. "I was on the fourth or fifth team," he recalled. "That was very disappointing because I had never been on any team other than the first team, so I thought, *Whoa, there's something wrong here.*"

Hoping to get some helpful hints on the finer points of the pro game, Edgerson approached some of the veterans but learned quickly that they were just as concerned about their jobs as he was about his. "I did ask for some help," he recalled, "and they looked at me like I was stupid. They said, 'Are you crazy? We aren't going to teach you how to beat us out of our jobs.' To me, that was a terrible attitude to have, that you're not going to tell a rookie things to do. It hindered my progress because I went up and played the game the way I thought I should play it, and I got burned a couple of times."

When Edgerson took his concerns to the coaches, he was advised to just be patient. "It was hard to be patient," he recalled, "especially when I'm looking at some of these guys, and obviously you always think you're better than somebody else anyway. So I was patient and finally they gave me an opportunity to start on the first team, and that's where I was from that point on."

Edgerson ended up picking off six passes in his rookie year and over the next seven seasons was a cornerstone of the formidable defense that led the team to four straight postseason appearances

(1963–66) and two league titles (1964, 1965). He snagged 23 interceptions in his time with the Bills, returning two for touchdowns. But just as important as his duties as an active member of one of the AFL's best defensive secondaries was Edgerson's role as a quasi player-coach to his teammates, having learned through his own experiences just how vital that tutelage can be to younger players.

"Booker was my player-mentor," remembered Edgerson's companion corner, Butch Byrd, who came to the Bills in 1964. "We would get together before games and he would tell me about different quarterbacks' strategies and tendencies, wide receivers' strategies and tendencies, because this was the first time I was facing them."

"When Butch came in," said Edgerson, "I coached him. I told him, 'Here's the things you do, what to watch for, how to play your position.' [Cornerback] Robert James was the same way. I sat and talked with Robert. People would say, 'Why are you teaching him that?' I said, 'Hell, he's going to replace me or Butch at some point.'"

"I learned a lot from Booker," recalled another cornerback, Hilton Crawford, who joined the Bills in '69. "I played on the same side with him—I played behind him. The main thing that I learned from Booker was that height doesn't matter, size doesn't matter—it's heart. Booker wasn't a tall person, and to me he played like he was."

Edgerson put his natural leadership skills to good use in his post-football life, helping shape the future of thousands of individuals at Erie Community College in Buffalo, where he served as the director of equity and diversity from 1982 until his retirement in 2007. He remains one of the most respected members of the Bills family and is very active in the community both privately and through the team's alumni association. He was honored in 1993 with the Ralph C. Wilson Jr. Distinguished Service Award, given annually to former Bills players for outstanding service to the organization and the community. In 2010, he and Butch Byrd were reunited as co-recipients of the Kent Hull Hard Working Man Award, presented annually by Hanes Supply Inc. of Buffalo to a past or present Western New York sports figure for exceptional leadership on and off the sports field.

Though he was only selected to play one All-Star Game (1965) and only received one All-AFL mention (1969), Edgerson has been honored for his on-field achievements on several occasions. He is enshrined in the Western Illinois Athletics Hall of Fame, the Quad-City Sports Hall of Fame, and the Greater Buffalo Sports Hall of Fame. In 2010, he became the 26th man enshrined on the Bills' Wall of Fame at Ralph Wilson Stadium.

 **Chuck Knox**

The 1970s had not been going well for the Buffalo Bills, despite three winning campaigns riding the back of O.J. Simpson. By the end of the '77 season, the team had compiled an overall record of 39–71–2, with only one playoff appearance during the decade. It was clear that major changes were in order, and they began with the firing of head coach Jim Ringo, who had overseen two straight losing seasons after taking over for Lou Saban in early 1976. The search for Ringo's replacement began immediately, and among those rumored to be on the short list of candidates were Monte Clark (former 49ers head coach), John Ralston (formerly with Denver), and Bill Walsh (Stanford University). But the speculation ended on January 11, 1978, when the team made the surprising announcement that it had signed former Los Angeles Rams coach Chuck Knox to a six-year contract worth $1.2 million.

Fans and players alike were thrilled to hear that Knox was coming to Buffalo. He was a proven winner, having won five straight division titles in five years with the Rams, employing a conservative, run-oriented offense the media dubbed "Ground Chuck."

Guard Joe DeLamielleure saw the signing as the first step toward the Bills' return to respectability. "He's one of the top football coaches," he said at the time. "Right up there with John Madden, [Don] Shula, and Bud Grant. And now we've got him. The encouraging thing to me is that a guy of his stature would come here to Buffalo. He must think there's something here."

Knox made it clear from the get-go that he was taking the Bills in a new direction. His first major personnel move was trading the aging Simpson to San Francisco for a batch of draft choices. Those picks would prove valuable over the next few years in helping stock the team with young, talented players. Behind the same back-to-basics, no-nonsense approach that proved wildly successful with the Rams, the Bills responded by improving to 5–11 in Knox's first year.

As 1979 approached, there was a buzz surrounding the Bills that had not been felt in at least four years. Fans were buoyed by what appeared to be a strong draft—in which the club selected future stars Jerry Butler, Jim Haslett, Jeff Nixon, and Fred Smerlas—and the surprising acquisition of Isiah Robertson, the six-time Pro Bowl linebacker who had anchored Knox's stingy defenses in Los Angeles. The blend of veteran experience and youthful energy was proving successful, and the Bills improved to 7–9.

Things broke open in 1980. Just as Lou Saban had done in his two stints with the club, Knox continued to acquire players—either proven pros or through the draft—who fit into his grand design. Reliable veterans—such as linebacker Phil Villapiano and guard Conrad Dobler—were brought in along with two more players Knox knew and trusted from his days with the Rams: safety Bill Simpson and wide receiver Ron Jessie. Via the draft, the Bills acquired guard Jim Ritcher and, with one of the picks received from San Francisco for O.J. Simpson, multithreat halfback Joe Cribbs.

If any further proof was needed that these were not the same old Buffalo Bills, that evidence was provided on opening day when they defeated Miami for the first time since 1969 (a stretch of 20 straight losses). The team won its next four games and finished the season at 11–5, claiming its first division crown since 1966. But the dream season ended in heartbreaking fashion with a 20–14 loss to San Diego in the AFC divisional playoff. Despite the club's first-round ouster, Knox earned NFL Coach of the Year honors from the Associated Press and *The Sporting News*.

Knox and the Bills continued their winning ways in 1981, but the final record of 10–6 was only good enough for a wild-card spot in the playoffs. The Bills won a 31–27 thriller over the Jets in the first round but lost 28–21 to eventual Super Bowl representative Cincinnati in the divisional round.

After consecutive playoff seasons in 1980 and '81, the Bills were favored by some experts to take it to the next level—the Super Bowl—in 1982. The team was loaded offensively, with All-Pro–caliber wide receivers in Frank Lewis and Jerry Butler, along with two-time 1,000-yard-rusher Joe Cribbs, being led by veteran quarterback Joe Ferguson. The defense was even better, having given up the second-fewest points in the AFC the previous year (276). Barring some unforeseen calamity, this would be the Bills' year.

But after getting off to a 2–0 start, the NFL players voted to strike and remained on the picket lines until mid-November. By that time, seven regular-season games had to be excised from the schedule, and the Bills lost the momentum they had at the start of the campaign. The team managed to win just two of its seven post-strike games and finished at a disappointing 4–5 and fourth place in the division.

Knox had a year remaining on his contract but resigned when he and owner Ralph Wilson failed to reach an accord on a new deal. Many players expressed disappointment, even anger, when the popular coach left. His work, they felt, wasn't finished, and there is no doubt that another shining chapter in the team's history left with him.

A day after his resignation from the Bills, Knox signed on to coach the Seattle Seahawks and had them in the playoffs in his first year with the club. When the Seahawks won the AFC West in 1988, Knox became the first coach in NFL history to win a division title with three different franchises. He finished his career with a three-year return stint with the Rams (1992–94).

Although Knox left abruptly without completing his program, his .507 winning percentage at Buffalo places him third on the team's all-time list, behind only Marv Levy and Lou Saban.

73 The Buffalo All-Americans

On October 30, 2011, the San Francisco 49ers attracted national attention for tying an obscure record that had lasted for more than 90 years. The record was for most games at the start of a season with at least one rushing touchdown scored, while not allowing a rushing touchdown. The long-standing record of seven games was set in 1920 by the Buffalo All-Americans.

Huh?

Many fans, no doubt, were scratching their heads, wondering, "The Buffalo *whats?*" The Buffalo *All-Americans*—Buffalo's first NFL team.

When the American Professional Football Association began play in 1920 (it was renamed the National Football League in 1922) with teams such as the Akron Pros, Canton Bulldogs, Columbus Panhandles, Dayton Triangles, Decatur Staleys, and Rochester Jeffersons, the Buffalo All-Americans were there. Led by quarterback-coach Tommy Hughitt and a bevy of actual college All-Americans such as guard Swede Youngstrom, tackle Lou Little, end Murray Shelton, and halfback Ockie Anderson, Buffalo might have had the most aptly named team in the history of the league.

The team was actually an outgrowth of a local semipro outfit called the Buffalo Niagaras, who in 1918 had won the Buffalo Semi-Pro Football League title. A year later, the Niagaras' core players formed a new team, called the Prospects. The Prospects carried on the tradition of success, taking the New York state championship in its first and only season.

After claiming local and state titles in successive seasons, Buffalo's gridders were eager to try their luck with the new national league they had read about. Having missed the initial league meetings, a letter requesting membership was submitted to the league founders, and the Queen City's team was welcomed as a charter member.

Much of the early legwork for the Buffalo team was performed by Howard E. "Barney" Lepper, a former member of both the Niagaras and the Prospects. All of the early press announcements refer to Lepper as the team's manager, and it was Lepper and local businessman (and Lepper's eventual successor as team manager) Frank J. McNeil who signed the lease for the team to play their home games at the Canisius College Villa. One of the first players signed up was a feisty 27-year-old quarterback out of the University of Michigan named Ernest "Tommy" Hughitt, a teammate of Lepper's on the Niagaras and Prospects. After guiding those teams to respective championships, the diminutive Hughitt—all of 5'8" in height and weighing 150 pounds—was the obvious choice to call the signals for the All-Americans.

Polo, Anyone?

When the New York Jets hosted the last pro football game ever played in New York's historic Polo Grounds on December 14, 1963, it was only fitting that the Buffalo Bills were the opponent. After all, it was Buffalo's original pro team, the All-Americans, that played the first-ever pro game there—against the Canton Bulldogs in 1920. The All-Americans narrowly defeated the Bulldogs—led by Hall of Famers Jim Thorpe and Wilbur "Fats" Henry—by a 7–3 score. Swede Youngstrom was the hero, blocking a Thorpe punt and recovering in the end zone for the winning points.

The All-Americans established themselves as one of the elite teams in the early days of the APFA, finishing within one game of the title in each of the first two seasons of the league. In 1921, the All-Americans actually claimed the title but lost it to George Halas' Chicago Staleys in an executive decision.

They had gone undefeated in their first nine games that year, and after defeating the Dayton Triangles at the old Canisius Villa to end their season on November 27, the All-Americans claimed the league title with a record of 8–0–2. But for some unknown reason, team manager McNeil had scheduled his team to play two more games that, he told local papers, would have no bearing on the team's claim to the title.

Enter George Halas. Halas' Staleys (who became the Chicago Bears a year later) had amassed a record of 7–1–0, with their only loss coming against Buffalo on November 24 (Thanksgiving Day). He scheduled a rematch with Buffalo at Chicago for December 4, hoping to exact revenge against the team that had marred his perfect record. McNeil made the mistake of scheduling his team's two "postseason" contests on the same weekend, the first for Saturday, December 3, against the tough Akron Pros, after which his men would take an all-night train to Chicago to play the Staleys on Sunday.

After dispatching the Pros on Saturday, the All-Americans were off to Chicago, where they disembarked the next day in no condition to take on Papa Bear's hungry brutes. The All-Americans fought hard, but the Staleys took the game, 10–7.

McNeil still believed his team was champion and gave tiny engraved gold footballs to his players to commemorate the achievement. Halas had other ideas; he argued the title belonged to the Staleys, basing his claim on his belief that the second game of their series with Buffalo mattered more than the first. He also pointed out that the aggregate score of the two games was 16–14 in favor of the Staleys. McNeil insisted his team's last two games, including the one against Chicago, were merely exhibitions. It didn't matter. The league declared the Staleys champions.

McNeil spent the rest of his life arguing that his team had been bilked but was never able to get the league to reverse its decision. Some historians still agree that the title is rightfully Buffalo's, but it is very unlikely the city will ever see the 1921 decision overturned.

The All-Americans enjoyed winning seasons in 1922 and '23 but never again enjoyed the success they had in those first two years. McNeil sold the franchise in 1924 to a group led by Warren D. Patterson and Tommy Hughitt, who changed the team name to the Bisons. Hughitt lasted one more year before hanging up his cleats. Further changes in ownership and name occurred throughout the decade but to no avail. By 1929, Buffalo's first professional football team had run out of money and time.

74 Al Bemiller

If Al Bemiller hadn't had such good aim, he might not have been a center. He had begun his football career at Syracuse as an end, but when the team found itself in need of a pivot man, a certain talent he never knew he had put him into a position he never wished to play.

"I didn't want to be a center," he recalled. "When I was in high school I was an end—a tall, skinny end. Prep school—tall, skinny end. Went to Syracuse—tall, skinny end my freshman year. In my sophomore year, one day we were playing basketball in the gym—that's how we got in shape. Coach Dailey came in and he said, 'Okay, I've got a football here. Any of you [who] can center this damn ball?' We all said, 'We'll try.' So he marked it off and said, 'There's a doorknob. Whoever hits that doorknob is gonna be my center.' I [hiked the ball and] hit the doorknob. From that time on, I was a center."

And a very good one, too. He became the anchor on Syracuse's formidable offensive line—dubbed the "Sizable Seven"—that led the Orange to an undefeated season and the national championship in 1959. Though Syracuse dropped to 7–2 in Bemiller's senior season (1960), he still garnered enough attention to earn All-East honors.

Bemiller was drafted in the seventh round by the Buffalo Bills of the AFL and the same round by the NFL St. Louis Cardinals. He ultimately chose the Bills for two reasons: "I didn't know how good I was," he explained. "I figured I had a better shot at making the [Bills]. Then I had a coach up at Syracuse who used to play here [Rocco Pirro], and he was telling me how great the town is, how great the people were, and so on."

The Bills already had a pretty good center in Dan McGrew, who had been an All-League selection in 1960, but Bemiller supplanted McGrew before the end of training camp. "One night we had a rookie party," Bemiller recalled. "We all went out partying, drinking, and I ended up bringing him home. So from that time on, I knew that I was going to make the team. I was a good Pennsylvania boy—we drank beer from the time we were little."

Bemiller started all 14 games as a rookie, but the Bills finished below .500 for the second straight season, and head coach Buster

Ramsey was let go. Lou Saban, a firm believer that a successful team is constructed with the offensive line as its foundation, took over in 1962 and a year later had the Bills in the playoffs for the first time.

In 1964, the Bills won their first of two straight AFL championships, defeating San Diego 20–7 in the title game. That was also the year in which Bemiller proved his value to the team when he was moved to right guard after the Bills acquired veteran center Walt Cudzik from Boston. Bemiller played guard throughout the following season as well, but when an injury prevented regular center Dave Behrman from playing in the championship game (a rematch with the Chargers), Al slid over and came through with a flawless performance. His presence served as a stabilizing factor after All-League guard Billy Shaw was knocked unconscious on the opening kickoff, and the Bills won 23–0.

Saban resigned after the 1965 season and was replaced by Joe Collier, who made Bemiller his permanent center. The Bills once again found themselves in the championship game at the end of the year but came up short against the Kansas City Chiefs, who thus earned the honor of representing the AFL in the very first Super Bowl.

"That was a real letdown for me," Bemiller recalled, "because in high school we won our conference championship. I [went] to college and [won] a national championship. And then we won the AFL championship. Now I had this step yet to go that would have completed all my steps."

Throughout his career, Bemiller was one of the Bills' most versatile performers, which probably worked against him when it came to All-Star voting. For three years he was a center, then for two years he was a guard, and then he went back to center again. Midway through the 1967 season, he was even asked to fill in at tackle when the offensive line was decimated by injuries.

Where the heck did he fit in? The true answer is, anywhere he was needed.

And he was durable, too, never missing a game in his nine years with the Bills. In fact, Bemiller's first and only major injury as a professional football player turned out to be his last. In the 1969 season finale against San Diego, Al suffered a severe knee injury while covering a punt. He was determined to come back, but the nine-year veteran was not in coach John Rauch's long-term plans. "The next year I went back and I was fully recovered," he recalled. "I was in great shape, and Rauch let me go."

Despite having a few good years left on his 32-year-old frame, Bemiller decided it was time to transition into the next phase of his life. "I could have gone on, but I chose not to because I had my restaurant in Hamburg—Al Bemiller's Turfside. And it was going great guns. I had the restaurant for 15 years.... We always had live bands. [Then] disco came in, and all these other places started to pop up, and it went down the tubes."

His retirement ended a streak of 126 consecutive regular-season starts, which stood as the team record for 12 seasons. (What makes that streak more impressive is the fact that he also never missed an exhibition or playoff game, extending his number of starts to 173!)

"I always ran scared," he explained. "Somebody's looking for your job—I was very conscious of that all the time. When you're a marginal player like I was, you just want to keep playing. You don't want to get out of the game. You never take time off. As soon as somebody else steps in there, and especially in those days, if they did better than you, you were gone."

Bemiller remains one of the most respected members of the Bills family and is very active in the community through the team's alumni association. He was selected to the Bills Silver Anniversary Team in 1984. He and his wife, Wanda, live in Orchard Park, not far from the home of today's Bills, Ralph Wilson Stadium.

From Red, White, and Blue to Black and White

It is very rare indeed that a former NFL player becomes an on-field official after leaving the playing field. It is so uncommon, in fact, that only four players who were active during the Super Bowl era have gone on to do it. One of those players is former Buffalo Bills safety Steve Freeman.

Freeman came to the Bills as a rookie free agent in 1975. He had been originally selected by New England in the fifth round of that year's draft out of Mississippi State but was cut by the Patriots midway through their exhibition schedule. The Bills brain trust saw something special in Freeman and signed him on August 21. He turned out to be a reliable backup and special teams performer and even started several games when the defensive backfield was decimated by injuries. Freeman became the team's permanent starting strong safety in 1979, and it wasn't long before the 5'11", 185-pound Texas native established himself as one of the toughest players on the team. (In 12 years with the Bills, he missed just one game due to injury.)

Freeman enjoyed a breakout year in 1980, recording seven interceptions on what was the top-ranked defense in the league and helped the Bills to their first playoff appearance in six years. In 1983, Freeman made a seamless transition to free safety and enjoyed his best year as a pro, earning First-Team All-Pro honors from *The Sporting News*. The Bills moved Freeman back to strong safety in 1984 and '85 but switched him again to free safety in 1986. He was still playing solid ball, but at 33 years of age, he was not figuring into new coach Marv Levy's long-term plans and was traded to Minnesota during the off-season.

Steve Freeman works the Green Bay Packers and Cleveland Browns matchup in 2009.

Stripes

Of the four former NFL players from the Super Bowl era who have gone on to become on-field officials, only two are currently active. The other active official aside from Freeman is head linesman Phil McKinnely, formerly a tackle with the Atlanta Falcons, Los Angeles Rams, and Chicago Bears. Ironically enough, McKinnely serves on Triplette's crew alongside Freeman.

The other two players-turned-officials were Gary Lane, a quarterback with the Browns and Giants in the late '60s who later spent 20 years as a referee and side judge, and Pete Like, a quarterback for the Jets, Broncos, Eagles, and, very briefly, Bills (though he never appeared in a game for them) between 1964 and 1972 who worked as a back judge during the 1980s.

At the time he left Buffalo, Freeman held the team record for most regular-season games played with 178. He also holds the distinction of being the only Bill to have played under the three most successful coaches in team history (Lou Saban, Chuck Knox, and Marv Levy). As a Bill, Freeman intercepted 23 passes, three of which were returned for touchdowns. He also recovered eight fumbles.

Freeman retired after one season with the Vikings, having played 13 seasons and 190 regular-season games in his career. He began officiating football games at the high school level and then moved on to college, working games in the Southeastern Conference for several seasons. His development continued with three seasons in NFL Europe before graduating to the NFL in 2001. He currently serves as a back judge on referee Jeff Triplette's crew and bears the number 133 on his new uniform.

Freeman and his wife, Bo, reside in Oxford, Mississippi. He is an enshrinee of the Mississippi State University Sports Hall of Fame (class of 2000).

76 Blade

Bills record-setting defensive back Tom Janik, the man teammates nicknamed "Blade" for his slight build (he was listed at 6'3" and 190 pounds), began his professional career with little fanfare, being taken in the third round of the 1963 draft by the AFL Denver Broncos. A Little All-America selection as a two-way back and punter at Texas A&I, Janik languished for two years on a pathetic Denver team before being traded to Buffalo for a seventh-round draft choice in 1965.

After spending most of his first season with the Bills on special teams, Janik moved into a starting role in 1966 when regular left corner Booker Edgerson was sidelined with a knee injury. Janik responded with a fine season in which he intercepted eight passes, returning two for touchdowns. Surprisingly, he was passed over in the All-Star voting. Janik got everyone's attention the following year, however, when he was moved to strong safety after an injury felled starter Harold Clarke. He turned in a spectacular season in which he tied for the AFL lead with 10 interceptions, returning those for 222 yards and two scores and earning All-AFL honors.

Despite a record-setting day against the Jets on which he picked off three Joe Namath passes (returning them for a total of 137 yards, including one that went 100 yards for a touchdown), Janik's numbers were down considerably in 1968, due mainly to losing three games with a hairline fracture in his leg.

He was traded to Boston in 1969 for a sixth-round draft choice. Janik had always been listed in the Bills' media guides as the team's backup punter but was never actually used in that capacity. (The Bills, after all, had one of the best punters in the business in

Paul Maguire.) He finally got his chance with Boston and led the Pats in punting in each of his three seasons with the club.

Janik passed away in his home state of Texas in November 2009. He still holds Buffalo team records for most interception yards in a game (137) and remains tied for most picks in a game (three) and season (10), as well as interceptions returned for touchdowns in a season (two) and career (five).

Man Mountain

Sam Adams' first game with the Buffalo Bills was perhaps the most memorable debut in team history. Facing Tom Brady and the New England Patriots on opening day 2003, the Bills held a 14–0 lead early in the second quarter when Brady took a snap from center at his own 37-yard line and dropped back to pass. His throw was deflected into the air and came down to rest in Adams' welcoming grasp. The 6'4", 335-pound defensive tackle shifted immediately into his highest gear. Escorted by a convoy of blockers led by linebackers Jeff Posey and Takeo Spikes, Adams made his way toward the sideline and rumbled all the way into the end zone to give the Bills a 21–0 lead. It was a spectacular beginning to what would become a three-year love affair between No. 95 and Buffalo Bills fans.

Adams was already a nine-year veteran by the time he signed with Buffalo as a free agent in March 2003, having spent six years with the Seattle Seahawks, two with the Baltimore Ravens, and one with the Oakland Raiders. The Houston native was the Seahawks' first-round pick in the 1994 draft (eighth overall) after a standout career at Texas A&M in which he was a consensus All-American in his junior—and final—season. He also threw the shot put and javelin on the Aggies' track team. During his time in Seattle, "Man Mountain" (as he was called by his teammates) developed into one of the premier defensive linemen in the game and was chosen as an alternate for the 1997 Pro Bowl.

He signed with the Baltimore Ravens prior to the 2000 season and received his first trip to the Pro Bowl that year in recognition of his huge role in the success of the Ravens defense, which ranked first overall and keyed the team's victory over the Giants in Super Bowl XXXV. Another Pro Bowl appearance followed the 2001 season, and Adams' market value skyrocketed. He signed a free-agent contract with the Oakland Raiders in 2002 and made a return trip to the big game, but the Raiders lost to Tampa Bay in Super Bowl XXXVII.

The following spring, Adams joined the Bills, and the big man became an immediate sensation with his interception and touchdown against the Patriots in the 2003 season opener. He earned his third Pro Bowl nod in 2004 after recording 40 tackles and five sacks to pace the league's second-ranked defense and guide the Bills to their first winning season in five years.

Adams became a casualty of football economics following the 2005 season, as the Bills were forced to release the 12-year veteran in order to make room under the salary cap. He played one season with the Cincinnati Bengals before moving on to the Denver Broncos for a 14th, and ultimately final, season in 2007.

In addition to his participation on the field, Adams participated in the management side of the game when he became an owner of the Everett (Washington) Hawks of the National Indoor Football League in 2004. Two years later, Adams moved the Hawks to a new league, Arena Football 2, but the team folded after the 2007 season.

Adams was enshrined in the Texas A&M Athletics Hall of Fame in 2001. His father, Sam Sr., had an outstanding 10-year career in the National Football League as an offensive guard with the New England Patriots (1972–80) and New Orleans Saints (1981).

78 The Dirtiest Player

By all accounts, former Bills guard Conrad Dobler was a pretty good football player. During his days with the St. Louis Cardinals in the mid-'70s, he was a three-time Pro Bowler on a line that was considered the best in the NFL at the time. But despite the accolades, there was something for which Dobler was better known—something for which he claimed an equal amount of pride. Aside from being considered one of the league's top linemen, Dobler was the consensus choice for its dirtiest.

It didn't start out that way. Dobler had enjoyed a pretty good career at the University of Wyoming and impressed the St. Louis Cardinals enough to select the Chicago native in the fifth round of the 1972 draft. As with most rookies, Dobler was treated harshly by his veteran teammates, but he internalized their disrespect and used it as motivation on the field. After paying his dues for a year as a backup and on special teams, he became the starting right guard in 1973. He brought a *defensive* lineman's mentality to his position, concluding that it was better to attack than be attacked. But it wasn't until his third year in the league that Dobler began his descent into the "dark side" of the game.

When the Cardinals faced the Minnesota Vikings in the 1974 NFC divisional playoff, Minnesota defensive tackle Doug Sutherland accused Dobler of biting his finger, and the story spread like wildfire. Dobler never denied the charge, and he became the scourge of the league practically overnight. Teams preparing to play the Cardinals often requested, only half-jokingly, a rabies vaccination. Some of his biggest haters included Pittsburgh's "Mean" Joe Greene, whom Dobler once allegedly punched, and the Rams' Merlin Olsen, with whom Dobler carried an open, ongoing feud. Some of the dirty tactics Dobler admitted to include leg whips, tripping, eye-gouging, and, on at least one occasion, kicking an opponent in the face (Jack Youngblood, also of the Rams). But the one accusation to which he never owned up while still an active player was the biting, quipping that he "would never do such a tasteless thing."

Dobler reveled in the notoriety and was immortalized by *Sports Illustrated* in July 1977 with a cover story proclaiming him as PRO FOOTBALL's DIRTIEST PLAYER. But all the attention made Dobler a marked man, not just by opposing linemen, but also by officials. "In one game I was called for tripping a guy who was standing up," he joked. "Sure, I tried to trip him, but I didn't succeed, and attempted tripping is not illegal."

As his villainous reputation continued to grow, so did his stature among those whose opinions mattered most. As part of the offensive line that gave up a record-low eight sacks in 1975 (and included Hall of Fame tackle Dan Dierdorf), Dobler was named to his first of three consecutive Pro Bowls—and this was at a time when the coaches did the voting, not the players or the fans.

The Cardinals, tiring of Dobler's antics, dealt the recalcitrant guard to New Orleans in 1978. A severe knee injury forced him to miss most of his first season with the Saints, but he returned to action in 1979 and played well enough to earn All-Pro recognition from UPI. The following summer, the Buffalo Bills, anticipating the departure of All-Pro guard Joe DeLamielleure, traded a draft choice to the Saints to get Dobler. Chuck Knox, who had taken over as head coach of the Bills two years earlier, had been gradually restoring the once-proud franchise to its former glory and was looking for Dobler to provide veteran leadership on a squad teeming with young talent. DeLamielleure was eventually traded, and Dobler became the starting right guard, a spot he held down for most of the next two seasons. He played an integral role in helping the Bills reach the postseason both years, but his reputation had followed him to Buffalo, and Knox felt it necessary to bench Dobler late in 1981 when officials began throwing an inordinate number of flags in his direction. "I lived in a fishbowl," Dobler recalled. "The tackle next to me pulled a guy's jersey over his head, and they called me for holding."

It was just as well, however, for at that point in Dobler's career, it required a Herculean effort just to prepare himself to play each week. "My list of injuries by this time was really unbelievable," Dobler wrote in his autobiography. "The process I had to go through just to get ready for games was amazing. The icing, the deicing, the taping, the braces, the stretching, the painkillers—it was an adventure just getting my body to the point where I could suit up and play."

Those aches and pains followed Dobler into retirement and over time deteriorated into debilitating handicaps resulting in numerous surgeries, including at least 30 knee operations. He now relies on a cane and a heavy supply of medications just to help him stay upright. Still in need of further surgeries, Dobler, like many other disabled NFL veteran players, has been unsuccessful in gaining disability assistance from the league.

Compounding Dobler's post-football worries is the health of his wife Joy, who became paralyzed as a result of falling out of a hammock on July 4, 2001. The cost of health care has forced the Doblers into financial hardship. After seeing a segment about them on HBO's *Real Sports*, golfer Phil Mickelson offered to help the Doblers by putting their two youngest children—daughter Holli and son Stephen—through college.

Today, the Doblers make their home in Overland Park, Kansas. Dobler remains actively involved with the Gridiron Greats

Assistance Fund, which provides services and financial aid to retired players in dire need. He is as tenacious, if not more so, in his fight for retired players' benefits and stem-cell research as he was in protecting his quarterback on the playing field.

Legendary sportswriter Jim Murray once wrote that Dobler "didn't play football, he waged it." Considering the success that approach brought Dobler during his playing days, one can only expect that he will eventually prevail.

79 The Role Player

Longtime Bills fans mainly remember running back Roland Hooks for two things: his spectacular four-touchdown performance against the Cincinnati Bengals in 1979 and the last-minute Hail Mary pass he caught to beat the New England Patriots in 1981. For Buffalo coaches from Lou Saban to Chuck Knox, however, Hooks was a super-sub and consummate role player, filling in ably for every Bills back from O.J. Simpson to Joe Cribbs, notching three 100-yard rushing games along the way, and providing yeoman service on special teams whenever called upon.

Hooks was Buffalo's 10th-round draft pick in 1975, a stand-out running back out of North Carolina State. At that time, the Bills had perhaps the greatest running back who ever lived in O.J. Simpson, along with two holdover backups in Don Calhoun and Gary Hayman, so Hooks' odds of making the team were long at best. He was never really given a chance to find out, however. Hooks missed the first four weeks of the exhibition season after contracting hepatitis, then suffered a season-ending injury in the preseason finale.

When he returned for camp in '76, Calhoun and Hayman were gone, and Hooks made the most of his opportunity, playing well enough to secure the backup spot behind Simpson and becoming a valuable special teams performer.

After Simpson tore up his knee midway through the 1977 campaign, Hooks stepped in and played well, carrying the ball 128 times for 497 yards, including a superb performance at New England on November 6 when he rushed 27 times for 155 yards to spur a 24–14 Bills victory.

Chuck Knox took over as head coach in 1978, and Hooks became one of his most reliable players. His most notable individual outing came on September 9, 1979, when he scored four touchdowns (3, 32, 4, and 28 yards) in just five carries in the Bills' 51–24 rout of the Bengals.

Hooks' best year was 1981, as he enjoyed 100-yard performances in two consecutive weeks. The first came on November 22 when he compiled 111 yards on six catches against the Pats, including the unforgettable last-minute, game-winning touchdown catch affectionately known to Buffalo fans as "Big Ben." A week later, Hooks, filling in for the injured Joe Cribbs, carried the ball 19 times for 109 yards and two touchdowns as the Bills defeated the Washington Redskins 21–14. He also led the team in punt returning that year, bringing back 17 kicks for 142 yards (an 8.4-yards-per-return average).

In his seven seasons with Buffalo, Hooks gained 1,682 yards rushing and 12 touchdowns on 399 attempts (a 4.2-yards-per-return average). He was on the receiving end of 96 passes, good for 950 yards and three scores.

Hooks now lives in Reno, Nevada, and coaches the running backs on the Bishop Manogue Catholic High School football team. In 1996, he received the Ralph C. Wilson Jr. Distinguished Service Award for his efforts in helping retired players transition to life after football. He continues to support his brothers in arms through his involvement with the NFLPA former players chapter in Reno.

80 Ahmad Rashad

To sports fans across the country, Ahmad Rashad is recognized as one of the smoothest and most respected sportscasters in the business. Before he gained fame for his work in the studio and broadcast booth, however, Rashad was a standout wide receiver best remembered for his spectacular seven-year career as a member of the Minnesota Vikings. But long-suffering Bills fans will always remember Rashad for his one shining season in Buffalo (1974) in which he led the team in receptions and played a major role in the team's first playoff appearance since 1966.

Rashad (born Robert Earl Moore in Portland, Oregon) was a two-time All-America selection at the University of Oregon, where he caught passes from future Pro Football Hall of Famer Dan Fouts. He became the only player in Pac-10 history to lead the conference in scoring from two different positions (running back and wide receiver). The St. Louis Cardinals selected the 6'0" 205-pounder with their first pick (fourth overall) in 1972. It was around this time that he converted to Islam and changed his name to Ahmad Rashad, meaning "admirable one led to truth."

After two fine seasons in St. Louis during which he was selected to UPI's All-Rookie Team in 1972 and set an NFL record for the longest nonscoring completion with a 98-yard reception from Jim Hart in a game against the Los Angeles Rams, Rashad was dealt to the Bills for quarterback Dennis Shaw on January 26, 1974. The speedy, sure-handed wideout won instant fan approval with his two-touchdown performance in the season-opening defeat of the Oakland Raiders. He turned in his best game statistically on November 3 in the Bills' 29–28 win over the Patriots in which he caught eight balls for 115 yards and a touchdown.

Rashad led the run-oriented Bills in catches with 36 and played an integral role in the club's playoff run that year. Despite losing to the Steelers 32–14 in the AFC Divisional Playoff Game, the Bills appeared to be a team on the rise, with the top running back in the game—O.J. Simpson—and a stable of outstanding receivers including Rashad, Bob Chandler, and J.D. Hill. But the trio's potential was never realized, as Rashad suffered a severe knee injury in an exhibition game against Kansas City, sidelining the receiver for the entire 1975 season. He later became embroiled in a contract dispute that led to his departure from the team in May 1976, when he signed with the Seattle Seahawks (one of two expansion teams entering the league that year).

His time in Seattle was brief as well, as he was traded to the Minnesota Vikings after just two preseason games. It was during his time with Minnesota that Rashad's career flourished, with four Pro Bowl appearances (1978–81, including game MVP honors in '79) and a Super Bowl (XI) in seven years. He retired after suffering a second serious knee injury midway through the 1982 season, having caught 495 regular-season passes (10th on the NFL's all-time list at the time) for 6,831 yards and 44 touchdowns.

Rashad made a seamless transition from the playing field to the broadcast booth beginning in 1983, covering the NFL and other sporting events for NBC. In 1985, Rashad proposed to actress Phylicia Ayers-Allen, costar of NBC's popular sitcom *The Cosby Show*, before 40,000,000 witnesses during the pregame broadcast of the Thanksgiving Day game between the Detroit Lions and the New York Jets. Fortunately for Rashad, Ayers-Allen said yes, and the two married a month later, with Rashad's former Buffalo teammate O.J. Simpson serving as best man.

In 1990, Ahmad became the host of NBC's *NBA Inside Stuff.* The show later moved over to ABC and evolved into *NBA Access with Ahmad Rashad.* He has been nominated for six Emmy Awards for his television work and won one for writing in 1988. He is also the author of *Selected from Rashad: Vices, Mikes, and Something on the Backside.*

Rashad was inducted into the National College Football Foundation Hall of Fame in 2007 and is a member of the Minnesota Vikings 50th Anniversary Team.

Draft Busts

Every off-season, so-called experts from each of the 32 NFL teams gather to draft players from that particular year's pool of eligible college talent. Each team is looking to improve itself by acquiring a player who can fill a need or, in some cases, fill a stadium. But when it comes to the drafting of football players, there are no guarantees. It seems that for every first-round success story, there are at least 10 guys who crash and burn. The former are the ones who make personnel men look like geniuses. The latter—the ones referred to as "busts"—can cost them their jobs.

When it comes to the Buffalo Bills, there have been plenty of both. Some of the great No. 1 picks include Hall of Famers O.J. Simpson, Joe DeLamielleure, Jim Kelly, and Bruce Smith and numerous Pro Bowl performers, including Shane Conlan, Ruben Brown, and Eric Moulds.

Then there are the ones who never quite lived up to their lofty selection status, among whom the 10 listed below are the most glaring. Let the debate begin!

10. Jim Davidson, T, Ohio State (first round, 1965 AFL). A First-Team All-American for Woody Hayes' Buckeyes in 1964, Davidson never played a down for the Bills or any other pro

team (but then again, only one of the Bills' first eight selections that year wound up playing for the club: linebacker Marty Schottenheimer).

9. Tom Cousineau, LB, Ohio State (first round, first overall, 1979). The most famous holdout in team history, Cousineau never agreed to terms with the Bills and wound up playing for the Montreal Alouettes in the CFL. But it wasn't all for naught. The Bills later traded his rights to the Cleveland Browns and used the draft choice they received to select quarterback Jim Kelly in 1983.

8. Walt Patulski, DE, Notre Dame (first round, first overall, 1972). In a way, it's a bit unfair to put Patulski on this list, given the fact that he played four seasons with the Bills and recorded (unofficially) 23.5 sacks during that time. Still, he was never the dominant force the Bills hoped the Lombardi Award–winner and Heisman candidate would be and was eventually traded to St. Louis, where he ended his career in 1977.

7. Perry Tuttle, WR, Clemson (first round, 19th overall, 1982). In two seasons, the man the Bills hoped would duplicate the success of fellow Clemson alum Jerry Butler hauled in a whopping 24 passes and scored just three touchdowns. He split his final NFL season (1984) between Atlanta and Tampa Bay, adding one more reception to his grand career total.

6. Al Cowlings, DE, USC (first round, fifth overall, 1970). The Bills used their first selection to pick Cowlings, at the urging of his former USC teammate O.J. Simpson. But after three unproductive seasons, Cowlings was sent packing. His association with Simpson would bring him greater fame many years later.

5. Tom Ruud and Bob Nelson, LBs, Nebraska (First and second round, respectively; 19th and 42nd overall, 1975). The Bills drafted fellow Cornhuskers Ruud and Nelson with their first

two picks in 1975, but the gimmick proved an abject failure. A lengthy contract dispute delayed their development, and neither ever amounted to anything in Buffalo. Ruud started just three games in three years with the team. Nelson was gone after two seasons, never having started a game. He later won two Super Bowl rings as the starting right inside linebacker for the Oakland/Los Angeles Raiders.

4. Erik Flowers, DE, Arizona State (first round, 26th overall, 2000). In two seasons with the Bills, Flowers made only six starts and recorded just four sacks. He later played for Houston (2002) and St. Louis (2003–04).

3. Mike Williams, T, Texas (first round, fourth overall, 2002). Many longtime observers rank Williams as the Bills' biggest draft bust ever, but he *did* stick around for four seasons (2002–05) and started 47 games. He may not have lived up to his All-Pro and Hall of Fame potential, but he still did better than the two players chosen above him on this list. He even managed to make a brief comeback in 2009 with the Washington Redskins.

2. Phil Dokes, DT, Oklahoma State (first round, 12th overall, 1977). Dokes was the standard by which all Buffalo busts were measured—at least until Mike Williams came along and made everyone forget him for a while. But truthfully, Dokes was the bigger letdown, lasting two seasons in which he started only 10 games.

1. Aaron Maybin, DE, Penn State (first round, 11th overall, 2009). An undersized defensive end projected to be a pass-rushing terror, Maybin was a colossal disappointment in his two seasons with the Bills. He appeared in 26 games, starting just one, and recording no sacks. By the end of his second year, he was a frequent healthy scratch. He was released prior to the 2011 season and drew chuckles from Bills fans when signed by the New York Jets a few weeks later. But Maybin

Aaron Maybin may well be the worst draft pick in franchise history.

had the last laugh, netting three sacks in seven games by the time he and the Jets faced Buffalo on November 27 that year. To the Bills' embarrassment, Maybin recorded two sacks of quarterback Ryan Fitzpatrick in leading the Jets to a 28–24 win. Ouch!

A Hard Rain

Folks in Western New York are accustomed to dealing with all kinds of weather. Snow, rain, hail, wind, cold...you name it. But when the Bills hosted the New York Titans on the night of September 22, 1962, they experienced punishing weather conditions of a completely different sort.

The Bills, after stumbling through their first two AFL seasons with a combined record of 11–16–1, had replaced original head coach Buster Ramsey with former Boston head man Lou Saban. But two games into the 1962 season, the team was 0–2 and looking no better than they had under Ramsey. Fans were becoming impatient and were ready to run this Saban guy out of town on a rail. If something didn't change quickly, that frustration was bound to boil over.

In Week 3, the Bills were set to host the 1–1 New York Titans, whose quarterback Lee Grosscup had been acquired just days earlier and had met his new teammates for the first time the morning of the game. The Titans couldn't expect to be in sync with virtually no time to prepare. The inept Buffalo defense, however, made the Titans offense look as if they had been playing together for years.

The Bills actually looked good when they drove all the way to the New York 11 on their first possession. Halfback Wayne Crow then scored what would have been the game's first touchdown, but the play was nullified by a holding penalty. Then, in an odd twist, former Titans quarterback Al Dorow (now calling the signals for the Bills) threw an errant pass that was intercepted in the end zone by former Bills defensive back Billy Atkins (who had been sent to the Titans in exchange for Dorow), killing the promising drive. The New Yorkers then drove 78 yards down to the Buffalo 2, from where Dick Christy scored to give the Titans a 7–0 lead. The Bills got on the board late in the second quarter when Warren Rabb connected with Elbert Dubenion for a 24-yard touchdown strike, but the extra-point try was no good, and the Bills trailed by one. The Titans responded with an eight-play, 73-yard drive that Grosscup capped with a six-yard scoring pass to Thurlow Cooper, making it 14–6 as the teams headed to the locker rooms.

The second half was a dull affair, with former Bills kicker Bill Shockley providing the only points on a 35-yard field goal in the third quarter to extend New York's lead. When the game ended, the score read New York 17, Buffalo 6, and the War Memorial Stadium crowd was not happy. They let the winless Bills know it with a downpour the likes of which no one had ever seen—one made up not only of boos, but also of booze.

"Apparently we were supposed to win," recalled Bills linebacker Mike Stratton, who was playing in his first regular-season game with the team that night. "The fans were quite upset, and they let their [displeasure] be known in voice and their arm."

"We were walking off the field, and the beer cans come flying out of the stands," said guard George Flint, "bouncing off our shoulder pads, our helmets, the whole deal."

"They cleaned our clocks," said Chuck Burr, the Bills public-relations director. "I'm standing up in the press box, and Lou Horschel, who handled the concessions for L.M. Jacobs, came in and said, 'Hey, we sold an awful lot of beer tonight. Look at those cans.' Then all of a sudden he stopped and said, 'Hell, we don't sell beer in cans!' All of those beer cans had come in from the saloons adjacent to the stadium. People brought them in. Nobody bothered to search for anything like that. We only sold beer in cups. The ground crew estimated there were 2,500 or 3,000 cans on the field."

"We looked terrible, and we had all of these beer bottles starting to fly out onto the field," recalled Saban. "Ralph [Wilson] was standing right next to me, and the game was over, and we had to duck some of these things to get back into the locker room. I happened to pick up a bottle, and it was full! So I said to Ralph, 'This guy had to be drunk, because why else would he throw away a full bottle of beer?'"

Apparently the new coach had not yet learned just how seriously Buffalo fans take their football. Three days later, he put in a waiver claim for an injured San Diego quarterback named Jack Kemp, and the Bills' forecast suddenly looked much sunnier.

Tom Dempsey

By the time Tom Dempsey signed with Buffalo as a free agent in 1978, he had already etched his name in the NFL record book by kicking the longest field goal in league history. This he accomplished on November 8, 1970, while a member of the New Orleans Saints, nailing a last-second 63-yarder to beat the Detroit Lions at Tulane Stadium. The most amazing thing about that kick (aside from the incredible distance, which bested the previous standard of 56 held by Baltimore's Bert Rechichar) was that Dempsey was born without the toes on his right foot—the same foot with which he kicked. Dempsey wore a modified shoe that, when laced up, had a flattened surface across the front that gave the appendage the appearance of a sledgehammer and, some asserted, gave Dempsey an unfair advantage.

"If not having any toes is an unfair advantage," Dempsey would counter, "I have an unfair advantage." He was even accused of having a steel plate embedded in the shoe! "They X-rayed it; it was just a thin piece of leather."

Despite being born with neither the toes on his right foot nor the fingers on his right hand, Dempsey did not allow himself to be limited. He played high school football at San Deguito High in California, though he did not kick until he was a collegian at Palomar College. After narrowly missing a 65-yard field goal—which reportedly had the distance but sailed wide—the coach of the opposing team brought Dempsey's name to the attention of Vince Lombardi, legendary coach of the Green Bay Packers. Dempsey was signed but never appeared in a game for the Packers. He eventually found his way to New Orleans and beat veteran Charlie Durkee for the place-kicking job in 1969. Teammates became accustomed to watching as Dempsey routinely launched field goals of 60-plus yards in practice. It didn't seem all that improbable to them when, down to the Lions by a point with two seconds to go and the ball at their own 45-yard line, they heard head coach J.D. Roberts—making his debut in that role—order the kicking team out to attempt a would-be record-setting field goal.

Despite his historic kick, Dempsey converted only 52.9 percent of his field-goal attempts that year and was cut by the Saints in the next preseason. He was signed by the Philadelphia Eagles in 1971 and enjoyed a four-year run that included a 106-point season in 1973. Coach Chuck Knox brought Dempsey to Los Angeles in 1975, where he helped the Rams get to the NFC Championship Game in both of his seasons with the club. After a brief turn with Houston in 1977, Dempsey was reunited with Knox, who had taken over as the Bills' head coach in 1978.

Dempsey's defining moment as a Bill came in the 1979 season opener against Miami. In the final seconds of the fourth quarter, the Bills, trailing 9–7, had driven to the Dolphins 18, giving Dempsey an opportunity to kick a 34-yarder that would have snapped the Bills' record streak of losses to Miami at 18. But Dempsey's kick sailed wide of the left upright, and the despised Dolphins notched their 19th straight.

Long-suffering Bills fans could not forgive Dempsey for the miss, and neither could Coach Knox. The struggling kicker lasted just two more games with the team before being waived in favor of Nick Mike-Mayer.

Dempsey's one-and-a-quarter-year stint in Buffalo was to be his last in the NFL. His record kick still stands, though it has been equaled twice, first by Jason Elam of the Denver Broncos in 1998, then in 2011 by Sebastian Janikowski of the Oakland Raiders.

84 Buffalo: Coach U?

As of 2012, five former Bills players have gone on to become head coaches in the National Football League.

Tom Flores came to the Bills late in his career, having spent his prime years calling signals for the Oakland Raiders before being traded to Buffalo in 1967 as part of the blockbuster deal that sent Daryle Lamonica to the Raiders. In three seasons with the Bills, he threw nine interceptions and no touchdowns. He was released midway through 1969 but landed happily as Len Dawson's backup on the Super Bowl–winning Kansas City Chiefs.

Flores returned to Buffalo in 1971 as quarterbacks coach. He later became an assistant coach with the Oakland Raiders and was named head coach upon John Madden's resignation in 1979. He led the Raiders to Super Bowl wins twice in his first five years with the team. Flores left the Raiders after 1987. He returned to the sideline in 1992 with the Seattle Seahawks but after three losing seasons was finished.

Flores holds the distinctions of being the first Mexican American starting quarterback *and* head coach in the league, as well as the first man to win a Super Bowl as a player and as a head coach. He is also one of only two men who have won a championship as a player, assistant coach, and head coach. Mike Ditka is the other.

Overall record: 97–87–0 (.527). Postseason: 8–3. Two Super Bowl victories.

Marty Schottenheimer came to the Bills in 1965 as a seventh-round pick out of Pittsburgh. As a player, he was terrific on special teams and a reliable backup to starting middle linebacker Harry Jacobs. He played a total of four years with the Bills and two with the Boston Patriots.

His first coaching experience came in 1974 as linebackers coach for the Portland Storm of the World Football League. Schottenheimer entered the NFL ranks in 1975 as an assistant with the New York Giants. In 1978, he became the linebackers coach for the Detroit Lions. He moved on to the Cleveland Browns in 1980 and was named head coach midway through 1984. Schottenheimer coached four full seasons in Cleveland and had the Browns in the playoffs each year, including two trips to the AFC Championship Game. He moved on to Kansas City in 1989 and over the next 10 seasons had the Chiefs in the playoffs seven times. In 2001, he was named head coach of the Washington Redskins but was fired by frenetic owner Dan Snyder after a single 8–8 season. Schottzy wasn't out of work long, as the San Diego Chargers hired him in 2002. His San Diego teams reached the postseason twice during his five-year tenure, but he was abruptly fired after a 14–2 campaign in 2006.

As a head coach, Schottenheimer was wildly successful in the regular season, but his teams consistently fell short in the playoffs. He holds the dubious distinction of having the most regular-season wins of any NFL coach not to make it to a Super Bowl.

Overall record: 200–126–1 (.613). Postseason: 5–13.

Sam Wyche's career in Buffalo was very short indeed. He was acquired in October 1976, and although he suited up, he never appeared in a game for the team. In 1979, Wyche was hired as an offensive assistant by Bill Walsh of the San Francisco 49ers. He accepted the head coach job with the Indiana Hoosiers in 1983 and one year later assumed the helm with the Cincinnati Bengals. He guided the Bengals to the Super Bowl in 1988 but lost to Walsh's 49ers. While with the Bengals, Wyche was credited with pioneering the no-huddle offense that the Bills later developed into their K-Gun attack. Wyche and the Bengals parted ways after the 1991 season, but he was immediately hired by the Tampa Bay Buccaneers. After four losing seasons, he was fired. Sam spent 2004 and 2005 as the quarterbacks coach with the Bills under Mike Mularkey, mentoring No. 1 draft choice J.P. Losman.

Overall record: 84–107 (.442). Postseason: 3–2. One AFC championship.

Jim Haslett was drafted by the Bills in the second round in 1979 out of Indiana University of Pennsylvania. He was an immediate hit with fans, who loved his aggressiveness on the field and fun-loving spirit off it. Jim played seven seasons as a linebacker in Buffalo and one with the New York Jets.

His first coaching gig was as an assistant at the University of Buffalo (1988–90). His first NFL assignment came as linebackers coach with the Los Angeles Raiders. He later served as an assistant with the New Orleans Saints and defensive coordinator with the Pittsburgh Steelers. Haslett was named head coach of the Saints in 2000 and guided them to a 10–6 regular-season record, the first playoff victory in franchise history, and was named NFL Coach of the Year. He was fired after going 3–13 in 2005 but was hired as defensive coordinator by the St. Louis Rams prior to 2006. In 2008, he was named the Rams' interim head coach for the remainder of the season but managed only two wins in 12 games and was not retained. He is currently defensive coordinator with the Washington Redskins.

Overall record: 47–61–0 (.435). Postseason: 1–1.

Kay Stephenson spent his college years backing up quarterback Steve Spurrier at Florida. He was signed as a free agent in 1967 by San Diego, where he backed up John Hadl. When Jack Kemp was hurt in the 1968 preseason, the Bills traded a draft choice to San Diego to get Stephenson. But after suffering a separated shoulder against Miami on November 10, Stephenson's career was over.

He began his coaching career as an assistant on Chuck Knox's staff with the Los Angeles Rams. When Knox took over as head coach with the Bills in 1978, he brought Stephenson along as his quarterbacks coach. When Knox bolted after the 1982 season, Stephenson was given his job. But the team he inherited was aging, and Kay enjoyed only one decent season (8–8) before it all went downhill. The Bills went 2–14 in 1984, and after starting the following year with four straight losses, Stephenson was fired. He never received another shot as a head coach in the NFL but resurfaced in the World League of American Football in the early 1990s and guided the Sacramento Surge to the league championship in 1992. He later spent time with three teams in the CFL.

Overall NFL record: 10–26–0 (.278).

85 Bobby Burnett

Buffalo's Bobby Burnett was the AFL Rookie of the Year in 1966, but his bright star faded almost as quickly as it rose. Within a year of winning the award, his promising career was essentially over after a severe knee injury. Instead of being the franchise's next

Cookie Gilchrist, as some predicted, Burnett became another in a long line of Bills heartbreak kids—players who, whether due to injury or illness, never got the chance to fully realize their potential on the field.

The Bills selected the Arkansas halfback in the fourth round in 1966, the third back taken by the team after first-round pick Mike Dennis of Mississippi and second-rounder Jim Lindsey, Burnett's backfield mate with the Razorbacks. But after Dennis and Lindsey opted for the NFL, the baton was passed down to Burnett.

"I didn't come in with my nose up in the air," Burnett remembered. "I came in with my head down a little bit. Billy Shaw, in one of the very first practices, told me, 'You want to be All-Pro?' I said, 'Yeah.' He said, 'You get on my butt and you follow me where I go. I'll make you All-Pro.'"

Burnett took Shaw's advice literally. "There were many times that I was tackled 10 or 12 yards down the field, and I was lying on top of Billy. I took his words to heart. He told me, 'You get on my ass and you stay with me.' And boy, I did!"

Running behind Shaw and the rest of the Bills' formidable offensive line, Burnett put together perhaps the finest season of any Bills rookie running back to that point, leading the team in rushing and compiling a total of 1,185 yards from scrimmage. He had his finest day in the 17–17 tie with San Diego on October 16, when he rushed for 138 yards on 27 carries and caught a touchdown pass. With the speedy Burnett setting the pace on the ground, the Bills returned for their third straight appearance in the AFL title game at the end of the year. Burnett had a spectacular game, catching six passes for 127 yards, but it wasn't good enough, as the Bills fell, 31–7, and the Chiefs advanced to play the Green Bay Packers in Super Bowl I.

For his efforts, Burnett was a consensus All-AFL selection and named Rookie of the Year. By 1967, however, the Bills were in serious decline, getting off to a dismal 3–5 start. Burnett, too, started slowly after suffering cracked ribs in the preseason and losing his starting job to Keith Lincoln, whom the Bills had acquired in an off-season trade. He saw his first significant action of the year against the New York Jets in Week 9 when defensive back Johnny Sample ended his campaign with a devastating tackle.

"He caught my leg low, and it totally dislocated my knee joint," Burnett recalled. "That was the end of it. I knew when I looked at my leg and my leg literally was out of joint out there on the field. It was hyperextended—it was dislocated out the wrong direction. I was lying on the ground, and I was looking at my foot almost in my eyeball—my foot was right up in my mouth. I was hurting—I was screaming and yelling. I tore the holy crap out of my knee. I tore the ligaments, I tore [cartilage] and [I] broke the tibia."

The Bills, unsure whether Burnett could make a full recovery, left him unprotected in the 1968 expansion draft. He was claimed by the Cincinnati Bengals but was released before ever playing a down for the team. He signed with the Denver Broncos in 1969 but appeared in only three games before calling it a career.

"I was thrilled that I made the [Broncos] roster," he said. "I had a good training camp, but when I got that football, I could tell that I wasn't running with no fear. That's your edge. You are looking at other people about to hit you and you are subconsciously protecting that leg. When a back loses a step, or he loses the edge, it's over. I don't care how much you get it back—you've lost the edge, you're done. I had to step up and say, 'It's over.'"

Today, Burnett works in real estate near Denver, Colorado, but remains a loyal follower of the Bills. "I die with the Bills when they don't play very well," he says. "I am a fan, and I always will be. That's where my heart is—how [could] it not be? That's where I had the time of my life. I died all four times they went to the Super Bowl."

86 So Just Who the Heck Was Chuck Green?

Avid football card collectors might notice as they look through their collections that the 1961 Fleer set contains an entry of a Buffalo Bills player identified as John (Chuck) Green. That player, of course, is actually Johnny Green, a strong-armed quarterback out of Tennessee-Chattanooga who called signals for the Bills in 1960 and '61. The odd thing about the card, however, is the parenthesized inclusion of the name "Chuck." Odd, since no one ever called him that.

But he has a theory as to how the error might have occurred. "All I can figure is [the card] was made during the week the first year we were there," said Green. "Chuck Burr was the publicity guy. I don't know if he thought he was giving everybody nicknames or what, but he's the one who did the card and the whole thing... unless he just gave me *his* name."

The error was corrected in the 1962 Fleer set. The inadvertent nickname eventually faded from memory, but for a while there, he joked, "I caught hell from all kinds of people."

Green's tenure in Buffalo was indeed short, but he is remembered for being the first Bills QB to throw for more than 300 yards in a game (334 in the 25–24 triumph over Houston on October 30, 1960). He also recorded more victories (five) than any other Bills starting quarterback during those first two seasons, and is one of only two (out of six) who threw more touchdown passes (16) than interceptions (15).

He was traded to the New York Titans for quarterback Al Dorow during training camp in 1962. He played parts of the next two seasons with the Titans before calling it a career.

87 A 50th Anniversary Team That Makes Sense

It might not be a popular sentiment, but to this writer, the Bills 50th Anniversary Team was a joke. Let's face it...no O.J. Simpson...four guards on the offensive line.... Seriously? True, the team certainly did not want to give the impression that they were glorifying a former player who has become one of the most reviled people in the country (Simpson), and voters were constrained by the stipulation that in order to be eligible a player had to have spent at least four seasons with the Bills (which effectively disqualified such players as Cookie Gilchrist or Bryce Paup, the 1996 NFL Defensive Player of the Year!). But the way the team was configured (i.e., four guards and no tackles on offense, 3-4 alignment on defense) and excluded certain players for political reasons (Simpson and Gilchrist) smacks of gerrymandering of the lowest order.

It is not this writer's intention to dishonor any of the greats who were selected to the Bills' all-time team. On the contrary, the 50th Anniversary Team selected here includes all of the players who made the official team. The list below, however, uses offensive and defensive formations that make sense (two backs, two receivers, two guards, etc., on offense; four-down linemen and three linebackers on defense), and includes a first and second squad, which allows, rather appropriately, for the honoring of 50 players in all.

The official 50th Anniversary Team, announced in June 2010, looks like this:

Offense: Jim Kelly (QB), Thurman Thomas (RB), Andre Reed (WR), Eric Moulds (WR), James Lofton (WR), Pete Metzelaars (TE), Billy Shaw (G), Joe DeLamielleure (G), Ruben Brown (G), Jim Ritcher (G), Kent Hull (C), Steve Christie (K). Defense: Bruce Smith (DE), Fred Smerlas (DT), Tom Sestak (DT), Darryl Talley

(LB), Cornelius Bennett (LB), Mike Stratton (LB), Shane Conlan (LB), Butch Byrd (CB), Nate Odomes (CB), George Saimes (S), Henry Jones (S), Brian Moorman (P), and Steve Tasker (ST). Marv Levy was selected as the coach.

The unofficial team, chosen by this writer, is as follows. It should go without saying that Marv Levy deserves coaching honors.

The Offense

First Team	Pos.	Second Team
Andre Reed	WR	Bob Chandler
Stew Barber	T	Howard Ballard
Billy Shaw (HOF)	G	Ruben Brown
Kent Hull	C	Al Bemiller
Joe DeLamielleure (HOF)	G	Jim Ritcher
Will Wolford	T	Joe Devlin
Ernie Warlick	TE	Pete Metzelaars
Eric Moulds	WR	James Lofton (HOF)
Jim Kelly (HOF)	QB	Jack Kemp
O.J. Simpson (HOF)	RB	Cookie Gilchrist
Thurman Thomas (HOF)	RB	Joe Cribbs
Steve Christie	K	Rian Lindell

The Defense

First Team	Pos.	Second Team
Bruce Smith (HOF)	DE	Ron McDole
Fred Smerlas	DT	Sam Adams
Tom Sestak	DT	Ted Washington
Ben Williams	DE	Phil Hansen
Mike Stratton	OLB	Bryce Paup
Shane Conlan	ILB	Harry Jacobs
Darryl Talley	OLB	Cornelius Bennett
Butch Byrd	CB	Antoine Winfield
George Saimes	S	Steve Freeman
Tony Greene	S	Henry Jones
Robert James	CB	Nate Odomes
Brian Moorman	P	Paul Maguire
Steve Tasker	ST	Mark Pike

88 The Super Bowl That Wasn't

In 1990, the high-flying 49ers of San Francisco were aiming for a three-peat championship that would likely pit them against the explosive Buffalo Bills in what promised to be a Super Bowl for the ages. Instead, the smashmouth New York Giants derailed both high-powered offenses, so it would be another two years before that anticipated offensive showdown occurred.

The game did not disappoint. When the Bills faced the 49ers at Candlestick Park on September 13, 1992, neither team attempted a punt throughout the entire game! In the 70-plus years since the founding of the National Football League in 1920, there had never been a game in which neither team punted. And it hasn't happened since.

Perhaps a look at the stat sheet will provide some insight as to the reasons why. Hall of Fame quarterbacks Jim Kelly and Steve Young staged a good old-fashioned shootout that produced a combined 51 first downs, 852 passing yards, and 1,086 yards of total offense. Kelly completed 22 of 33 passes for 403 yards, three TDs, and one pick. The Bills had two receivers with at least 100 yards (Andre Reed, 10 catches for 144, and Pete Metzelaars, with a career day of four catches for 113) and nearly a third (Thurman Thomas, four catches for 94).

Young was nearly flawless, completing 26 passes out of 37 attempts for 449 yards, three touchdowns, and one interception for a passer rating of 127.0, all without much help from Hall of Fame receiver Jerry Rice, who left the game with an injury in the first quarter. It marked just the third time that two quarterbacks threw for more than 400 yards in the same game.

Despite Young's slight statistical advantage, it was Kelly who walked off the field victorious. The Bills entered the fourth quarter trailing 31–27. After an exchange of interceptions, Kelly put together a drama-packed, textbook drive that covered 72 yards in 12 plays and ended with Thurman Thomas scampering 11 yards for a touchdown with 3:04 remaining, giving the Bills a 34–31 lead that stuck as the final score.

It was one of the wildest games in the annals of the league and one of the most exciting in the history of the Buffalo Bills. But then again, as Bills center Kent Hull impishly pointed out, "Fans of the punting game got screwed." Indeed, the team's punters, Chris Mohr of the Bills and Klaus Wilmsmeyer of the 49ers, never got onto the field, and since neither held the ball for place kicks or performed any other on-field function, their names did not make it onto the game's active roster.

"On the plane trip home after the game," quipped Bills head coach Marv Levy, "I took a stroll back into the area where Chris Mohr was sitting. I told him that he shouldn't expect to receive his weekly paycheck the next day after we returned to our facility in Buffalo.

"I still don't know if he ever showed to pick it up!"

89 John Rauch

John Rauch was a winner. In three years as head coach of the Oakland Raiders, his teams went a combined 33–8–1 (a winning percentage of .805!), appeared in the postseason twice, and played in a Super Bowl. So when Ralph Wilson signed Rauch to coach the

Buffalo Bills in 1969, it was a major coup. "Personally, I thought that was a tremendous move," said Butch Byrd. "It seemed to me that we got a guy coming from a winning team who knew how to win and had some of the answers that obviously our coaching staff didn't. I thought it was very positive."

Jack Kemp agreed: "He had had a lot of success in Oakland. We all thought he was a very smart offensive coach, so most of the guys, at least at first blush, were in favor of John Rauch."

But the optimism that greeted the team as they returned to camp that summer slowly dissipated, as Rauch's personality—and system—rankled the veterans. "After the first couple of weeks," recalled Booker Edgerson, "it was like a bad dream. He was the worst coach that I ever had. The guy was terrible."

Rauch had been brought in to turn around a franchise that had gone from three consecutive appearances in the AFL title game to the worst in pro ball in a matter of two seasons. It was obvious that changes had to be made—some of them hard. But Rauch seemed intent on overhauling the entire works, including the area of the team's greatest strength—the defense. His system forced even All-Pro caliber players to modify their styles.

"John was tough," Ron McDole recalled. "The biggest problem was that he came in and tried to change everything. We had guys playing on the defense who could have been coaches. We were in our thirties. It got to the point where, I remember one time he said to [Jim] Dunaway, 'Do it the way [Tom] Keating does.' Dunaway said, 'Why don't you just get Keating?' He couldn't do what Keating did. So we ran into a lot of that."

Rauch's changes weren't reserved strictly for the defense. "Coming into a situation like he had come into in Buffalo," said quarterback Dan Darragh, "change in the offense was necessary. The offense the Bills had was out of date and ineffective. But in order to run the original West Coast offense that he adapted from Sid Gillman, he needed people across the board that had the skills that were necessary to execute it. Frankly, the team that he took over didn't have enough people with the right skills to run his offense. His offense did not focus on a single running back being the primary ball carrier. What he wanted to do with his offense didn't fit the players he had."

Rauch had the good fortune of joining the Bills at the most important juncture in the team's short history. By virtue of the previous year's 1–12–1 finish, the Bills had earned the top choice in the upcoming draft. As expected, they used the pick on O.J. Simpson, the Heisman Trophy–winning halfback from the University of Southern California. Simpson, a shifty runner who possessed world-class speed and deceptive power, was perhaps the most heralded back to come out of college since Red Grange. Rauch, however, felt Simpson could best serve the Bills not by carrying the ball, but as a decoy. Since opposing defenses would be keying on Simpson, Rauch reasoned, that would create opportunities for the other backs and receivers. He insisted, "I'm not going to build my offense around one back, no matter how good he is."

"We knew [Simpson] had a lot of ability," said Paul Costa, "but the way Rauch was using him was weird. You've got a rookie running back and he's got a lot to learn, and you've got a coach that's insecure, so they didn't really hit it off. I don't think he had any confidence in O.J.'s running ability, because he didn't use him right—decoy, wide receiver, and all that."

There was more. For the first time in team history, camp sessions were closed to the public. According to Rauch, other clubs sent spies to camps throughout the league. He cited his former team, the Raiders, as one such team that benefited from spying on the Bills.

"I think he was paranoid after working for Al Davis in Oakland for so long," remarked trainer Eddie Abramoski. "Everything was secretive to him. Rauch was suspicious of everybody in the organization except the people he brought in. He would send the doctor and the trainer and the equipment man outside while he talked to the team, like we were outsiders."

"Some of the college guys came in, and there were no weights," added Edgerson. "They started asking for them, but Rauch was trying to put us on isometrics. That was when I screwed up my back. A lot of other guys got screwed up, and it was just a mess."

It all added up to an ugly first season for Rauch, with the Bills limping to a 4–10 final record. In his second year, Rauch lost many of the most reliable players he had—such as Jack Kemp, Billy Shaw, and Stew Barber—to retirement while others, like Al Bemiller, George Saimes, and Harry Jacobs, were traded or cut. The result was an even worse record of 3–10–1.

Rauch responded by clearing out even more of the team's veteran players, including Butch Byrd and Ron McDole. As his third camp with the Bills was getting under way, Rauch found himself in Ralph Wilson's doghouse after the owner learned of unflattering remarks the coach had made about McDole and recently retired punter Paul Maguire on a local radio program. When Wilson informed Rauch that he planned to go public with a defense of the two former stalwarts, Rauch knew he was in a no-win situation, both literally and figuratively, and tendered his resignation. By that time, the team was in total disarray. Harvey Johnson, who had filled in after Joe Collier's firing in 1968, took over but, given the circumstances, never had a chance. The Bills finished 1–13.

There's no telling whether things could have gone better had he arrived a year earlier or maybe two years later, but as it stands, John Rauch's tenure in Buffalo is viewed as one of the lowest points in the history of the franchise.

90 For Whom the Bell Trades

Through the years, the Buffalo Bills have had a number of players who have been labeled "what-ifs," players whose careers with the team, for a variety reasons, never quite reached their full potential. Whether due to injury, bad timing, character issues, off-the-field problems, or salary disputes, the list of the team's what-ifs seems to grow with each passing season. One of the biggest what-ifs in Bills history is running back Greg Bell. What's more, he is one of those whose career, like so many of the others, enjoyed a near-miraculous revival after moving on to another team.

By 1984, the Bills were a team in decline. After making the playoffs under coach Chuck Knox in 1980 and '81, the team had finished 4–5 in the strike-shortened 1982 season and then went 8–8 in 1983, their first year under Kay Stephenson. Making matters worse for the Bills was the loss of their three biggest offensive weapons (wide receiver Jerry Butler to injury, wide receiver Frank Lewis to retirement, and three-time 1,000-yard rusher Joe Cribbs to the USFL). The Bills went into the draft looking to fill the void Cribbs had left and believed they had done so by selecting Bell out of Notre Dame with their first pick.

Bell was an immediate starter, but through the first four games of the season, the team was 0–4 and Bell's stat line looked more like a flatline, showing a pallid 77 yards and no touchdowns on 27 carries (a 2.9-yards-per-carry average). But as if jolted by a defibrillator, Bell came to life in Week 5, gaining 144 yards on 29 carries against the Colts. Over the last 12 games of the season, he rushed for 1,023 yards on 235 attempts to finish with 1,100 yards. His best performance came in Week 12 when he rushed 27 times for

What If, Indeed!

There are two sides to this "what-if." What if the Bills had not agreed to the deal that sent Bell to the Rams and brought Cornelius Bennett to Buffalo? Well, it's very likely that the defense would not have been as dominant as they were over the next four seasons. What's more, the Bills might not have drafted a certain Oklahoma State running back named Thurman Thomas with their first pick in the 1988 draft.

206 yards to lead the 0–11 Bills to their first win of the year over the powerful Dallas Cowboys.

He had another fine season in 1985, augmenting his 883 rushing yards with the 576 he picked up on 58 pass receptions. But Bell's fortunes went into a downward spiral in 1986, when a groin injury limited him to just six games. Injuries continued to plague Bell in 1987, and many close to the team began to question his toughness and dedication. Some of his harshest critics, such as Bills nose tackle Fred Smerlas, began referring to him as "Tinker-Bell."

"Bell was one of the biggest wastes of talent we ever had," observed Eddie Abramoski, the Bills' veteran trainer who taped the ankles of every Bills player between 1960 and 1997. "Bell was a great athlete. His problem was—although he probably wouldn't admit it—he really didn't like football that much. At least not enough to be a full-time professional. It's a tough game when you don't like [it]."

Bell made perhaps his greatest contribution to the Buffalo Bills off the field—by being part of the blockbuster trade that brought linebacker Cornelius Bennett to the team on October 31. The Bills gave up Bell, their first-round draft choice in 1988, and their first and second choices in 1989 in exchange for the rights to Bennett, who had been holding out after being chosen second overall by Indianapolis in the 1987 draft. The Colts then sent Bell and the draft picks they had acquired from Buffalo, along with their own first and second picks in 1988, a second-round pick in '89, and running back Owen Gill to the Los Angeles Rams for superstar halfback Eric Dickerson.

Fortunately, most Bills fans were too busy following their own team's resurgence in 1988 to notice that Bell was having the best season of his career with the Rams, finishing with 1,212 yards and 16 touchdowns and being named NFL Comeback Player of the Year. He followed that performance with another solid campaign in 1989, gaining 1,137 yards and scoring 15 touchdowns, becoming the first back to rush for 1,000 yards and 15 touchdowns in consecutive seasons since Jim Taylor did it for the Green Bay Packers back in 1961 and '62.

Despite two outstanding seasons with the Rams, Bell became expendable when the team acquired running back Curt Warner from Seattle, and he was subsequently dealt to the Los Angeles Raiders prior to the 1990 season. He saw limited action with the Raiders—who already had Marcus Allen and Bo Jackson on their roster—appearing in just six games that year, his final NFL season.

91 Learn Marv Levy's Fight Song

It all started on October 2, 1994, as the Bills were getting drubbed by the Chicago Bears at Soldier Field. Though the 20–13 outcome does not suggest a shellacking by any means, losing has a way of magnifying those little humbugs that coaches and players might be inclined to ignore when they win. And despite the fact that the Bears only scored four times in this game, what happened after each of those scores caused Buffalo coach Marv Levy great irritation. With each score, the strains of the Bears fight song, "Bear Down, Chicago Bears," blared through the stadium's public-address system. It got to be more than the 69-year-old Levy could bear.

As a way of lightening things up after the loss, Levy promised his team that he would write a fight song if they won their upcoming game against Miami. Duly inspired, the players did their part by defeating the Dolphins 21–11 the following Sunday, and the coach was on the hook. "I didn't think they'd take me seriously," he said. "The pressure was on."

What his players didn't know was that Levy was in familiar territory. The Chicago native was a close follower of college football while growing up—a time when the collegiate version of the sport was more popular than the pro. "As a kid I was always fascinated by college fight songs," he recalled. "There was a Saturday night radio sports broadcast in Chicago in which the announcer, in overly dramatic tones, would announce the winners and the game details of every college game played that day. After each game's summary, the station would play the winning team's fight song. I learned them all, as did many of my friends."

A few years later, Levy and some of his high school teammates at South Shore High School applied that knowledge to composing a fight song for the football team called "Fight On, You South Shore Seahawks." Decades later, during his tenure as head coach of the Kansas City Chiefs, Levy penned a fight song for the team called "Give a Cheer for Kansas City," unfortunately now long-forgotten.

So it shouldn't have surprised anyone that it took Levy, who holds a bachelor's degree in English literature from Coe College, just one day to compose the lyrics for his Bills song. He performed an a cappella version of "Let's Win for Buffalo" at the team meeting the next day (Monday, October 10). "When I presented the song to

"The Bills Make Me Want to Shout"

Every time the Bills score a touchdown or field goal at Ralph Wilson Stadium, "The Bills Make Me Want to Shout" is played to the delight of the frenzied masses. But the song, used by the team since September 13, 1987 (a 31–28 loss to the New York Jets), is not really a fight song in the traditional sense of the term. Whereas fight songs are usually unique to each team and used to inspire or pump up the home crowd, "The Bills Make Me Want to Shout" is more celebratory in nature and was adapted from the classic "Shout," originally performed in 1959 by the Isley Brothers.

our players," Levy recalled, "they truly embraced it." Defensive end Bruce Smith even asked the coach to do a rap version.

"I told him I don't do rap," said Levy.

Later that evening, the coach gave a spirited rendering of the ditty on his local cable television show. The studio audience gave a rousing ovation, but local radio commentators were not so kind when it aired the next day.

Though the lyrics were Levy's alone, the melody was borrowed from an old summer camp tune he sang as a college-aged counselor. Not realizing that the camp song had actually been adapted from "Go Lane, Go!"—the fight song of Lane Technical High School in Chicago—Levy applied his lyrics to the song's melody. "After it received some publicity," he recalled, "I received a call from the school's principal. He told me how delighted he was to have me do that adaptation."

To Levy's disappointment, the team never officially adopted "Let's Win for Buffalo" as its official fight song. "I never did present it to Mr. Wilson," he explained, "but I did to our marketing department, and although they expressed interest and I kept asking them to, they never really pushed it as a substitute for 'The Bills Make Me Want to Shout.' I still believe it would be even more inspiring."

Let's Win for Buffalo

(Lyrics by Marv Levy; melody from "Go Lane, Go!" by Jack T. Nelson)

Go Bills! For we are here to cheer for you
Go Bills! We are your fans so true
With victory in sight
We'll yell with all our might
So, Go Bills! Fight Bills! Go!
C'mon, let's win for Buffalo!
Go Bills! We're with you
Fight Bills! We're with you
Go Bills! Let's win this game
We'll raise up all our voices high
The Bills team spirit will not die
So, Go Bills! Fight Bills! Go!
C'mon, let's win for Buffalo!
Go Bills! For we are here to cheer for you
Go Bills! We are your fans so true
With victory in sight
We'll yell with all our might
So, Go Bills! Fight Bills! Go!
C'mon, let's win for Buffalo!

(Lyrics reprinted by permission)

92 Take in the Bills GameDay Experience

Billed as "the largest indoor tailgate party in the NFL," the Buffalo Bills GameDay Experience combines entertainment, concessions, and music with interactive games, exhibits, and displays to bring fans an exciting way to kick off game days in the Bills Fieldhouse, situated across the parking lot from Ralph Wilson Stadium. The revelry begins three and a half hours prior to game time during the regular season and is guaranteed to get even the most casual fan into the spirit by the time the Bills hit the field.

Every Sunday morning, there are two youth football games played on a miniature football field inside the fieldhouse—the first starts at 10:00 AM and the second at 11:30 AM. Fans young and not-so-young can show off their own talents in various football-themed skill games. How far can you kick, throw, or punt? Would you make a good wide receiver? Run a pattern and catch a pass!

Guests can get an autograph or have their picture taken with one of the many Bills alumni who are always on hand.

Finally, memorabilia collectors and souvenir hunters will find everything they're looking for at the Bills Store, a 2,000-square-foot retail shop located at the front of the Fieldhouse. The Bills Store alone is worth the trip, especially when looking for the perfect birthday or holiday gift for that special Bills fan in one's life.

Now, go enjoy the game!

93 The Buffalo Bills vs. the *Hamilton Tiger-Cats*?

One of the more bizarre episodes in Bills history took place on August 8, 1961, when the team traveled to Hamilton, Ontario, Canada, to open their preseason against the Hamilton Tiger-Cats of the Canadian Football League. A crowd of approximately 12,000 were present at Civic Stadium to witness what was the first, and ultimately last, game played between a CFL team and one from the upstart American Football League.

The game was played under Canadian rules, which was confusing to most of the Bills players, save for the fortunate handful—Wray Carlton, Johnny Green, and Mack Yoho—who had actually spent time in the Canadian league. Even guard Billy Shaw, a future Hall of Famer playing in his first game as a pro, was victimized by the strange rules. "I got a penalty early in the game," he recalled. "We were receiving a punt and there was some rule about blocking, and I got a penalty. [Head coach] Buster [Ramsey] chewed my butt out."

"I don't know who was responsible for that," Bills guard Don Chelf said of the arrangement, "but I'm not sure that was the greatest thing that ever came down the pike. If you're going to play with 12 men, three downs, and a wider field, you were getting some fundamentals, but you certainly aren't getting a hell of a lot of offensive planning and defensive planning."

"I was just a rookie," recalled center Al Bemiller. "I went along with any program they said. I was more than happy just to play in a game. I think they were just trying to get some publicity in the area—trying to get some of their fans and so forth. It was an exhibition game, and it was more or less to go up there and try to make the team—each individual—as far as we were concerned."

The Tiger-Cats had the benefit of playing by familiar rules, and they took advantage of the unwitting Bills early in the first quarter. After a Hamilton quick-kick of 77 yards pinned the Bills down on their own 10, Buffalo quarterback Johnny Green threw an interception to Butch Rogers, who returned it 22 yards for the game's opening score. The Tiger-Cats had an opportunity to widen the lead later in the period, but Ron Miller's 27-yard field-goal attempt was wide. Willmer Fowler fielded the kick in the end zone and—per Canadian rules—attempted to bring it out. But Fowler was tackled behind the goal line, and Hamilton was awarded a one-point rouge, putting them up 8–0. Butch Rogers picked off another Green pass early in the second stanza, giving Hamilton possession at the Buffalo 13. Moments later, Hamilton's star quarterback, Bernie Faloney, connected with Hal Patterson for the touchdown, making it 15–0 Hamilton. The Bills then got on the board when Billy Atkins tackled Don Sutherin in the end zone for a two-point safety. The Tiger-Cats responded with Tom Dublinski hitting Garney Henley with a 36-yard strike. The conversion attempt was blocked, leaving Hamilton with a 21–2 lead. On the last play of the half, Richie Lucas ran nine yards to the Hamilton 39, but an unnecessary-roughness penalty against the Tiger-Cats moved the ball to the 24. Lucas then hit tight end Monte Crockett for the touchdown with no time left on the clock. The conversion attempt failed, and the Tiger-Cats took a 21–8 lead into the locker room.

The Tiger-Cats extended their lead early in the third when Faloney hit Paul Dekker for a touchdown, making it 28–8. The Bills answered back later in the period, with Johnny Green guiding the offense down to the Hamilton 3-yard line before rookie full-back Art Baker punched it in. On Buffalo's next possession, Green hit Crockett from eight yards out for his second touchdown of the game, and the Bills were suddenly back in it at 28–21. But that was as close as they would get, as the Tiger-Cats added a field goal and a late touchdown to ice a 38–21 triumph.

"The Bills," cracked the *Hamilton Spectator*, "had nothing to declare as they cleared Buffalo customs last night but an assortment of bruises and a scrambled ego. Hospitality here was so shabby that besides the 38–21 licking, the president of the Bills was, at first, turned away at the gate [and] the American flag hung below the Canadian ensign (and had but 48 stars)."

"I didn't like it," said safety Jim Wagstaff. "There were people running all over in the backfield and all that—pretty tough to try to work and design. We played a lot of one-on-one type stuff back in the secondary. If you got a guy going, you'd go with him. I don't know who even got us into that thing—I wasn't in management. It was a fiasco."

94 Grab Your Whammy Weenie (If You Can Find It)

The Whammy Weenie has got to qualify as one of the strangest, if not *the* strangest, promotions in the history of professional sports. "What was a Whammy Weenie?" you, gentle reader, might ask. It is a green, hot dog–shaped rattle that was marketed by Bells Supermarkets in 1982 for Bills fans to shake at opposing teams at Rich Stadium. According to the ad copy, the Whammy Weenie "is rancid, rotten, and green...the symbol of all the foul, downright disgusting, and repulsive distaste we have for the opposition. When waved in the face of an opponent, its moldy green odor and menacing sound is guaranteed to cause sudden sloppiness, frequent fumbles, inopportune interceptions, and downright disorganization. Bills opponents will shake in the wake of the Whammy Weenie."

The Whammy Weenie was, in essence, Buffalo's answer to Pittsburgh's "Terrible Towel." The weenies were made of hard

The elusive Whammy Weenie. Courtesy of the Greg Tranter Collection

green plastic molded into the shape of a jumbo-sized hot dog, with "Whammy Weenie" emblazoned on the side in gold paint. Each contained a couple of ball bearings inside the hollow shell to make it rattle when shaken.

The promotion rolled out at the start of the 1982 season, with full-page ads appearing in the *Buffalo Evening News* featuring members of the team's famed Bermuda Triangle (Jim Haslett, Shane Nelson, and Fred Smerlas) holding their own Whammy Weenies aloft. Fans could purchase a weenie at Bells for a mere 49 cents or get one free with a $5.00 purchase. One could also purchase Whammy Weenie beanies, Whammy Weenie bumper stickers, Whammy Weenie foam cushions, Whammy Weenie T-shirts, and other sundry Whammy Weenie–related items.

So what became of the Whammy Weenie? Well, the *official* story goes something like this: Three weeks into the regular season, rumors began to circulate that the yellow paint used for the weenie's logo contained high levels of lead. When tests confirmed that the paint indeed contained extremely high lead levels, literally thousands of the little green hot dogs were pulled from the shelves and destroyed.

Now, the rumor swirling through the stadium concourse was that the questionably shaped artifact was kiboshed by Bills management after seeing several obnoxious fans using it to make rude gestures toward opposing players (and each other!). Given the shape of the Whammy Weenie, it's astonishing that no one foresaw the inevitability of such shenanigans.

Although seen as a colossal marketing flub back in the day, the weenies that managed to escape destruction have over the years become coveted collector's items. According to Greg Tranter, owner of the largest Buffalo Bills memorabilia collection in the world, a Whammy Weenie in excellent condition could today be worth as much as $50!

95 Three Forgettable Weeks

Everyone—the players, the management, the media, the fans— knew there was going to be a strike at some point in 1987. For Bills fans, however, the thought of a strike was especially galling, given the fact that the team *finally* seemed to be heading in the right direction after three straight losing seasons. This wouldn't be the first players' strike, of course. Only five years had passed since a work stoppage cut a 57-day swath through the middle of the 1982 season. But this strike was going to be different. The owners weren't about to let something as trivial as a lack of talent keep the turnstiles from revolving. The games were going to continue—with or without the players.

A day after dispatching the Houston Oilers 34–30 in Week 2 (a game that featured the first fourth-quarter comeback win of Jim Kelly's illustrious career) the players voted to join their NFL brethren on the picket line. A day later, the Bills, along with every other team in the league, began the task of scouting players to replace the striking regulars. Just as it had been during the Bills' first training camp back in 1960, the locker room was filled with every type of wannabe one could imagine—from schoolteachers to truck drivers to grocery clerks—whose long-dead dreams of playing pro football had been magically revived. Indeed, a visit to the team's locker room during the next three weeks was quite literally like walking into the past. There were even a couple of actual old-timers—quarterback Dan Manucci and center Will Grant—who came in from the pasture in search of one last moment in the limelight.

After canceling the games scheduled for Week 3 in order to give teams time to shake off the cobwebs and learn their playbooks, the season resumed with the "counterfeit Bills" meeting the bogus Indianapolis Colts on October 4. With 9,860 fans of comedy in attendance, the Colts, led by quarterback Gary Hogeboom and wide receiver Walter Murray (two Colts regulars who opted not to honor the strike) crushed the Manucci-led Bills 47–6. Hogeboom left the game in the third quarter having completed 17 of his 25 passes for 259 yards and five touchdowns, while Manucci—calling signals for the first time since he was a member of the USFL Arizona Wranglers back in 1983—completed just seven of 20 passes for 68 yards and two interceptions.

Three days later, the picket line began to crumble as two regular Bills, Carl Byrum and Durwood Roquemore, crossed over and reported to work. They were of little help, however, as the Bills fell to the Patriots 14–7 in pouring rain the following Sunday. Mississippi Valley State quarterback Willie Totten, who had led the team to its only touchdown against the Colts a week earlier, got the start for the Bills, completing nine out of 21 passes for 84 yards and a score.

In the week leading up to the third and what would be the final replacement game, several more Bills broke ranks and reported in, including Robb Riddick, Leon Seals, and Keith McKeller. The New York Giants, the Bills' upcoming opponent, were buoyed by the arrival of superstar linebacker Lawrence Taylor. With player solidarity in a state of rapid dissolution, NFLPA president Gene Upshaw called an end to the strike that Friday, but there was not sufficient time to cancel the weekend's scheduled games. The replacement players would get one last shot at glory.

"I began to develop a liking and respect for these young men who were living a dream they never imagined would become a reality," Marv Levy later confessed. "They were playing in the NFL! How about that?"

In what the coach described as "the worst-played game in NFL annals," the teams fumbled, bumbled, and stumbled their way through a scoreless first half in which center Will Grant—whose veteran presence was supposed to stabilize the Bills offensive line— was flagged for a half-dozen holding calls.

"What in the world is going on out there?" Levy asked Grant in the locker room at halftime. "You have been called for holding six times in just one half!"

"Hey, Coach," Grant replied, "that's really good, because I've been holding on every down."

The faux Bills overcame all of the gaffes and blunders to defeat Taylor and the Giants 6–3 in overtime. Orchard Park's own Todd Schlopy was the hero, kicking a 31-yard field goal to tie the game in the fourth quarter and a 27-yarder in overtime for the win.

As the real Bills returned to Rich Stadium the next day to reclaim their lockers from the likes of Manucci, Totten, Schlopy, Grant, Sheldon Gaines, Thad McFadden, and Rick Schulte, some admitted that they had been quietly rooting for their replacements to defeat the Giants. They would have been foolish not to, however, since the strike games were counting toward each team's final record. Despite the win, the replacements ultimately did more harm than good, winning just one of their three games. The Bills finished the season at 7–8, barely missing the playoffs.

96 Naming the Bills

The city of Buffalo has had an on-again, off-again courtship with pro football dating back to the formation of the American Professional Football Association (forerunner to the National Football League) in 1920. The Buffalo All-Americans (later known as the Bisons and Rangers) were the city's first "pro" team and a member of the APFA/NFL from the league's founding through the 1929 season (with the exception of 1928).

A decade later, Buffalo returned to the pro gridiron with a franchise in a minor football association called the American Football League (the third league, but certainly not the last, to use the name). This particular AFL survived just two seasons before folding, and Buffalo's entry, known as the Indians in 1940 and Tigers in 1941, was thus relegated to footnote status in the annals of pro football.

In 1946, a new major league known as the All-America Football Conference was formed, and the Queen City was again a participant. Buffalo's team was called the Bisons in its first year, but that name had already been used by the city's original NFL team and was also being used by its minor league hockey and baseball teams. In an effort to distinguish itself from those other franchises and generate fan interest, the Bisons held a contest in which fans were asked to submit their ideas for new nicknames for the team. More than 4,500 suggestions were received, including Bullets, Nickels, and Blue Devils. The name "Bills" received multiple submissions, but a gentleman named James F. Dyson was ultimately credited with coming up with the name based on his essay comparing the team, owned by Jim Breuil (who

Tried and True

The Buffalo Bills are among three of the eight original AFL franchises to still have its original name (the Denver Broncos and Oakland Raiders are the others). The Los Angeles Chargers became the San Diego Chargers in 1961. The Dallas Texans moved to Kansas City and were renamed the Chiefs in 1963. That same year, the New York Titans were renamed the Jets. The Boston Patriots moved to Foxborough in 1971 and became known as the New England Patriots. The Houston Oilers moved to Nashville, Tennessee, in 1997, and two years later were renamed the Tennessee Titans.

just happened to be the president of Frontier Oil), to a posse of "Buffalo Bills," a reference to legendary buffalo hunter and frontiersman William "Buffalo Bill" Cody.

The AAFC team was fairly successful in its four-year existence, which included three seasons of .500 ball. In 1948, the Bills played the Cleveland Browns for the league championship, but they were crushed 49–7. Despite their successes and ardent fan support, the Bills were refused admission into the National Football League when it absorbed the AAFC in 1950. (Only the Browns, San Francisco 49ers, and Baltimore Colts were accepted into the new, expanded NFL.)

When Ralph Wilson founded the current franchise in 1959, one of the first orders of business was to give the team a name. A similar contest was conducted in which numerous names were submitted. After much consideration, Wilson decided to honor the team that had represented the city in the AAFC, and on November 30, 1959, his new team officially became known as the Buffalo Bills.

97 Superman Was a Buffalo Bill

Well, sort of.

Superman was *almost* a Buffalo Bill. But it wasn't Kryptonite that killed the Man of Steel's budding football career. No, Superman's downfall was something that made him appear as human as any one of us—a knee injury.

Superman, it turned out, was a mere mortal, and disguised as Dean Cain—a mild-mannered defensive back from Princeton University who came to the Bills as a free agent in the summer of 1988—he suffered a knee injury that ended his NFL career before it had a chance to begin. But then again, if it wasn't for that injury, it's quite possible that Cain would be known today for his career with the Super Bowl–era Buffalo Bills rather than as the greatest superhero of all time.

Cain grew up in Santa Monica, California, the son of actress Sharon Thomas and the adopted son of film director Christopher Cain. He did some acting prior to entering Santa Monica High School but put acting on the back burner in order to concentrate on schoolwork and athletics, playing on the football and baseball teams. (By the way, Cain's Santa Monica H.S. baseball teammates included Rob Lowe and Charlie Sheen.)

After graduating in 1984, Cain received several athletic scholarship offers but chose Princeton despite the fact that the Ivy League school was the only one that could not offer a scholarship. He was captain of the volleyball team and played free safety on the football team. In 1987, he set an NCAA 1-AA record by racking up 12 interceptions in a single season and was selected First-Team All-American.

Cain graduated from Princeton in 1988 with a degree in history. Though he went undrafted, he was intent on pursuing a career in the NFL and landed a free-agent contract with the Buffalo Bills. Unfortunately, his career didn't last long. Just days before he was scheduled to compete in his first preseason game, he suffered a severe knee injury while practicing at the team's training camp in Fredonia. Just like that, Cain's football career was through.

But the screen-idol-handsome Cain had a backup plan. He returned to Hollywood, and the rest, as they say, is history. He appeared in such films as *Best Man* with Drew Barrymore and *Futuresport* with Wesley Snipes but caught his big break when he landed the career-defining role of Clark Kent in *Lois & Clark: The New Adventures of Superman*. The show, which costarred a beautiful young actress named Teri Hatcher, enjoyed a successful five-year run on ABC (1993–97). Cain later found success as the host of the documentary television series *Ripley's Believe It or Not*, which ran for four years (2000–03) on TBS.

He has since starred in several made-for-television movies, including *The Perfect Husband: The Laci Peterson Story* (2004), *A Mile in His Shoes* (2011), and all three *The Dog Who Saved...* movies. His film roles continue to increase, but to an entire generation of TV viewers, Dean Cain will always be Superman. And every Buffalo Bills fan should know that Superman was very nearly a member of their beloved team.

98 Attend Draft Day at the Stadium

The NFL Draft, first held in 1936, is the annual trip to the fountain of youth for the league's 32 franchises. It was the brainchild of Bert Bell, then a co-owner of the Philadelphia Eagles, who felt it was the best way to ensure the fair distribution of talent among the teams and thereby create a more competitive league. Up to that point, players graduating from college could sign with any team in the league they wished. Predictably, the top college players tended to go with top pro teams, continuing their dominance and ensuring that the teams at the bottom of the heap tended to stay there.

The draft itself has since become big business. It was first televised in 1980, when the fledgling sports network ESPN secured permission from a skeptical Pete Rozelle, the NFL commissioner at the time. By 2010, 39 million fans were tuning in. That was also the year the draft became a three-day affair. Day one (Thursday) is the main event, when the first-round picks are made. Day two (Friday) encompasses rounds two and three, with the final four rounds occurring on day three (Saturday).

Hard-core fans who can't make it to New York City to attend the draft in person stay glued to ESPN or the NFL Network—or perhaps Twitter or some other social-media format—all weekend in eager anticipation of their team's next selection. For some, the draft is a perfect reason for a tailgate party in the middle of April. Mock drafts and office draft pools add to the fun in the weeks leading up to the big weekend.

NFL teams have taken to opening their facilities and turning the event into a weekend-long celebration, with local sports radio talk shows providing live remote broadcasts all day Thursday and Friday. Fans fortunate enough to secure admission can follow the draft on huge television screens inside the Ralph Wilson Stadium Fieldhouse while mingling with members of the Buffalo Jills, team alumni, and media. The fieldhouse itself is transformed into a glorified two-day tailgate party space, with an abundance of food, beer and fellowship. Fans can also take a tour of the stadium that includes a walk through the Bills' locker and weight rooms. And of course, the Bills Store and ticket office are open throughout the entire event.

But not just any fan can take part in Draft Day festivities. The main event takes place on Thursday evening, and admission is limited to club seat holders and other select VIPs. The next two rounds are made on Friday, at which time all other season-ticket holders are welcome.

99 The Original Wide Right (or, How the Kicker Met His Public)

One of the most colorful characters in the annals of the Buffalo Bills is Booth Lusteg, the team's place-kicker in 1966. Lusteg had the misfortune of being the one chosen to fill the shoes of the departed Pete Gogolak, the team's specialist in 1964 and '65 who was well known as the first soccer-style kicker in pro football. Things had gone moderately well for Lusteg until the sixth game of the season when he shanked three out of four attempts in a 20–10 loss to the Boston Patriots, causing the Bills to fall to 3–3. Fans were not happy. The rookie booter had a golden opportunity to atone for his poor outing when the Bills faced the San Diego Chargers in Week 7, but what transpired instead has become one of the franchise's enduring legends—and it's all true!

The War Memorial Stadium crowd of 45,169 saw two games in one that week—the first that had the Chargers taking a commanding 17–0 lead before intermission, and the second that saw the Bills rebound and almost pull off one of the greatest comebacks in team history. The Bills defense, little more than an impediment in the first half, came to life in the second, holding the high-voltage Chargers to zero offensive yards. First-year halfback Bobby Burnett also responded to the call, playing his finest game as a pro.

"We were behind 17–3 at halftime, and I hadn't done much," Burnett recalled. "But in the second half, I ran wild." He sure did. Burnett—who would be chosen AFL Rookie of the Year at season's end—finished the day with 138 yards on 27 carries and also caught a three-yard touchdown pass from Daryle Lamonica in the third quarter to bring his team to within seven.

Late in the fourth, Lamonica engineered a 60-yard drive that took the Bills to the San Diego 1. He finished off the drive himself with a quarterback sneak, and Lusteg's conversion tied the game with 3:47 remaining. The Bills managed to get the ball back on their own 45-yard line with less than three minutes on the clock. Lamonica maneuvered his team to the Chargers 16 with six seconds left. Coach Joe Collier then sent Lusteg in to attempt a 23-yard field goal that would cap a sensational 20–17 come-from-behind win and redeem the kicker's dreadful performance from the previous week. As Lusteg lined up to make the attempt, the Chargers, in an obvious effort to rattle the rookie, called a timeout. Moments later, Lusteg returned to his place behind holder Lamonica. Center Al Bemiller's snap was perfect. Lamonica gave his kicker a perfect hold. Lusteg approached. The kick was on its way and...no good! Lusteg's kick had sailed wide right!

"We came back and tied that game up at 17 and literally drove down the field to win it," said Burnett, "and Booth Lusteg missed a stupid 23-yard field goal."

"He felt bad," Daryle Lamonica remembered. "He kicked a pretty good kick. I thought we had a good hold, but we just missed. I say 'we' because we did that collectively, as a team. I never, ever thought a game was won or lost on one play."

But it's not so much the stomach-churning tie that resulted from Lusteg's miss that warrants its inclusion in this book as it is the bizarre events that occurred in the hours that followed. The story goes that Lusteg was so dejected by his miss that he decided the best way to unwind was to walk home from the stadium. As he made his way down Delaware Avenue, a car pulled up and screeched to a halt. Two young men, presumably enraged fans, emerged from the vehicle and confronted Lusteg in broad daylight on one of Buffalo's busiest streets. Though reports at the time indicated that he had been roughed up, Lusteg wrote in his autobiography several years later that only two punches were thrown—with neither finding their target—before the hooligans returned to their car and fled the scene. "One took a punch that only brushed me," wrote Lusteg, "while the other sent his fist right at my face. I ducked and he missed. It was all so ironic. He missed the punch like I missed the kick. If I hadn't been so depressed, I would have yelled 'wide right!'" The embattled kicker, mentally shaken but otherwise unharmed, declined to press charges.

Controversy seemed to be Lusteg's closest companion as he made his way through the 1966 season with the Bills. In addition to the postgame scuffle, there was a little matter that came to light the last week of November, as the Bills were getting ready to play the Patriots at Boston. Ted Barron, a local businessman and owner of the Boston Sweepers semipro football team, threatened legal action to prevent Lusteg from playing in the game. According to Barron, Lusteg—a member of the Sweepers in both 1964 and '65—was still under contract with the team as a result of an option clause. Barron was also threatening to sue the Patriots, whom he claimed had reneged on a promise to provide players for the Sweepers. The spurned owner then claimed the Bills owed him $500 for Lusteg's rights. He was threatening to sue the Bills and Lusteg for $50,000 [each] for breach of contract. Fortunately for both, Barron eventually relented and Lusteg was allowed to proceed with his AFL career.

But as Lusteg attempted to put Ted Barron and the Boston Sweepers behind him, the Bills arrived in Boston on December 3 to find newspaper headlines proclaiming their kicker's dirty little secret. The previous day's edition of the *Boston Traveler* had carried a front-page story revealing that Booth Lusteg was an impostor! He was not *Wallace* Booth Lusteg from Boston College as he had claimed, but rather *Gerald* Booth Lusteg from the University of Connecticut. Lusteg had used his younger brother's identity when he tried out for the Bills because he believed a professional football team would be reluctant to sign a 28-year-old rookie, especially one who had never even played college ball. Wallace Lusteg was younger at 25 and had actually played football at Boston College (never mind that it had only been for a single day). Gerald Lusteg had attended the University of Connecticut, but the only sport he had played there was baseball.

In spite of it all, Lusteg was able to carve out a fairly successful four-year career in the AFL and NFL. In his one and only tumultuous season with the Bills, Lusteg tied for the AFL lead in scoring among kickers with 98 points on 19 field goals and 41 conversions. Nevertheless, the Bills, undoubtedly eager to rid themselves of all the headaches, released Lusteg before the start of the '67 campaign and replaced him with veteran Mike Mercer, whom the team had loaned to the Kansas City Chiefs prior to '66.

After leaving Buffalo, Lusteg spent 1967 with the Miami Dolphins, 1968 with the Pittsburgh Steelers, and 1969 with the Green Bay Packers. He resurfaced in 1974 for one last go-round with the Portland Storm of the ill-fated World Football League. His post-football life included, fittingly enough, a stint as a bit actor in Hollywood, appearing in such films as *Airport '77*, *The Greatest*, and *Black Sunday*.

100 Super Mario!

The Buffalo Bills gave their long-suffering fans something to shout about on March 15, 2012, when they signed All-Pro defensive end Mario Williams to a six-year, $100-million contract, making the pass-rushing star the highest-paid defensive player in league history. Williams, the No. 1 overall pick in the 2006 draft, had played his entire career with the Houston Texans and was considered the top free agent available after recording 53 sacks in 82 career games and appearing in the Pro Bowl in 2008 and 2009.

The Texans had raised eyebrows when they selected the North Carolina State All-American with the first pick in 2006; everyone expected that USC's sensational halfback Reggie Bush would be taken first. The so-called experts that scoffed at the selection were lining up to say "told you so" after a modest rookie campaign in which Williams recorded 47 tackles and just 4.5 sacks, but the 6'6" 290-pounder came into his own with a strong season in 2007, making 59 total tackles and 14 sacks. A year later, Williams recorded 53 tackles and 12 sacks en route to his first Pro Bowl nod.

He made the Pro Bowl again in 2009 but was slowed by a nagging groin injury that forced him to miss three games in 2010, and though he still managed to record 8.5 sacks, he missed the Pro Bowl.

He returned fully healthy in 2011 but was moved to outside linebacker in new defensive coordinator Wade Phillips' 3-4 scheme. Ultimately, a torn pectoral muscle suffered in the fifth game of the season versus Oakland once again forced him to be placed on injured reserve. When his contract with the Texans ran out at the end of the season, he became the most sought-after free agent on the market. The contest eventually boiled down to two teams—the Bills and the Chicago Bears. Buffalo general manager Buddy Nix flew to North Carolina, accompanied by defensive coordinator Dave Wannstedt, to pick up Williams and bring him back to Orchard Park. The Bills applied a full-court press, wining and dining Williams and his fiancée while offering absurd amounts of money and assuring him that the team was committed to switching to a very sack-friendly 4-3 defense. During his two-day stay, the Bills also arranged to have Williams and his fiancée spend some time at the home of Hall of Famer Jim Kelly and his wife, Jill. The visit with the Kellys proved very persuasive in convincing Williams that Western New York would provide a stable community in

A blockbuster acquisition, the Bills are looking for Mario Williams—shown here with Bills coach Chan Gailey (right) and GM Buddy Nix (left)—to be a defensive leader.

which to live and raise a family. "Seeing Jim Kelly was a big plus for me, and he did some heavy recruiting,"

"He's a complete player," remarked Dave Wannstedt of Williams. "He's got power or speed. That's what separates great defensive ends, pass rushers. If you're slow getting off the ball, he's got the ability to run by you. He's going to make an offensive tackle be honest. If you give him an edge, he's got enough intelligence and athletic ability to take advantage of it."

The Bills are looking to improve a defense that finished 26th overall and recorded just 29 sacks in 2011. With star-in-the-making Marcel Dareus and Pro Bowler Kyle Williams holding down the defensive tackle slots, Mario and fellow free-agent defensive end Mark Anderson (who recorded 10 sacks as a member of the New England Patriots in 2011) should be able to wreak havoc on opposing offenses and give the Bills what could be the best defensive line in the entire league.

Indeed, with a healthy offense and this defense, 2012 should be a very exciting year for the Bills and their fans!

Bibliography

Books

Abramoski, Eddie, and Milt Northrop. *Tale of the Tape: A History of the Buffalo Bills from the Inside.* Orchard Park, New York: The Buffalo Bills, Inc., 2002.

Carroll, Bob, Michael Gershman, David Neft, and John Thorn. *Total Football II: The Official Encyclopedia of the National Football League.* New York: HarperCollins, 1997.

DeLamielleure, Joe, and Michael Benson. *Joe D's Tales from the Buffalo Bills.* Champaign, Illinois: Sports Publishing, LLC, 2007.

Dobler, Conrad, and Ross Bernstein. *Pride and Perseverance: A Story of Courage, Hope, and Redemption.* Chicago: Triumph Books, 2009.

Felser, Larry. *The Birth of the New NFL: How the 1966 NFL/AFL Merger Transformed Pro Football.* Guilford, Connecticut: The Lyons Press, 2008.

Levy, Marv. *Where Else Would You Rather Be?.* Champaign, Illinois: Sports Publishing, LLC, 2004.

Levy, Marv, and Jeffrey J. Miller. *Game Changers: The Greatest Plays in Buffalo Bills Football History.* Chicago: Triumph Books, 2009.

Lusteg, G. Booth. *Kick Rejection...and Win!!.* Baltimore, Maryland: Publish America, 2001.

Maiorana, Sal. *Relentless: The Hard-Hitting History of Buffalo Bills Football.* Lenexa, Kansas: Quality Sports Publications, 1994.

———. *Relentless II: The Hard-Hitting History of Buffalo Bills Football.* Coal Valley, Illinois: Quality Sports Publications, 2000.

Maxymuk, John. *Quarterback Abstract: The Must-Have Ratings Guide for NFL Quarterbacks*. Chicago: Triumph Books, 2009.

Miller, Jeffrey J. *Buffalo's Forgotten Champions: The Story of Buffalo's First Professional Football Team and the Lost 1921 Title*. Philadelphia: Xlibris Corporation, 2004.

———. *Rockin' the Rockpile: The Buffalo Bills of the American Football League*. Toronto: ECW Press, 2007.

Pitoniak, Scott. *Buffalo Bills Football Vault: The First 50 Seasons*. Atlanta: Whitman Publishing, 2010.

Smerlas, Fred, and Vic Carucci. *By a Nose: The Off-Center Life of Football's Funniest Lineman*. New York: Simon & Schuster, 1990.

Tasker, Steve, and Scott Pitoniak. *Steve Tasker's Tales from the Buffalo Bills*. Champaign, Illinois: Sports Publishing, LLC, 2006.

Newspapers and Periodicals

Buffalo Bills Media Guides
Buffalo Courier-Express
Buffalo Evening News
Dallas Morning News
Fort Worth Star-Telegram
Jacksonville Times-Union
Niagara Gazette
New York Times
Rochester Democrat and Chronicle
Sports Illustrated
Washington Post

Websites

Buffalo Bills (www.buffalobills.com)

National Football League (www.nfl.com)

Pro Football Hall of Fame (www.profootballhof.com)

Professional Football Researchers Association
  (www.profootballresearchers.org)

—

About the Author

Jeffrey J. Miller is an award-winning writer whose previous books include *Game Changers: The Greatest Plays in Buffalo Bills Football History* (with Marv Levy), *Rockin' the Rockpile: The Buffalo Bills of the American Football League*, and *Buffalo's Forgotten Champions: The Story of Buffalo's First Professional Football Team and the Lost 1921 Title*. He lives in Springville, New York, with his wife, Cathaline, and their son, Benjamin.